IOII3644

Hidden Powers of State in the Cuban Imagination

UNIVERSITY PRESS OF FLORIDA

Florida A&M University, Tallahassee
Florida Atlantic University, Boca Raton
Florida Gulf Coast University, Ft. Myers
Florida International University, Miami
Florida State University, Tallahassee
New College of Florida, Sarasota
University of Central Florida, Orlando
University of Florida, Gainesville
University of North Florida, Jacksonville
University of South Florida, Tampa
University of West Florida, Pensacola

Hidden Powers of State
in the Cuban Imagination

KENNETH ROUTON

University Press of Florida
Gainesville · Tallahassee · Tampa · Boca Raton
Pensacola · Orlando · Miami · Jacksonville · Ft. Myers · Sarasota

Copyright 2010 by Kenneth Routon
All rights reserved

All figures in this book are reproduced courtesy of the author,
unless otherwise noted.
Printed in the United States of America. This book is printed on Glatfelter
Natures Book, a paper certified under the standards of the Forestry
Stewardship Council (FSC). It is a recycled stock that contains 30 percent
post-consumer waste and is acid-free.

First cloth printing, 2010
First paperback printing, 2011

Library of Congress Cataloging-in-Publication Data
Routon, Kenneth.
Hidden powers of state in the Cuban imagination / Kenneth Routon.
p. cm.
Includes bibliographical references and index.
ISBN 978-0-8130-3483-6 (alk. paper)
ISBN 978-0-8130-4196-4 (pbk.)
1. Cuba—Politics and government—1959–1990. 2. Cuba—Politics and
government—1990–93. Political culture—Cuba. 4. Socialism—Cuba.
5. Exceptionalism—Cuba. I. Title.
F1788.R595 2010
972.9106'4—dc22   2010001921

The University Press of Florida is the scholarly publishing agency for the State
University System of Florida, comprising Florida A&M University, Florida
Atlantic University, Florida Gulf Coast University, Florida International
University, Florida State University, New College of Florida, University of
Central Florida, University of Florida, University of North Florida, University
of South Florida, and University of West Florida.

University Press of Florida
15 Northwest 15th Street
Gainesville, FL 32611-2079
http://www.upf.com

To Lisbeth and Beny

Contents

Figures

Acknowledgments

I gratefully acknowledge support from the Fulbright-Hays Program, the Fernando Ortiz Foundation in Havana, Cuba, Southern Illinois University at Carbondale, and an Andrew W. Mellon Postdoctoral Fellowship at Wesleyan University in Middletown, Connecticut. These programs and institutions provided crucial material and institutional assistance during both the researching and writing up of the ethnographic material presented here.

Although this book is the product of my own intellectual labor, it would not have been possible without the help and support of a number of individuals and institutions. In Boone, North Carolina, Greg Reck, Jeff Boyer, Susan Keefe, and Patricia Beaver's passion for anthropology inspired me to make that great leap from the anonymous comforts of undergraduate learning to the disciplinary rigor of professional graduate training. I would also like to thank my philosophy professors: Patrick Rardin, who unwittingly provoked my enthusiasm for the phenomenology of Maurice Merleau-Ponty, and William Hutchins, who first introduced me to the marvelous, life-affirming beauty of Ben Okri's writing and the existential riches of West-African religions and philosophy.

Jonathan Hill has been a pillar of support throughout my efforts to navigate the bureaucratic red tape that any U.S. scholar doing research in Cuba has to face. His theoretical and ethnographic interests in the study of culture, power, and history have influenced my own intellectual development beyond measure. John McCall helped calm my initial intellectual apprehensions by selflessly lending an ear to my occasional rants and always offering sound advice. His seminars on the body and space provided an open forum through which to explore the descriptive richness of sensuous ethnography. I thank David Sutton for his guidance and wisdom as I went through various stages of professional development as well as for teaching me that theoretical/philosophical abstractions never suffice when a good ethnographic vignette will do. I am grateful to Anthony Steinbock for his fascinating and provocative seminar on the phenomenologist Maurice Merleau-Ponty. Finally, I want to thank Don Rice for always supporting my efforts to carry out research in Cuba.

Without the help and support of a great number of people in Cuba this book would never have been written. I trust that they all know who they are and, therefore, will understand my decision not the name them here.

This work has also benefited greatly from conversations and feedback received from a number of people over the years. I would like to thank the following people (in no particular order) who, in one way or another, knowingly or unknowingly, helped me by asking the tough questions, encouraged me to consider other lines of thought and interpretation, and inspired me to pursue other avenues of ethnographic representation: Liza McAlister, Stephan Palmié, Mick Taussig, Ariana Hernández-Reguant, Bonno Thoden van Velzen, Raquel Romberg, Leo Vournelis, Connie Sutton, Jalane Schmidt, Ann Wightman, the anonymous reviewers of *American Ethnologist*, and all the other anonymous reviewers who took the time to read and comment on earlier drafts. Any shortcomings in this work, of course, are entirely my own.

I would also like to thank my wife, Lisbeth, and our son, Beny, for their patience, unconditional love, and for always picking me up when my resolve was waning. I dedicate this book to them. Finally, I want to express my deepest gratitude to my mother for providing the love of an entire family and for all of her enduring support over the years.

The Magic of the Revolution

CHAPTER *1*

"The fantasy of our people," the Cuban ethnographer Lydia Cabrera once wrote, "holds that all our presidents had a *brujo* [sorcerer] or spirit medium backing them from the shadows" (1979: 209). During my fieldwork in Havana between 2003 and 2006, and again during a brief stay in 2009, I collected a number of these tales regarding the hidden powers of state, filing them away in a make-believe archive comprised of "stray facts, manic theories, and well-told lies."[1] But there was one in particular that I kept returning to over and over again in my field notes, and again while writing this ethnography—a seemingly absurd yet enthralling moral artifact of the popular imagination. This was the phantasmagoric image of an *nganga* (fetish or magical object), long rumored to belong to the nation's now-ailing yet larger-than-life former president.

"Ever since I was a little girl," La Mariquilla tells me, "I've heard that he has his nganga. No one really knows, but they say he keeps it in a room somewhere in that big José Martí monument or one of those government buildings in the Plaza of the Revolution. All his bones of the dead are there, spirits that do anything he orders them to do. And it doesn't eat goats and chickens like the people's nganga. It eats bulls because they are strong. There hasn't been beef in the *bodega* [government rationing stores] in years but his nganga never goes hungry."

A typical nganga is a cast-iron pot which serves as a receptacle for natural substances, man-made objects, and human remains, a postcolonial variation on the fetish objects first made by slaves and maroons on the island. Today's nganga are a complex assemblage of materials that condense a host of spirit-forces and magical properties. They are microcosmic worlds unto themselves, characterized by their own internal forms of social organization and power structure that evoke the labor regime of plantation slavery, marronage, military command and reconnaissance, and wage labor. Presided over by an authoritative spirit of the dead, captured or contracted from a local cemetery, the nganga are nevertheless subject to the directives and manipulations of their living owners. The living activate their nganga by entering into a pact with the dead, harnessing their otherworldly powers to fulfill specific tasks or goals in the material world. The nganga thus congeal fantasies of total control.[2]

Allegedly subject to periodic ritual feedings with the blood of imported bulls, the Comandante's nganga, among other hidden forces, is credited with all sorts of monumental powers and undertakings. It has thwarted hundreds of assassination attempts on his life (734, to be exact, according to the president himself), a U.S.-backed foreign invasion, and been the secret power behind his monstrous charisma, his marathon speeches, his uncanny ability to move the masses with just a wave of his hand, and his disproportionately enormous influence on world affairs.

Even more striking is that this nganga may have a history that stretches far back into the island's colonial past. One tale has it that General Fulgencio Batista, the dictator whose regime the Comandante's 1959 revolution toppled, purchased a legendary nganga that once had belonged to a group of runaway slaves who used its magical powers to evade slave-hunting militias in the mountains of Escambray. Following his sudden and unusual rise to power in the 1930s, General Batista went looking for the maroons' nganga, believing it would bolster his power and keep his enemies at bay. After a difficult negotiation over the price, he came into possession of the renowned fetish, and every year thereafter fed it the warm blood of a sacrificed bull. Years later, when revolutionary forces were closing in on him, the General quickly fled the country, accidentally leaving the prized nganga behind. When the rebel army raided his country estate, some soldiers found it hidden by the door and carried it away. From exile, Batista made repeated efforts to have the nganga smuggled out of the country, offering hundreds of thousands of dollars to anyone who could return it to him. However, the Comandante, some say, decided to keep it and harness its powers to new, revolutionary ends.

Whether real or imagined, the image of this presidential fetish offers an exceptional vantage point from which to consider the ways in which popular idioms of power feed the moral and political imaginary sustaining the revolutionary state in Cuba, and vice versa. What powers might such a presidential fetish contain? What ghostly forces of the past might it unleash in the present? How might its magical capacities be harnessed to the national agenda and machinery of the state?

A knee-jerk reaction to such popular fabulations would be to simply brush them aside as mere ethnographic curiosities, fictions of the cultural imagination that, while interesting, are ultimately unfit for a serious and sober analysis of power. Yet it has become abundantly clear in recent years that state functionaries and eminent revolutionary scholars have been taking popular idioms of power all too seriously, harnessing their dream-images and magical capacities to the national agenda, and especially to the notion of Cuba as a bastion of resistance against capitalist imperialism. The late Joel James, former director of the Casa del Caribe, for instance, enshrined the image of revolutionary society's heroic flight from the snares of global capitalism when he made the bold claim that the Cuban nation itself was a "great nganga" (2006: 27–28). Like the nganga, whose spirits of the dead and magical capacities were ostensibly harnessed by runaway slaves to escape the terrors of colonial society and live a precarious yet liberated existence in the bush, the Cuban nation, James suggested, also harnesses the invisible powers of the dead—all those who died during conquest and anticolonial struggles; all those that gave up the ghost slaving away in the cane fields or running from slave-hunting militias; all those who perished at the hands of ruthless, U.S.-backed dictators during the republic; all those who fell defending the revolution from mercenaries funded by Yankee gold. According to James, the Cuban nation conjures these dead to both redeem their struggle and enlist their powers to escape from the horrors of neoliberal imperialism and thereafter live a precarious yet liberated existence in the global wilderness.

I envision this book as my own kind of nganga, an ethnographic archive of the metaphorical and magical constructions of power circulating back and forth between popular culture and the socialist state in post-Soviet Cuba. Drawing on recent theoretical approaches that bring together anthropology and history in the study of power, this ethnography examines the magical pathos of politics and everyday life in post-Soviet Cuba. I describe not only how the monumentality of the socialist state arouses popular images of its hidden powers, but also the ways in which revolutionary officialdom has, in recent years, tacitly embraced vernacular fantasies of power and harnessed them to the national agenda. Popular culture and the state, I suggest, are deeply entangled within a promiscuous field of power, taking turns siphoning the magic of the other in order to embellish their own fantasies of authority, control, and transformation.

Money, Morality, and Magic in the Special Period

When I began my fieldwork in May 2003, most Cubans were still suffering from the economic hangover that followed the worst years of the so-called Special Period.[3] Lasting throughout the 1990s, but with no definite end, the Special Period was the Cuban government's euphemism for the economic crisis and warlike austerity that came to define everyday life on the island following the collapse of the Eastern European socialist regimes. The sudden loss of subsidies and trade with the former Soviet bloc, which until then had propped up the island's economy, led to massive shortages of fuel, food, and many other basic goods. Cuba, so it seemed, was a country under siege. Facing the threat of total economic ruin, the Cuban state was forced to momentarily suspend its micromanaging of the domestic economy as it struggled to find new sources of revenue. As the state faded into the background of everyday life, so did much of the socialist ethos it had spent the better part of three decades trying to cultivate in the populace. With citizens left to pursue their own survival strategies, a thriving black market soon emerged and an older ethos of sharing (*compartir*) soon began to give way to an emerging culture of wheeling and dealing (*resolver*) (Hernández-Reguant 2002: 6–7).

For many, hustling became the only viable means of daily survival in the sinking economy. Fierce competition over scarce resources, however, had an often detrimental effect on everyday social life. With everyone struggling for themselves, altruism seemed to be becoming a thing of the past. An air of uncertainty and distrust lingered over even the most seemingly innocent social interactions and exchanges. Suspicions and fears regarding the hidden designs and aggression of others—the most menacing of which took the form of magic and sorcery—made everyday social relations not only a precarious, but a potentially dangerous affair.

Meanwhile, the state began pushing through a series of economic reforms to confront the growing crisis. Foreign investment and international tourism, which the socialist state had always spurned, were now embraced as the most promising strategies to settle the country's economic woes. By 1996, market reforms seemed to be turning things around. Yet both the official and underground economy continued to stir up a great deal of anxiety. While some groups had clearly benefited from the changes—those who received dollar remittances from family and friends living abroad, those lucky enough to land a job or scrape out a living hustling in the tourist sector, those with the capital to start their own businesses, and those who managed state enterprises and government institutions, for example—others were still languishing, especially those with no or only limited access to hard currency. Market reforms had created a double economy—one based on the massively devalued Cuban *peso*, the currency in which most state salaries were paid, and the other founded on hard currency like the U.S. dollar and, later, the convertible peso, which circulated mostly in government-run dollar stores, the tourist zones, and, of course, the black market. Unable to make ends meet on meager government salaries, most had no choice but to find ways of tapping into the new market economy. It now seemed that everything had a price—"not only material objects," as Hernández-Reguant notes, "but time, labor, and affect" (2009: 8). The flirtation with market reforms had begun to leave its mark—self-interest, unbridled accumulation, and ostentatious display suddenly appeared in every nook and cranny of society, not only threatening to erode the socialist values of self-sacrifice, hard work, and solidarity, but also making the moral authority of the socialist state increasingly suspect.

By the end of the decade, however, the country appeared to have survived the worst of the crisis. As economic conditions improved, the government began curbing many of the market reforms that had led to the recovery. The state began reasserting its control over everyday life, making a concerted effort to reign in the autonomous economic and social spheres that had sprung up in its absence and to purge any real or imagined public challenges to its authority. Some of the measures adopted by the government entailed heavily taxing independent entrepreneurs, firing state managers in an effort to root out corruption, imposing harsher penalties for petty crime, rounding up and jailing dissidents en masse, and launching new propaganda campaigns. The state, it seemed, was returning to politics as usual.

What perhaps distinguished the period in which my fieldwork took place from the previous decade was that, by the time I conducted my research, all hope that market reforms would lead to more openness and ease some of the heavy-handedness by which the government sought to restrict political discourse and economic self-determination had been replaced by a kind of gloomy pessimism. The state, many believed, had no intentions of pursuing any changes that would erode its status as the absolute center of moral authority and power. Yet things were not the same; the country had changed. Limited market reforms and the development of the tourist industry had ushered in a new era and, for many, there was no going back. Cuba was undergoing an uncertain transformation. And if the state had any hope of reviving revolutionary political fervor it would have to improve the way it engaged with civil society and, in particular, popular culture. If the state had learned any lesson from Eastern Europe, it was that the existence of autonomous economic sectors and forms of popular expression posed one of the most serious threats to its policing powers and socialist ethos. Not only could these sectors easily convert their wealth into political capital but, given their economic independence, they could also shun displays of revolutionary allegiance that for others were absolutely essential to political citizenship and upward mobility.

One of these sectors was the underground ritual economy that gravitated around the cult houses of Afro-Creole religions on the island. In the early 1990s, when the government initially retreated from everyday economic life, these religions underwent a kind of public florescence, gaining in popularity not only among the country's black and mulatto population, but among all social sectors—whites, educated professionals, party members, government bureaucrats, not to mention visiting foreign tourists. The most obvious factors driving this religious revival were economic and social. As economic conditions worsened, many people's chances of survival were directly correlated to their access, or lack thereof, to the black market economy. The informal social and economic networks that link, however loosely, various cult houses across the island have always enjoyed some measure of autonomy, even if their activities were sometimes closely monitored by the government. With the economic crisis, however, local cult houses took on an even more expanded economic role by becoming important centers of informal distribution and exchange within the ever-expanding black market economy.

But this was not all these ritual centers provided. As local cults of affliction, they also offered spiritual protection from the social ills that now plagued society. The economic crisis had not only inflamed morally suspect activities such as hustling, prostitution, stealing, and other petty crimes, it had also fueled what many believed to be an unprecedented rise in predatory forms of *brujería* (magic and sorcery). State-managed market reforms that had resulted in some measure of social stratification only reinforced these perceptions. Tales of people who turned to sinister forms of ritual work—either to enrich themselves at the expense of others or due to the envy and jealousy they felt at seeing others do better than themselves—became a common feature of local lore during the Special Period. Afro-Creole religion, then, became a kind of refuge for those seeking its healing powers and protection from the hidden aggression of others. In a social environment beleaguered by fears of victimization, both magical and mundane, a situation that made even family and friends the object of suspicion, local cult houses offered not only protection, but an alternative form of social support. Rather than leave social relations to chance, here they could be ritually defined and managed.

But this only tells part of the story. For some, Afro-Creole religions also held the prospect of financial reward. The lure of hard currency may have also piqued popular interest because, once initiated, individuals could then go on to oversee the initiation of others and thus accumulate sizeable amounts of capital from inflated ritual fees. Given the immense interest of foreign tourists in local exotica, especially Afro-Creole religion, one could potentially make thousands of dollars by overseeing tourist initiation into local cult houses. Popular religion, it seemed, had become big business, and suddenly even local cult leaders and devotees were no longer immune to accusations of hustling and sorcery, frequently being suspected of using religion as a vehicle for profit. Moreover, given the economy's increasing dependence on foreign tourism and dollar remittances from abroad, ritual initiation and other rites also provided a means of domesticating or whitewashing new wealth—especially important since the accumulation of this wealth, and the forms of conspicuous consumption that accompany it, were seen as morally suspect (compare Holbraad 2004).

Afro-Creole religions gained important new functions in other spheres as well. As the promise of socialist modernity waned, which effectively diminished the state's moral authority and its hold over the public imaginary, these religions and their magic offered a wealth of imagery upon which to base new visions of power and authority. Like other forms of popular expression, such as music, popular religion provided a space for social critique. Brujería, an inseparable component of these religions, for example, is just as much a ritual arena as it is an informal political discourse concerning the circulation of power in society and a social chronicle of the misfortunes, afflictions, and struggles of everyday life. Moreover, as an informal arena of social critique, brujería not only deals with tales about the concealed predations of ordinary citizens, but, as the image of the Comandante's nganga illustrates, also includes a great deal of speculation and rumor regarding the hidden designs and powers of public figures, political leaders, and the state itself.

It would not take long for the regime to get the message. In the early 1990s, the state began responding to mounting tensions in the body politic in part by softening its hard-line emphasis on political community (that is, the socialist project) through reforms and campaigns designed to promote national unity and cultural identity (Hernández-Reguant 2002: 105–107). Some of the state's efforts were clearly intended to both validate and include the Afro-Creole religious community to help reinvigorate grassroots support for the revolution. Although the religious revival of the 1990s initially suggested that religion remained an arena beyond state control, the Special Period has witnessed some often incongruous state attempts to co-opt Afro-Creole religions into the national agenda. In the early 1990s, for example, the state began licensing and funding cultural associations run by ritual specialists and, in 1992, lifted the ban prohibiting religious devotees from membership in the Cuban Communist Party (PCC). These measures seemed to breathe new life and meaning into banal political mantras such as, "INSIDE THE REVOLUTION, EVERYTHING! OUTSIDE THE REVOLUTION, NOTHING!" Now, fellow comrades could be openly recognized as both socialists and spirit mediums, party members and priest-healers, *fidelistas* (followers of Fidel Castro) and "fetishists."

The Cuban state's effort to revive the magic of the revolution by domesticating the "wild" energies and profuse powers of Afro-Creole religion, however, often only served to bolster perceptions of revolutionary omnipresence—that is, the sense that the state is everywhere present in the myriad details of everyday life. Yet, as we will see, it also fostered perceptions of a state eager to tap into the magical capacities of popular religion in order to revive and nourish its own power and authority.

The Spirits of Revolution Square

25 December 2005: Today we made our way to a political festival organized by the Union of Communist Youth (UJC) and, little did we know, straight into the middle of a revolutionary fairyland. What we were about to witness was a massive political spectacle that seemed to revel in the surreal, placing on public display a monumental montage of state iconography and popular images of magical power and the occult.

El Gordo's 1956 Buick coughed and sputtered long after he removed the key from the ignition, the plastic effigy of San Lázaro on the dashboard shaking violently in response to the car's grumpy protestations. We stopped several blocks away from Revolution Square in order to avoid the hordes of policemen swarming the streets. El Gordo ran an unlicensed taxi service out of Guanabacoa, a fairly mundane illegal activity made far more conspicuous by the presence of the yuma ethnographer.[4] We got out fast and followed the sound of timba (percussion-driven Cuban salsa) blaring from a public address system in the square.

By the time we arrived, the festival celebrating the "47TH ANNIVERSARY OF THE TRIUMPH OF THE REVOLUTION" was already under way. As we walked through the oversized public square—the most important ritual center of state power on the island—the monumental emblems of the revolution were everywhere on display. On one side of the square sits the José Martí Memorial, a 358-foot star-shaped tower flanked by a 59-foot marble statue at its base, a soaring monument dedicated to Cuba's legendary anticolonial hero. On the other side lies the Cuba Ministry of the Interior building whose front is stamped with a huge, iconic iron portrait of Ernesto "Che" Guevara, the guerrilla fighter and revolutionary hero who helped topple the Batista regime. In front of Che's effigy, artists staged didactic performances for children who showed their enthusiasm by waving little Cuban flags in the air. There were sports exhibitions, a circus, and a screening of the animated film Vampires in Havana.[5] That afternoon, a carnival procession led by a police motorcade paraded down the avenue followed by musical performances on a large stage erected in front of the José Martí National Library.

While we awaited the bigger concerts scheduled for that evening featuring Paulito FG and Los Van Van, La Mariquilla, whose family I had been staying with for some time in Guanabacoa, suggested we get something to eat. After finishing our pork sandwiches, we bought some beers and accompanied Caridad in browsing the vendor kiosks lined up along the periphery of *the plaza. Caridad had been instructed by Arcaño, a self-described brujo or sorcerer, to look for a small toy airplane to give as an offering to her Elegguá, an Afro-Creole oricha or "saint" (santo) described as the owner of the cross-roads, messenger of the gods, and supernatural broker of fate.*[6] *Caridad had plans of leaving the island to go live abroad with her foreign fiancée. She had received the coveted "letter of invitation," navigated the labyrinthine socialist bureaucracy, and paid its exorbitant fees with money transfers from abroad. All she had left to do was acquire that final government rubber-stamp on her passport, literally phrased in capital letters, reading: "PERMISSION TO LEAVE." Caridad desperately needed her Elegguá to grease the bureaucratic wheels or "open the roads" (abrir los caminos), as Cubans say.*

As Caridad and her mother continued rummaging through the cheap plastic trinkets and toys, Antonio turned to me and asked, in all seriousness, "Do you know where the Comandante lives?"

"No," I responded, "but they say he never sleeps in the same place twice."

"I know where he lives," Antonio said, a mischievous look in his eyes. "He lives up there," he said, pointing to the top of the monstrous marble monument to José Martí. "He's watching us this very moment!" he exclaimed, his body convulsing with laughter.

As night began to fall, we planted ourselves over by the stage area. The police were now moving through the gathering crowd, sizing up its shifting dynamics as the daytime revelers were gradually overrun by their nocturnal counterparts, a potentially combustible assortment of partygoers (fiesteros), salsa-lovers (salseros), people associated with the illicit desires of the street (callejeros), pickpockets (carteristas), hoodlums (guapos), hustlers (jineteros), and, of course, scores of smiling, bright-eyed foreign tourists. The police went around checking national identification cards and confiscating rum bottles, which had been strictly prohibited since they could easily be converted into deadly weapons in a brawl. La Mariquilla suggested we bribe one of the security or entertainment personnel to let us in behind the police barricades that surrounded the stage, sensing that we would be safer there than out in the crowd. She spotted an acquaintance and, after a couple minutes of inconspicuous haggling, we slipped him two dollars and were allowed to pass through.

"¡Ay, mamá!," La Mariquilla suddenly murmured in restrained bewilderment. Deliberately keeping her voice down and drawing the syllables out slowly, her subdued response was not unlike the way Havana residents soften

1.1. The Union of Communist Youth's mural depicting José Martí holding an effigy of Elegguá.

their speech for dramatic effect when they catch wind of some scandalous neighborhood gossip. To the right of the stage, a large mural had been erected for the festival whose arresting images had us all mute for a few seconds until La Mariquilla broke the silence. At the center of the mural was an image of José Martí, the most revered ancestor in the national revolutionary pantheon, seated in a simple wooden chair and holding an effigy of Elegguá in his left hand (Figure 1.1). With her eyes still fixed on the mural before her, and without trying to hide the baffled look on her face, La Mariquilla's reaction perfectly captured the sense of surreal shock conjured up by this composite image of revolutionary power.

"Nno, tremendo arroz con mango!" [literally "tremendous rice with mango"], she exclaimed. "Rice with mango" is a popular Cuban expression denoting a sticky mess, total confusion, or something out of the ordinary that results from mixing things that do not go together.

Is this mural a political or religious image, or both? Martí, dressed in a statesman's black suit, looks drowsy, as if he had been woken in the middle of the night to pose for an impromptu portrait. He props himself up with one arm and in the other holds an effigy of Elegguá Laroye (that is, the effigy Cubans place behind their doors to act as supernatural sentinels which protect la casa—the house—from the invisible "dirt" or dangerous magic associated with la calle—the street). Martí is flanked on either side by two majestic, blood-red roosters. To his left, a fluttering Cuban flag melts into the figures of doves and the water below them. A boy runs in play. To Martí's right stands an Abakuá masquerade. Dressed in a conical-headed costume of black-and-white geometric patterns and a belt from which several cowbells hang, the masquerade holds a branch of bitter broom, used to sweep away harmful spirits and sorcery, and a cloth-adorned rod, pointed in the direction of Martí, upon which a tocororo *has perched before taking flight. Four distinct ritual signatures are scattered about throughout the image. Barely visible, two hands inscribed with intersecting lines resembling a cross emerge from the border on the far left, recalling the ritual scarifications of Palo initiation rites. Two infants with closed eyes, the guardian angels of the revolution, hover in the air above.*

How carnivalesque! Martí assumes supernatural status as the symbolic Eleggúa of the revolutionary nation-state. Eleggúa is cast in the role of cosmic revolutionary, the invisible motor of national history. Here, national history and the invisible world of spirit forces mutate into the surrealism of a political dreamworld. We briefly catch a glimpse of an unabashedly promiscuous world where the cult of Afro-Creole "saints" and revolutionary monumentality mingle freely, where cosmology, history, and political community coalesce into one.

It is a clever and seductive image, and one surely intended to resonate with those groups who initially provided support for the 1959 revolution; namely, black communities and the poor. After all, Martí "opened the roads," so to speak, that eventually led away from colonialism and toward national sovereignty, only fully realized after the revolution, the leadership contends. The fetish power of such imagery lies in its blurring of state monumentality with the magical capacities and numinous authority of spirit-forces and the dead. While the mural may appear to acknowledge both the value and contemporary vitality of popular imaginaries of power and their magic, which is in itself a significant departure from earlier cultural policy, it does so by wresting these dream-images away from the populace and harnessing them to the ideological apparatus of the party and state. Martí and his Eleggúa, then, conjure up a number of thorny questions about the ways in which images of power are refracted through historical memory, popular culture, and political community.

Popular Culture and the State

The relationship between popular culture and the state has been a central issue in the anthropological study of power in recent years. Antonio Gramsci's notion of hegemony (see *The Prison Notebooks*) did much to provoke anthropological preoccupations with the circulation of power between governing elite and the masses. Gramsci was interested in how dominant social groups were able to impose their authority on society without resorting to force. He was concerned with how it was that both dominant and subaltern groups not only accepted their position within the social hierarchy, but also naturalized the arbitrary rules and constructions of power propagated by the elite as matters of "common sense." Gramsci called this phenomenon hegemony and suggested that by accepting the dominant order, subaltern groups were willing participants in their own oppression.

One of the problems of Gramsci's work, however, is that the sphere of the state is so expanded, reaching so far into the nooks and crannies of civil society, that the distinction between the two almost evaporates entirely. Nevertheless, as Stuart Hall notes, Gramsci's work constitutes a virtual Copernican revolution in Marxist approaches to the state: (1) He stressed not only the repressive functions of the state, but its productive aspects as well; (2) He placed questions of culture, especially popular culture, at the very center of the state's sphere of activity (Hall 2006: 361). Gramsci argued that a major goal of the state is to harness civil society to the imperatives of economic development and political acquiescence. The state therefore mediates between cultural formations and class relations, drawing these into particular configurations and harnessing them to specific ideological agendas and political imaginaries.

But what about the critical capacities of popular culture? Here, Russian philosopher and literary critic Mikhail Bakhtin's work on carnival is particularly suggestive. Bakhtin argued that the vulgar aesthetics of carnival constitute an implicit critique of power in which subjects or citizens, to borrow a phrase from Michel de Certeau, "subvert the fatality of the established order" (1984: 17–18). Bakhtin's work is not limited to those public festivals in which the status quo and power arrangements of a society are momentarily suspended, allowing people to openly mock those in power through vulgar displays. Rather, his insights apply to any social practice in which carnivalesque rituals of reversal, mockery, vulgarity, and the grotesque are central. He suggested that the aesthetics of carnival are always available to be appropriated by dominated groups as counterpoints to the established order, demonstrating that although they may not hold the reigns of power, and may be subject to the state's machinations, such domination can never completely contain the subaltern imagination.

In a critique of Bakhtin, Achille Mbembe suggests that rather than being an arena exclusively for the expression of counter-hegemony, carnivalesque idioms of power are also available to the elite (1992). He argues that popular culture and the state in postcolonial Africa share a similar "aesthetics of power," which results in what he calls their mutual "zombification"—that is, a stagnant relationship that leaves both politically impotent, incapable of fully realizing their goals. In order to make sense of the imagery and efficacy of postcolonial relations of power, Mbembe argues, the often overlooked "intimacy" or "promiscuity" that characterize the relationship between popular culture and the state require that we dispense with the binary categories used in typical interpretations of domination (resistance versus passivity, subjection versus autonomy, civil society versus the state, hegemony versus counter-hegemony). According to Mbembe, we can no longer interpret the power and authority of officialdom merely in terms of surveillance and the politics of coercion. In postcolonial Africa, popular culture and the state are involved in a kind of casual and indiscriminate relationship in which each absorbs and reflects the aesthetics of power and political imaginary of the other, refashioning them to fit their own agenda. Nor can we read the practices of ordinary citizens in terms that exclusively stress their opposition to or disengagement from the state. Rather, Mbembe suggests, we should examine the "logics of conviviality" and "the dynamics of domesticity and familiarity" that embed both the state and popular culture within the same aesthetic and epistemological field of power (1992: 14).

In a brief yet provocative rejoinder entitled "Machiavellian, Rabelaisian, Bureaucratic?" Dain Borges considers the relevance of Mbembe's argument to Latin America. Although African "belly politics" resonate with political culture in many postcolonial Latin American nations (for example, the nineteenth-century caudillo and Belle Epoque dictatorships, the populist demagogues that emerged beginning in the 1930s, and the "bureaucratic-authoritarian" military regimes of the 1960s and '70s), Borges suggests that there is no single style of commandment or aesthetics of power shared by civil society and the state in this region. According to Borges, something beyond mere intimacy appears to mark the relationship between popular culture and the ruling classes in Latin America. For instance, whereas the popular dictator novels of the 1970s, such as Gabriel García Márquez's *Autumn of the Patriarch* (1975), may have reveled in scatological mockery to represent power in all of its nervous potency, their tone was ultimately nostalgic—that is, they were looking back into the past at larger-than-life political figures that could no longer serve to condense and centralize power in the present. Nevertheless, he notes, "Latin Americans' masochistic taste for Machiavellian political maneuvers is particularly appreciative of Rabelaisian wiles, and the people answer in kind" (Borges 1992: 111). Although vestiges of Machiavellian excess still linger on in the region, especially among those political figures that embody something of the political style of the classic caudillo, Borges claims that Rabelaisian vulgarity seems to be present only in those city-state tyrannies "where it is impossible to conceal Who Rules" (Borges 1992: 109–12).

Although Borges is persuasive in noting the coexistence of differing aesthetics of power in postcolonial Latin America, recent ethnographic studies suggest that the promiscuity between popular culture and the state in this region has been grossly underappreciated. In a remarkable study of spirit possession and the state, Michael Taussig, for instance, offers a fascinating account of "the logics of conviviality" at work in modern Venezuela (1997). Exploring the ways in which the dead are harnessed for state purposes, Taussig argues that popular religion and the Venezuelan state are trapped in what he describes as a "perfidious contagion of power." The metaphorical and magical constructions of power that characterize spirit possession, on the one hand, and the state, on the other, betray their particular situatedness in these cultural domains by coming to seduce and fuel the imaginary of the other (1997: 5).[7] For example, the very fetishized historical figures upon which the state relies for its own legitimatization are dramatically brought to life in the bodies of citizens during spirit-possession ceremonies. Spirit mediums channel the spirits of national icons such as María Lionza and Simón Bolívar in often melodramatic and kitsch spectacles of nationalist fervor. As Taussig makes clear, the mediums themselves are not so much empowered by the magic of these dead as they are by the state's embellishment and exaltation of them. Spirit possession—in this context, at least—brings to life, and therefore makes "real," what are normally just inert, metaphorical representations of state power.[8]

What makes Taussig's study so profound is that it clearly demonstrates how the "fictional reality" of the state serves as a screen for both political desire and fantasy (compare Aretxaga 2003). As an elusive ensemble of power relations and institutions rather than an organic unity, the "state" as such does not exist outside of our representations of it. Rather, like spirits or race for instance, the state is what we might call a moral artifact—a phantasm that nevertheless acquires the character of the real by virtue of the fact that the imagery used to represent it often comes to play such a profound role in shaping everyday social experience and praxis. Yet representations of the state have to be popular in order to be useful. This is what makes popular culture such an important site for the mediation of social tensions and conflict (Sharma and Gupta 2006: 357). Taussig's ethnography provides a striking example of this—he not only calls attention to how the magical capacities of history, or the "slumbering powers of the dead," as he puts it, are harnessed to contemporary political imaginaries, but he also reveals how popular and official constructions of power are both implicated in representations that fetishize the state. The magic of the state, he suggests, is not just the real effect of official manipulations of the public imaginary. Nor is it merely the projection of popular fantasy onto officialdom. Rather, the fetish power of the state is rooted in the complex play of seductions, reflections, and mutual appropriations that flow back and forth between these spheres.

Ethnography on an Awkward Scale

The chapters that follow address a number of questions concerning the magical elan of power and everyday life in late-socialist Cuba. How are the discourses and practices associated with magic implicated in the socioeconomic changes taking place on the island? How do official representations of state monumentality arouse popular images of its fetish powers? How do popular idioms of power feed the moral and political imaginary sustaining the revolutionary state? What role does historical memory play in these metaphorical and magical constructions of power?

This is "ethnography on an awkward scale" (Comaroff and Comaroff 1992), ethnography that follows cultural constructions of power as they snake their way nervously through those awkward spaces where local and global political imaginaries and moral economies cross paths—to the local barrio where socialist and market values intersect against a backdrop of economy austerity and moral decay, and where the magical capacities of both vernacular and state vigilance intermingle; to the composite images of power that circulate back and forth between domestic ritual arenas and the public spaces of revolutionary political spectacle; to local constructions of the past and global projects of public memory; to the emergent economies of desire and cosmopolitanism in the tourist zones.

I begin by exploring everyday intersections of politics and domesticity in one Havana barrio. Chapter 2 examines how two forms of surveillance and social control, one political and the other magical, articulate with one another in everyday life. The relationship between these two forms of vigilance defies typical and overly simplistic interpretations of domination as an opposition between clearly distinct centers of power. Rather, this chapter illustrates the deeply symbiotic nature of political and magical forms of vigilance and social control in contemporary Cuba. In Chapter 3 I examine popular rumors and images of the hidden, magical powers of Cuban political leaders. I suggest that popular perceptions of the magical prowess and supernatural mystique of political figures are emblematic of a particular cultural understanding of power. This chapter carefully teases out these implicit meanings and ambiguities by placing them within the broader context of a political imaginary deeply rooted in the eccentricities of Cuban history. From here, I move on to exploring specific instances of the state's appropriation of popular imaginaries of power by looking at the intersections of ritual and revolutionary representations of slavery. Chapter 4 describes how ritual images of slavery have been harnessed to revolutionary ideology. Although the particular way in which ritual officiants "represent the ghost" dramatically diverges from the moralizing tenor and ideological agenda of official commemorations of slavery, some contemporary adepts appear to be reimagining the historical origins of these ritual images and practices in ways that directly incorporate romantic revolutionary reifications of slave resistance.

Chapter 5 examines how the distortions of a dollarized tourist economy introduced into Cuban social relations come to be represented as "mystically managed" and "manageable." My focus is on a heretofore unexplored dimension of the literature on the Special Period—namely, the ritual management of desire via the use of love magic in the tourist-driven economy of Havana. The promiscuity between official and extra-official manipulations of the global economy of desire linked to tourism in Havana has either been ignored altogether or at least overlooked. Ethnographically tracing some of the ways in which love magic is both talked about and practiced in Havana, I argue that the national economy is not only subject to, but nourished by the magical manipulation of tourist desire. I follow this with a look at how the revamping of international tourism may be arousing popular interest in subaltern historical icons. Chapter 6 describes a little-known spirit-possession ceremony known as *rumba de cajón al muerto*, roughly meaning "box-drum rumba for the dead." Celebrating Creole rather than African-born spirits of the dead, these "spirits who like rumba" are national caricatures—for instance, the sweet and seductive *mulatta* and the treacherous, elderly black brujo. The popular theater of spirit possession is shown to resonate and, to some extent, overlap with the kitschy theater of state power and representation of local exotica in the tourist zones.

Chapter 7 focuses not on narrative constructions of the relationship between ritual and state power but on the actual courtship of the Ifá divination priesthood by the revolutionary Cuban state. In this chapter I describe the struggle between various factions of Ifá divination priests (*babalaos*) over control of the annual divination ceremony known as the Letter of the Year. Although the ceremony has been performed since the early twentieth century, its prophecies were until recently largely confined to Ocha-Ifá religious communities on the island. After the collapse of the former Soviet bloc, however, the oracle's sometimes controversial prophetic announcements soon began attracting the attention of the wider Cuban public as well as the international community. Ocha-Ifá's increasing public visibility and contestations over the political meanings of the Ifá oracle have not only led to a power struggle among different factions of divination priests, but have also been harnessed by the state in order to revive revolutionary political fervor. Finally, the epilogue ties together these various discursive strands by reflecting on the broader theoretical problems and questions that the ethnography brings to the surface.

The Eye and the Tongue

CHAPTER 2

What might a make-believe inventory of the Comandante's nganga look like? What stately artifacts, images, and remains would an archaeologist specializing in the excavation of popular imaginaries find interred there?

Although any human remains will do, Lydia Cabrera informs us, those most highly prized in the construction of an nganga are the finger bones (so they can do things), toe bones (so they can move), leg bones (so they can run), and skull (so they can think) (1983: 122). After being amputated to identify his corpse, the hands of Ernesto "Che" Guevara were rumored to have been preserved in a glass jar, shipped to Havana, stored in the Palace of the Revolution, and displayed to only the most esteemed of guests (Castañeda 1998: 418). Following the repatriation of his corpse from Bolivia in 1997, many began to speculate about whether the remains were in fact Che's. Some believed that the state had deliberately deceived the public into thinking that the legendary guerrilla hero had been returned to the revolutionary society he helped bring about in order to revive political fervor during a time of great economic decline and moral decay. Others suggested that his remains had not really ended up in a mausoleum in Santa Clara, where an elaborate state funeral had taken place, but were instead stored in some secret location closer to the heart of state power in Havana. After all, when the president's beloved "White Udder"—the F1 bovine he had once hoped would feed the nation but which has since been replaced by imported cows to feed the tourists and, we might add, his nganga—passed away, he allegedly had it stuffed and placed in a storeroom inside the Museum of the Revolution.

All these fictional possessions, phantom body parts, and secret museum storerooms are so many variations on the same thing: the detritus of vernacular fantasies regarding the hidden powers of the state. To our make-believe inventory of the president's nganga we would have to add, in addition to the remains of revolutionary heroes, the millions of vigilant eyes, ears, and tongues of the body politic itself. The enormous sensory and informatory capacities of the revolutionary body politic were soon assimilated into the surveillance apparatus of the state in the form of neighborhood-based political watchdog committees. Blanketing the island in a pervasive network of vigilant corporate bodies, these committees greatly expanded the sensory prowess of revolutionary officialdom, an eye and ear on every street corner. Like the sentient trees that connected the secret thoughts of the townspeople to the president through a network of invisible threads in Miguel Asturias' famous novel (1963), the culture of vigilance that permeates revolutionary Cuban society is also the subject of wild fabulations depicting the uncanny reach of the state into everyday life.

The Eye and the Tongue

During the early months of my fieldwork I remember walking with a friend through a neighborhood in the Vedado section of Havana, where we came across a low concrete wall tattooed with state graffiti. The wall displayed a stark admonition, spelled out in big black capital letters: "THIS NEIGH-BORHOOD IS WATCHED BY THE COMMITTEE FOR THE DEFENSE OF THE REVOLUTION."[1] It was a warning to any actual or would-be counter-revolutionaries that their movements and activities were being carefully monitored, noted, and reported to state authorities. Warnings such as these, along with countless revolutionary slogans, are a banal feature of the urban landscape in Havana and are, indeed, present throughout the entire country. At the time I did not think twice about it, considering it just a commonplace advisory with little relevance to magic and folk healing, which is what I had come there to study.

Later, while walking through La Mariquilla's neighborhood in Guanabacoa, I noticed a small tin plate hanging from a local residence. The sign bore the image of a conjoined eye and tongue penetrated by a dagger, a single drop of blood hanging suspended below. An inscription beside the image,

2.1a. and 2.1b. Two examples of charm-images, posted on the outside of houses, that protect against evil eye and "bad tongue."

again in capital letters, read, "I AM WATCHING YOU!" (Figures 2.1a and 2.1b). It was not the first time I had seen this charm-image. In fact, it is an image you often encounter in Cuban homes, especially those of Afro-Creole religious devotees. The only difference was that this one had been placed on the outside of the door, making it a feature of local public space, rather than inside the first room of the house where they are normally displayed. These charm-images serve as a warning to anyone with malevolent intentions that the house and its occupants enjoy mystical protection. Given that they are such a mundane artifact of popular culture, it did not occur to me at the time that these images might have anything other than a ritual significance.

Several months would pass before the implicit relationship between these two images would suggest itself to me. That moment came in a casual conversation with La Mariquilla's next-door neighbor. "Apart from our problems with the blockade," he told me, "Cubans have just two enemies:

the eye and the tongue." Even though he did not mention names, it was clear that he was referring to the culture of vigilance that permeates everyday life in revolutionary Cuba. The primary function of the Committees for the Defense of the Revolution is political surveillance, but they are also major social conduits for the circulation of local rumor and gossip. A great deal of this informal talk has less to do with counterrevolutionary activity than with the semipublic expression of personal innuendo, scandal, and social tension. Images like the conjoined eye and tongue, however, provide magical protection from evil eye and, as I would soon learn, the ever-vigilant gaze and "bad tongue" (*mala lengua*)—unwarranted and often salacious rumor and gossip with the power to curse—of neighbors, family members, friends, and strangers.

In this chapter I examine the relationship between political and ritual forms of surveillance and social control in one Havana barrio. At one level, magical images, charms, and rites are clearly a means of diverting some of the nervous exuberance associated with revolutionary vigilance and perceptions of state omniscience. Yet to stop there would be to miss the more subtle and significant ways in which the two fuel and feed off the excesses of the other. Here, surprising juxtapositions of seemingly incompatible powers are not just mundane—they are an integral aspect of the moral and political imaginary sustaining the state in post-Soviet Cuba.

The Barrio of Brujos

I first met La Mariquilla when she was still hawking black market CD recordings to tourists for a local rumba group in Havana. At the time, I was renting a room from a family in Vedado, a living arrangement facilitated by the research foundation with which I was affiliated. Later, after making a joke about how the Vedado family knocked on my door dozens of times throughout the day to offer me coffee, so much so that it had become a nuisance, La Mariquilla told me without the slightest hint of doubt in her voice that they were doing some kind of magical work (*trabajo*) on me.

"Who drinks that much coffee? Even those white folks that say they don't believe in those things know how to do sorcery [*echar brujería*]," she said. "They just want your money; they don't want you to move from the house," she added.

A few weeks later, after telling my landlady that I had decided to base my research in Guanabacoa and would therefore be moving, she expressed her dismay by warning me that this municipality was an "underworld" (*bajo mundo*) of unemployed blacks who turn to sinister forms of magical predation to get what they want.

Such comments reverberate with decades-old colonial and republican associations linking blackness with criminal delinquency and the morally dubious world of sorcery and witchcraft. They also resonate with the way in which magical powers tend to be delimited topographically (Mauss and Hubert 1972: 38–39); that is, magical capacities are mapped onto the social landscape in such a way that isolated, marginal, or "inferior" races or cultures are given an ascribed reputation for sorcery (Tylor 1974). Those groups who occupied the lowest rungs of the colonial social hierarchy due to racially motivated perceptions of their "wildness" and "savagery," or proximity to nature, for example, were often believed by the elite classes to likely possess extraordinary powers to harm, heal, and significantly alter the course of misery and affliction (Taussig 1998: 446). Following typical prerevolutionary patterns, my landlady's comment located these extraordinary powers in the historically marginal, "black" barrios of the city. In fact, Guanabacoa is often referred to by both outsiders and residents alike as "the bewitched barrio" (*el barrio embrujado*) or "the barrio of brujos" (*el barrio de los brujos*).

The stereotypical image of the brujo in the Cuban cultural imagination is that of a dark and sinister figure who, drunk from his nightly sojourns in the bush among spirits and in the local cemetery hunting for bones, enriches himself by preying on the hatred, envy, and carnal desires of others (compare Cabrera 1979: 160). The brujo's vulgarity is magical; he is often depicted as the purveyor of a mercenary sociality, willing to capitalize on the most profane or morally corrupt human emotions and desires. Indeed, for the most part, the brujo still retains his character as a villain in the revolutionary imagination, but for reasons somewhat different than those of the colonial and republican past. My former landlady's allegations betray the expressed revolutionary distaste for magic as "pure production *ex nihilo*" (Mauss and Hubert 1972: 179). The utilitarian character of ritual work such as spirit possession and folk healing, the central occupations of the brujo, conflicts with the revolutionary emphasis on hard work and the ethos of the New Man because these skills "create the illusion that worldly needs can be satisfied by means of magic rather than hard work" (Ayorinde 2004: 122; Argüelles Mederos and Hodge Limonta 1991: 111).

La Mariquilla's counterclaim that the Vedado family was attempting to solidify its access to the tourist economy by concealing mystical predations in little cups of Cuban espresso, however, is much more than an ad hoc defense against racially motivated and historically situated constructions of otherness. Her suspicions reflect deeply entrenched cultural understandings of the uneven circulation of power in society and the central role magic plays in the production and negotiation of these social dynamics. If magic is society casting spells on itself (Taussig 1980), then the magic of the Special Period can tell us much about the social ills and dilemmas that now plague revolutionary Cuba.

Mercenary Sociality, State Surveillance, and the Grotesque Body Politic

As local, state-organized committees comprised of neighborhood residents, the CDRs are charged with the task of keeping a politically sensitive eye on their fellow comrades and reporting any suspicious activity to the municipal popular assembly (*Poder Popular*). Although they are responsible for organizing both local block parties on revolutionary holidays and neighborhood meetings to discuss pressing social concerns (for example, water shortages, housing conditions, the selective distribution of rationed telephones, and delegate candidates), their raison d'être is motivated by the conviction that the agents of hostile governments, especially the United States, lurk like spooks within the social landscape, secretly plotting to undermine and destroy the revolution. One of the earliest proclamations of the National Directorate, for instance, declared that, "The worms [counterrevolutionaries] are waiting, hidden in the shadows, to do their ruinous work of destruction and terror, paid for by the Yankee gold to which they have sold their hearts and consciences" (quoted in Fagen 1969: 72).

As I would soon learn after coming to live with La Mariquilla's family, however, the CDRs are also quasi-official organs for the production and circulation of local rumor and gossip, much of it having little to do with counterrevolutionary activity. Rather, the CDRs are often populated by local busybodies who indulge themselves daily in the sometimes sporadic and trite, sometimes salacious, and sometimes deliberately fabricated details of people's private lives and local scandal. It is the peculiar entanglement of the personal and the public that makes the CDRs such efficient social mechanisms for the production, exchange, and consumption of local rumor and gossip. As Richard Fagen noted less than a decade after their creation in 1960:

certain responsibilities of the CDR allow and even encourage the public expression of personal and social hostilities, antagonisms, and vendettas. Turning the watchdog responsibilities over to groups of citizens has made possible and even inevitable the use of public power for personal advantage, revenge, and catharsis. (Fagen 1969: 101–102)

Although Fagen was writing during the first decade of the revolution, his observations still resonate with the particular social dynamics of revolutionary vigilance today. The CDRs not only have the power to embellish local rumor and gossip by raising it to the level of counterespionage, enabling vindictive comrades to recast what are essentially interpersonal animosities through whispered allegations of the violation of revolutionary political morality—for example, "so-and-so does not work" or "doesn't go to political rallies and marches" or "has a yuma or foreigner staying in their house"— but they also contribute to local perceptions of state omniscience.

Cubans have a number of *dichos* (popular expressions) that allude to the culture of vigilance that pervades revolutionary society. "There's always an eye that sees you," one common expression warns. The sense of being the object of endless and near-preternatural scrutiny is so prevalent that some dichos suggest that the urban landscape itself is endowed with sensory organs. "Even the walls have ears and the floors senses," I often heard people say. These popular sayings instantiate the magical realism associated with perceptions of an omniscient state, as described by Miguel Angel Asturias in his novel *El Señor Presidente*:

A monstrous wood . . . separated the President from his enemies, a wood made up of trees with ears which responded to the slightest sound by whirling as if blown by a hurricane. Not the tiniest noise for miles around could escape the avidity of those millions of membranes. The dogs went on barking. A network of invisible threads, more invisible than telegraph wires, connected every leaf with the President, enabling him to keep watch on the most secret thoughts of the townspeople. (Asturias 1963: 39)

In Havana, however, it is not the sentient trees of the "monstrous wood" but the urban social landscape, and in particular the extraordinary sensory prowess of the local CDRs, that constitutes the "millions of membranes," the multitude of eyes, ears, and tongues linking revolutionary officialdom with the intimate details of the lives of its citizens. CDR members are much more than watchful neighbors in revolutionary Cuba; they are the sprawling sensory organs of the state itself, enabling it to extend its tentacles deeply into the most private conversations and most frivolous details of people's everyday lives.

It is not surprising, then, that popular discourse sometimes openly mocks the vulgarity of revolutionary vigilance and power by conjuring up images of a grotesque body politic. Moreover, these images, most often expressed in jest, also touch on political life and economic austerity during the Special Period. Take, for instance, the romantic image of the down-to-earth, self-sacrificing, working-man hero referred to as the "New Man" (*hombre nuevo*). As a model citizen, the New Man foregoes material incentives; his labor is never merely an economic resource, but rather a sincere expression of his moral commitment to the building of a revolutionary society. Yet, in popular discourse, he is sometimes mockingly depicted as a man of fantastic physical proportions and extraordinary sensory prowess. The New Man, Cubans joke, should have larger eyes so that he can see more, larger ears so that he can hear more, a fat and agile tongue so that he can be a more effective snitch, more than two hands so he can work and produce more, no stomach so that he will not get hungry, larger feet so that he can stand longer while listening to endless political speeches and endure arduous political marches in front of the U.S. Interests Section. Similar images of a grotesque body politic are also conjured up in depictions of local meddlers. "Busybodies," one expression goes, "cannot be deaf." The meaning is subtle: nosy people cannot be hard of hearing, for they must be gifted with extraordinary auditory powers, able to pick up on whispered conversations from a distance. Indeed, local busybodies are sometimes referred to as "elephants," referring to their metaphorically large ears, in other words, their uncanny ability to hear things the rest of us cannot.

The Poetics and Politics of Predation

The CDRs are not merely responses to but actually productive of the pervasive sense of social predation that haunts the popular imagination in contemporary Cuba. Although the forces that have historically threatened the sovereignty of the Cuban nation are undeniably real, revolutionary officialdom has clearly made every effort to sustain and inflate mass apprehensions of future invasion and harness the fears it incites in order to expand its reach into and control over everyday life and the imaginary of its subjects. The CDRs serve as a daily reminder that sinister forces lie in wait. Hidden within the dark nooks and crannies of the body politic, these forces prey on civil society like hungry hyenas, always prepared to take what is not rightfully theirs.

What is striking is the extent to which these state-sponsored fictions of the real resonate with neocolonial fantasies regarding the hidden social menace of magic and sorcery, especially those of African origin. Take, for example, the National Directorate's proclamation quoted above. If we replace the terms "worms" and "Yankee" with "brujo" and "Devil," respectively, the meaning hardly changes—"the [brujos] are waiting, hidden in the shadows, to do their ruinous work of destruction and terror, paid for by the [Devil's] gold to which they have sold their hearts and consciences." These two imaginations—that is, the political and the popular—in which the specter of mercenary sociality figures so prominently, incite and feed on the nervous exuberance of the other. In a society in which the pernicious gaze and bad tongues of one's neighbors are a daily source of anxiety and social tension, the lines separating political from magical forms of predation and vigilance become increasingly blurred.

A mulatta in her mid-forties, La Mariquilla was officially employed as a kitchen assistant in a local primary school. Her meager monthly income of about seven U.S. dollars at the time was barely enough to put food on the table. She, like many Cubans in her situation, supplemented her income by relying on her own creative wits and entrepreneurial skills within the ubiquitous black market economy. Despite significant efforts by the revolutionary government to eradicate race- and class-related disparities, the current economic crisis in Cuba has had a more devastating impact on the black and mulatto population. This is because they are far less likely than their white counterparts to have family abroad to send dollar remittances during hard economic times, and also because they have fewer ties to the dollar economy generated by the growing tourist industry (Pérez Sarduy and Stubbs 2000).

La Mariquilla's barrio is comprised of a fairly "typical" revolutionary mix of manual laborers, working-class professionals, military career men, party enthusiasts, ritual specialists, retired elders, and, of course, a motley assortment of unemployed petty entrepreneurs, hustlers, and the blessed recipients of dollar remittances from abroad. Located along a major thoroughfare that runs through the commercial and administrative center of the municipality, La Mariquilla's house is on any average day passed by literally hundreds of people. Given the tropical heat she, like most Cubans, keeps her front door open to allow for some ventilation, a commonplace which often fosters a very deceptive sense of neighborly openness and transparency. Walking down the street, for example, the sounds of the latest timba (percussion-driven Cuban salsa) and reggaetón (a youth dance music combining reggae, dancehall, and hip-hop) blaring from home stereos spill out into public space, neighbors sit on their front stoops talking or else in their living rooms watching telenovelas or black market videocassettes, and people generally come and go according to considerably more relaxed social norms, often foregoing courteous knocking by simply calling each other's names out. Lurking just beneath the surface of neighborly informality and openness, however, is a much more opaque world of social predation, frequently taking place through magical proxy and the concealed circulation of malicious rumor and gossip.

During the time I stayed with La Mariquilla's family, I was witness to (and, on a few occasions, partly the reason for) numerous spiritual "cleansings" of the house (limpiezas de casa) and the accumulation of a bewildering number of ritual "fortifications" and protective charms intended to safeguard the home and its inhabitants. Shortly after I came to live with her family, for example, La Mariquilla awoke one day to find coffee grinds spread out on the sidewalk directly in front of her house, so she quickly washed them away with a bucket of water before allowing anyone to leave. She was convinced it was the work of sorcery. La Mariquilla decided to go see Arcaño, a brujo specializing in the magic of Palo, an Afro-Creole religious formation with roots in the Congo. After telling him the situation, Arcaño agreed that the house was in need of a good "cleansing."

The following morning, Arcaño began by placing seven different kinds of herbs in two piles in front of the home's Elegguá. He then took some cane liquor and blew it on the altar and the two piles of herbs. He crushed up some chalk and dropped the dust on the pile. Then, beginning in the bathroom in the back patio and moving methodically through the rooms that led to the entrance of the house, he beat the walls violently with the herbs. When he finished he placed the two piles of herbs behind the threshold of the front door and drew two identical ritual "signatures" (firmas) on each of the two front doors—the sign of Lucero Mundo, an mpungu or spirit in the Palo pantheon said to share some affinities with Elegguá. Arcaño then retrieved a bottle from his belongings containing alcohol. Although gunpowder is preferred for such rites, it is often hard to come by, access depending entirely on one's connections with local policemen and military personnel. Arcaño poured the contents of the bottle in a thin stream leading from the herbs to the bottle, which he positioned to face towards the now-open front door, and then lit it. There was a small explosion. The "signatures" and the small explosion, he explained, would drive out or blow away any negative influence or presence (quimbasa), conjuring trick (trampa), or wickedness (maldá) in the house that were now concentrated in the herbs.

As if this was not enough, later that same day Arcaño got to work cutting a groove in the tile located in the threshold of the front door where he would place a small metal chain that he had soaked in various herbs and chicken's blood moments earlier. He said that the chain would guard the house by preventing the entry of magical dust and any uninvited spirits of the dead sent there to do harm. A few inches from the chain he hammered a railroad spike that had been "charged" with magical substances into the floor. The spike would warn of any suspicious movement by rivals or enemies. La Mariquilla then asked me to purchase a small turtle, which Arcaño placed in a water basin behind the front door. The turtle would help to "clean" the house of any contaminating or harmful magical substances (maldá). "The turtle," they said, "eats the bad magic."

All of these mystical agents, not to mention the ever-present Elegguá, represent the front line of defense in the daily fight to maintain the boundaries separating la casa from la calle; they provide a small but powerful mystical arsenal against the polluting substances that enter from the street and, by extension, the social predations of fellow comrades.

After suggesting that perhaps they were all just a little too paranoid about their neighbors' alleged aggressions, both magical and mundane, La Mariquilla defended her actions as absolutely necessary. "You don't understand because you are not Cuban," she said, speaking to me in the soft yet authoritative tone of an adult who wants to convey something important to a child,

It's not like before [the Special Period]. Now, there is no trust and a lot of interest [ulterior motives and the capitalistic desire for personal gain]. You can't trust your neighbor; you can't trust your coworkers; you can't trust the busybodies in the CDR. Life is hard. You can no longer rely on the state. You can only depend on yourself and your family. Here there is a lot of gaze, a lot of tongue, a lot of envy, a lot of malice. All Cubans are not the same. Some of them are wicked.

Caridad then told a story that corroborated her mother's perception of the links between magical predation, economic austerity, and moral decay during the Special Period. Before going to live in Miami, Rogelio, a white man who lived across the street, and his family had always had bad luck. Despite their best efforts, they were always destitute. Then, one of his sisters won the visa lottery and went to live in Miami. Rogelio began receiving dollar remittances from her and with that money underwent the lengthy and expensive initiation rites required to become a babalao (an Ifá divination priest).

"All of sudden," Caridad continued, "he shows up one day dressed in white; he made himself a babalao, and no one knew."

The first initiations Rogelio performed were for foreign tourists, fueling local accusations that he only wanted to enrich himself. Although the family benefited from this new income source, Rogelio still could not shake his bad luck. He wanted desperately to leave the island for Miami in pursuit of better economic opportunities, but so far his repeated efforts to win the visa lottery had failed. However, Rogelio's next-door neighbors, Ildamis and her daughter, had always been gifted with good fortune. While others had languished in deteriorating economic conditions, they had always had luck finding new income sources and meeting foreign tourists. So, when Rogelio offered to perform the ceremony known as "receiving" the warrior saints (those being Eleggúa, Ogún, Ochosi, and Osún)—a separate and distinct ceremony that may or may not be succeeded by full initiation ("making saint")—saying he would to do it for free, Ildamis and her daughter enthusiastically accepted.

A few weeks after the ceremony, the women's luck changed dramatically; they began to experience one great misfortune after another, including the death of a loved one and a rapid decline in their standard of living. Rogelio, on the other hand, soon won the visa lottery. Rumors then circulated in the neighborhood that he had ensorcelled Ildamis and her daughter through the medium of the warrior saints. Caridad referred to this kind of sorcery as "luck-switching" (cambia suerte), a creative twist on a rite known as "switching lives" (cambia vida) in which one tricks death by causing it to mistake a sacrificial animal for oneself. Rogelio now lives in Miami and sends dollar remittances to the family members he left behind. Two of them, a sister and a nephew, made saint during my stay. Rosita, his sister, is now a full-time santera, frequently performing ceremonies and other ritual work for her clients. Her ritual sincerity is also the subject of much local debate.

Fears of this kind of mystical victimization are exacerbated by countless other stories of hustling priest-healers and sorcerers who prey on their clients' vulnerabilities and exploit their financial resources. These behind-the-scenes brokers of desire are the subject of scorn in many popular jokes. Take, for example, the following passage from one of popular comedian Roberto Riverón's acts:

> You know that we [Cubans] have raised sorcery and witchcraft to a whole new level. Yeah, because if you go to Guanabacoa with a foreigner they will invoke the saint for him through the Internet! . . . When they tell a Cuban that they're going to get to travel [leave the country], the first thing they do is go to Guanabacoa. All of them! Their first visit before they even tell their mother, brother, wife is to the padrino [ritual godfather]! . . . You all know that one has to secure a trip no matter how much it costs. The Cuban goes to Guanabacoa and says to his ritual godfather, 'Padrino, the yuma is going to send me a letter of invitation [a form needed to secure an exit permit]. Open the roads for me!' When the padrino finds out there's going to be a trip, that there is money . . . you know how they are . . . at that very moment he says, 'I see a bad, bad, bad sign [osogbo]. There is a gray-haired white man making a shadow over your trip.' When a Cuban says, 'gray-haired white man,' he means the exploitive police boss of the sector! 'Padrino, what can I do in order for you to open the roads for me? I have to travel.' The padrino then tells him, 'stay calm, this can be resolved with four black hens, four white doves, and half a cow!' [2]

Riverón's bit prompted howls of laughter from my Cuban friends. Although they may be lost on foreign audiences, these comedic stabs at the island's ritual specialists and state functionaries resonate with domestic audiences for several reasons. First, he mocks those who would do just about anything, including using the Internet to conjure spirits, to satisfy tourist demand for local exotica. Second, he jokes that the bureaucratic red tape one has to overcome in order to go live abroad is so bewildering and the process so unpredictable that many who do receive a coveted invitation letter in fact go straight to their padrino rather than their family with the news. This is because they know they will need their padrino's magic to help remove the many obstacles posed by a notoriously slow and tangled government bureaucracy, on the one hand, and to protect them from the jealousy and envy of neighbors, friends, and family on the other. Yet the padrino has his own material interests. He appeals to racial sentiments by blaming the alleged bad luck of the would-be black traveler on the manipulations of an exploitive white police chief (jefe de sector)—that is, the official who checks in regularly with the CDR presidents to gather information on local residents, something the traveler will need to go well if he is to receive permission from the authorities to leave. In order to supposedly remedy the situation, the padrino makes the impossible demand of half a cow of the cash-hungry would-be traveler. Because resources are scarce in Cuba and beef happens to be tightly controlled by the state, reserved exclusively for the tourist industry, this payment is astronomically high.

Magic and the Culture of Vigilance

The irony of rites like the limpieza de casa, the bewildering accumulation of protective charms, and the employment of reptiles that "eat" bad magic borders on the surreal. Spurned by revolutionary officialdom as the fantasy of pure production out of nothing, magic becomes the only viable means of fighting against the social disorder and moral decay that exists beneath the public fiction of a tropical socialist paradise. Yet the state itself is a major player in these hidden struggles and magical battles. The sprawling surveillance apparatus of the revolutionary state is productive of local perceptions of a leadership gifted with a seemingly preternatural gaze and the magical propensity to be everywhere at once, and the people answer in kind. In short, the political economy of magic in post-Soviet Cuba is defined by a dialectical interplay of attributions and counter-attributions of power that bring popular culture and the state together within the same social field (compare Taussig 1980: 109).

27 June 2004: On the street corner stands one of the ubiquitous national shrines to José Martí. The shrine is kitsch—a simple, mass-produced white plastic bust atop a cement pedestal—but it stands in honor of the most revered ancestor in the national pantheon and the quintessential symbol of revolutionary political morality. Like some kind of ghostly white sentinel, a plastic panopticon, Martí invites local comrades to internalize his gaze; the revolution staring at itself. Around the shrine, two neighborhood children are absorbed in play, trailing behind them a makeshift kite fashioned out of a white plastic bag and the magnetic tape from an old cassette. The grandmother of the older one stands in her bathrobe on the sidewalk absorbing the latest gossip from a loose-tongued neighbor. A Russian Lada turns the corner, the latest timba briefly punctuating the dusky air—"La Habana me queda chiquita," Pachito Alonso intones.

As the night shadows spread over the barrio like spilled ink, the yuma ethnographer watches several pedestrians nearly stumble over a bundle of ritual debris left on the street corner, a banal reminder that Martí is not the only ghostly figure lurking within the urban social landscape. The street intersection is also the cosmological crossroads (cuatro esquina), the stomping-ground of Eleggua. Unlike Martí's shrine, which stands in public space, Eleggua's effigy is normally concealed behind domestic doors, where he stands guard on the floor, the first line of mystical defense in the daily battle to protect the security and communal benevolence of the home from the social and mystical pollution of la calle (the street). How does Eleggua, I wonder, receive his esteemed guest on the corner? What secrets does Martí whisper to the spirit-owner, secrets that no one else but them can hear? Do local residents ever ponder this surreal topography of power? Or does it only come across as marvelously strange to outsiders like me?

I believe it was the French surrealist André Breton who once made that enigmatic statement about Cuba being "too surreal a country to be lived in."[3] *One can almost hear the laugh of irony here. I am reminded of a tourist pamphlet I found on one of my Cuban friends' bookshelves. The writer enthusiastically embraces the utopian wonders of "tropical socialism." Nothing like the bleak and bone-chilling milieu of Moscow, Havana is a socialist capital in a tropical paradise, a "place of contrasts" that "assaults the senses." The ironies associated with these "contrasts," however, often implicate the tourist's romantic fantasies in a chamber of mirrors in which echo the vivacious howls of Rabelaisian laughter. Whereas bandanas, shirts, pants, baseball caps, and tattoos emblazoned with the image of the U.S. flag became fashionable among Cuban youth during the Special Period, it is the foreign tourist who is more likely to be seen sporting berets and t-shirts displaying Che Guevara's famous portrait, or the guayaberas associated more with state security agents and government officials than with the populace.*

The resplendent arroz con mango that is revolutionary Cuba today seems too banal to strike wonder in the hearts and minds of the citizenry. And the real question is how to write about the dream-like marvels of a social reality that is for the people who live it hopelessly mundane.

Opening the door just enough to peer out into the neighborhood, Arcaño murmured, seemingly to himself, "*Coño*, the gaze here is overwhelming!" He sensed in this brief glance that La Mariquilla and her family were the objects of a great deal of neighborly curiosity and scrutiny. "Here, you can feel the eyes touching you," he said.

"You don't know nothing," Caridad responded, repeating a couple of popular expressions I would hear over and over again, "here, people risk blindness looking for what is not theirs. And, from so much talking, their tongues fall to the floor [that is, they talk so much that their tongues grow so fat and distended that they fall out of the mouth and touch the floor]."

The sense of being the object of so much scrutiny and potentially dangerous talk is a banal aspect of everyday life. Suspicions of neighborly predations, however, are often provoked by specific incidents. On one occasion, for instance, La Mariquilla's attempt to magically "tie the tongue" (*amarrar la lengua*) of a neighbor targeted El Padrón, a devout follower of the Comandante's "religion," as one put it, and former president of the block CDR. Although retired, El Padrón still remained intimately involved in neighborhood affairs. Below, my field notes describe the incident that provoked La Mariquilla's anxiety.

13 August 2004: La Mariquilla has been planning a toque de santo (Ocha or Santería ceremony with batá drums) for weeks. But today is the Comandante's birthday and, worried that hosting such a ritual gathering on this day might be considered disrespectful, she went around feeling things out, returning, to my surprise, with a permission slip, complete with the appropriate rubber stamp, from the local branch of the National Revolutionary Police (PNR) saying that she could go ahead with her plans.

After the ceremony Antonio and I were sitting on the front stoop when El Padrón happened to pass by. Seeing us, he stopped. With a toothpick dangling from his mouth he said, looking at me, "You know, there is more freedom here in this country than anywhere in the world. This one," he said, tapping his cane on Antonio's knee (he is dark-skinned) while still looking fixedly at me, "he can be a lawyer, a doctor, whatever." Antonio remained courteous, but after El Padrón left he expressed his outrage at the incident. His perception was that El Padrón had heard the drums, waited for them to cease, and then decided to counter any misconceptions that the yuma ethnographer might have regarding "witchcraft" by reminding him that Cuba was a beacon of racial freedom and socialist modernity, quite unlike that imperial enemy to the north. Antonio was, at the time, unemployed. As many Cubans say, "it is not worth the effort" (no vale la pena) to work for meager government salaries when people can do better fending for themselves. Thus there was a concern that El Padrón might use his passionate distaste for "black things" (cosas de negro), such as "sinister" rituals involving drums, as a pretext to report Antonio's idleness to local authorities. La Mariquilla therefore "tied" his tongue.

Many other sources of La Mariquilla's recurring anxieties seemed to warrant the use of magic. Both my unexplained association with the household and Caridad's recent engagement to a foreigner were the cause of much neighborly speculation. Although I was not paying La Mariquilla to stay there, everyone assumed that I was, and since she was not licensed to rent to foreigners it became necessary to "tie the tongues" of local busybodies and snitches. My presence also fueled rumors falsely accusing La Mariquilla and Caridad of being *jineteras* (female hustlers of foreign tourists). These speculations associated them not only with prerevolutionary vices such as prostitution, but also with the petty entrepreneurism and incipient capitalist values that threaten to erode socialist modernity on the island. La Mariquilla was convinced that certain of her neighbors were envious of the family due to my close association with the household.

Protection against the potentially harmful effects of this rather intense neighborly vigilance and gossip would require much more ritual work. Arcaño felt that the family needed to take extra precautions. He told La Mariquilla and her daughter—the ostensibly weaker or more vulnerable members of the household—to purchase a protective charm called an *azabache*, or "The Eyes of Santa Lucía," to resist the influence of evil eye and, by extension, the vigilant gaze of envious neighbors. The charm is a small pendant of glaring eyes with two beads, one red and one black. They bought one immediately. La Mariquilla attached hers to her ritual necklace (*collar*) and Caridad pinned hers on the inside of her blouse.

A few days later, following Arcaño's advice, La Mariquilla placed a refashioned commercial doll (*kini kini*) garbed in a satin white dress and head scarf on a table facing the front door. Arcaño "charged" the doll with magical substances and La Mariquilla had it baptized in the local Catholic church, a common occurrence on the island. This spirit-doll, which can be seen from the street, whom La Mariquilla refers to as her "white Congolese girl" (*la conga blanca*), added another layer of vigilance over the house and neutralized any contaminating substances before they could harm its inhabitants. Arcaño returned a couple of days later to hang some plant material referred to as "cow's tongue" (*vaca lengua*) over the front door in order to protect against malicious rumor and gossip. Finally, I accompanied La Mariquilla to purchase a small plastic plaque, containing the image of a conjoined eye and tongue penetrated by a knife, which she hung in her living room.

These ritual precautions and magical protections, as numerous as they were, still did not quell La Mariquilla's anxieties concerning the pernicious gaze and bad tongues of her neighbors. I witnessed her on more than one occasion write the name of some suspicious neighbor or associate in pencil on an egg, which she then secretly threw to the ground on a corner of the street intersection (that is, a crossroads) by her house. On other occasions she wrote their names on *cartucha* paper, which she then rolled up in an herb called "hen's foot" (*pata de gallina*) and, after tying it with red and black thread, placed it alongside her Elegguá.

The Fictional Reality of State Vigilance

When I returned to Cuba in July 2009, La Mariquilla had removed the image of the conjoined eye and tongue from her living room. She had replaced it with a freshly painted charm-image that now hung just above her front door and was visible from the street. Driving and walking around the city that month I noticed more and more of these images—in Regla, Old Havana, and Marianao. What, I wondered, was behind the movement of these images from interior domestic space, such as living room walls, to the publicly visible exteriors of porticos and doors?

The repositioning of these charm-images, it seems, is directly linked to perceptions conflating the rise in forms of social predation with the amplification of state vigilance during the Special Period. Many spoke as if the country was besieged not by agents of imperial governments or invading foreign armies, but rather by hidden social forces and afflictions which arose domestically. As my neighbor had said, the country's most palpable enemy was its own penchant for meddling and gossip. As competition over scarce resources grew worse and forms of socioeconomic differentiation became ever more visible during the Special Period, the sense of being the object of constant and intrusive scrutiny by others was often cast in magical terms. The prying gaze and gossip of neighbors, friends, and family soon came to be seen as potential acts of predation that could bewitch and thus ruin one's already imperiled chances of moving forward in difficult and competitive economic conditions. This situation, then, seemed to require the novel use of old magic to protect oneself and one's family from the social predations and afflictions of a society in the midst of an uncertain transition.

The epidemic of evil eye and malicious rumor and gossip that began in the 1990s also directly implicated revolutionary officialdom. Much of the regime's survival over the past several decades is no doubt linked to what is, in fact, a massive and sprawling surveillance apparatus which includes a highly organized, nationwide network of neighborhood-based political watchdog groups. Since the 1990s, the country's economic woes have diminished the moral authority of the state in the eyes of many. Yet, so far, it appears that popular discontent with deteriorating economic and living conditions has not led to a significant erosion of the state's actual policing powers. The state, for instance, aware of its political vulnerability, actually stepped up surveillance efforts during the Special Period, even though it could not possibly attend to every violation of or potential threat to its power and authority in the early years of the crisis. Although the CDRs may have become more selective in reporting petty economic crime to the local police and popular assemblies—after all, their members are, by necessity, often full and willing participants in the black market economy—they remained on high alert, especially when it came to political matters. By the time of my fieldwork the state had returned to politics as usual—cracking down on unlicensed entrepreneurs, imposing heavy taxes and fines on independent economic sectors, rooting out corruption in state-managed enterprises, reasserting control over forms of popular expression such as music, and rounding up and jailing dissidents en masse. The state's rather heavy-handed reintegration into everyday economic and political life manifested itself as a visceral presence—its powers of surveillance were so real that you could "feel its eyes touching you."

Yet in some ways vigilance has also been partly a myth of the state. The sense that one's neighbors are forever watching and listening, ready to pick up on the slightest hint of ideological betrayal and report it to the authorities (as is their revolutionary duty), fuels popular perceptions and images of a state pregnant with the extraordinary sensory powers of the body politic. Moreover, given their tendency to personify the state rather than speak of it as an abstract entity, Cubans often locate the repository for all the information that flows in from these "millions of membranes" in the body and figure of one man—the Comandante. "He knows everything that happens here," and, "he is always watching and listening," people say. The specter of state vigilance haunts the public imaginary, arousing images of its magical capacity to see and hear everything and be everywhere at once. It is perhaps unsurprising, then, that Cubans sometime conflate the anxieties stirred up by images of an all-seeing state with suspicions and fears of becoming the victim of evil eye and the bewitching tongues of their neighbors. The state not only fuels popular anxiety regarding the menacing social forces that lurk in the shadows—recall, for instance, the imagery of worms used in one of the CDRs earliest proclamations—but by encouraging neighbors to spy and report on each other's private lives, it emphasizes the predatory nature of state vigilance itself. Forever lurking within the shadows of the body politic, it is always there—everywhere—lying in wait, ready at any moment to rear its ugly head and flex its political muscle.

Certainly protective charms, limpiezas, and other magic forces are being put to novel use in assuaging some of the nervous exuberance associated with this culture of vigilance. Yet to simply call their use "resistance" would be to miss the ways in which both popular and official imaginaries regarding the hidden social menaces that threaten the nation from within fuel and feed off the excesses of the other. The fictional reality of state vigilance, as this chapter illustrates, brings both popular culture and the state together within the same intimate and promiscuous field of political fantasy and desire. And, as will become increasingly clear, the imaginary center of state power around which many of these political fantasies and desires revolve is condensed into the figure of a single individual—the nation's ailing yet larger-than-life former president. It is ultimately the Comandante himself who serves as the screen upon which both vernacular and revolutionary imaginaries of power not only mingle but, in some cases, coalesce.

The Opacity of Power

CHAPTER 3

If, as Joel James suggested, the Cuban nation itself is a "great nganga," then it is one whose magical capacities are often envisioned in the popular imagination as personally conjured and harnessed to the machinery of state by the Comandante himself.

Recent changes in the political leadership on the island have so far done little to undermine the conflation of state power with the figure of the Comandante in the popular imagination. In 2006, the nation's iconic revolutionary leader suffered the onset of an undisclosed and apparently debilitating illness. Still a closely guarded state secret, the illness eventually led to his retirement and the transfer of power to his not-much-younger brother. Despite this momentous political development, tales of the Comandante's enduring control over national politics and the machinations of state, not to mention stories regarding his hidden powers and magic, continue to circulate in the form of local rumor and gossip. Given his sudden and mysterious absence from public life and the fact that many find it hard to imagine a world without him—convinced, for example, that he is still the one secretly calling the shots—the Comandante himself is now imagined to be a hidden presence animating national politics and wielding state power from within. "Have you seen the pictures?" a Havana resident asked me in June 2009. "He's a skeleton, a ghost. They've replaced all his organs with plastic ones but he still refuses to die. You never see him anymore but everyone knows he's still working things from behind the door."[1]

And so, slowly, there begins to emerge the image of an aging patriarch who, after nearly half a century of rule, suddenly vanished from the public stage, but whose figure still haunts the public imaginary like a living ghost. Stuffed with prosthetic organs and enhanced with his magic vitamins, this monumental phantom continues to work his giant nganga that is the slumbering power of the nation—its dreams and its dead—from somewhere behind the scenes, deep within the shadowy corridors of state power.

Unbridled Realities

This image of an illustrious yet solitary head of state roaming the dark halls of his palace and conjuring up all sorts of monumental fantasies, delusions, and pathologies is a familiar one. In some ways (but certainly not all), it resonates with Gabriel García Márquez's stunning portrait of an incredibly old and unnamed Caribbean tyrant, a lonely monster who—deftly skilled in the barren politics of survival and shrouded in the chimera of absolute power and colossal terror—wanders through his palace at night locking the doors, searching for assassins, and reading the graffiti on the walls of the servants' toilet like an oracle (1975).

Creating a composite image of countless Latin American and Caribbean despots, García Márquez refuses to disentangle fact from fiction in this tale of power. He seems to avoid any attempt to penetrate the aura of mystique that surrounds this fictional yet historically tangible head of state in the popular imagination. Rather, he paints a deliberately outlandish portrait, purposefully Rabelaisian in its excesses and distortions, depicting a world in which the role of the imagination in politics is a mundane quality of social experience, a reality shot through and through with the magical pathos of power. It should come as no surprise, then, that some of his critics accuse him of reveling in a surrealistic fantasy too lavish in tone to accurately convey the brutal realities of authoritarian power (see Kennedy 1976).

In his Nobel Prize lecture, García Márquez responds to these and other critiques. His comments are worth quoting at some length:

> Our independence from Spanish domination did not put us beyond the reach of madness. General Antonio López de Santana, three times dictator of Mexico, held a magnificent funeral for the right leg he had lost in the so-called Pastry War. General Gabriel García Moreno ruled Ecuador for sixteen years as an absolute monarch; at his wake,

the corpse was seated on the presidential chair, decked out in full-dress uniform and a protective layer of medals. General Maximiliano Hernández Martínez, the theosophical despot of El Salvador who had thirty thousand peasants slaughtered in a savage massacre, invented a pendulum to detect poison in his food, and had streetlamps draped in red paper to defeat an epidemic of scarlet fever. The statue to General Francisco Morazán erected in the main square of Tegucigalpa is actually one of Marshal Ney, purchased at a Paris warehouse of second-hand sculptures. . . .

Since then, the Europeans of good will—and sometimes those of bad, as well—have been struck, with ever greater force, by the unearthly tidings of Latin America, that boundless realm of haunted men and historic women, whose unending obstinacy blurs into legend. . . .

I dare to think that it is this outsized reality, and not just its literary expression, that has deserved the attention of the Swedish Academy of Letters. A reality not of paper, but one that lives within us and determines each instant of our countless daily deaths, and that nourishes a source of insatiable creativity, full of sorrow and beauty, of which this roving and nostalgic Colombian is but one cipher more, singled out by fortune. Poets and beggars, musicians and prophets, warriors and scoundrels, all creatures of that unbridled reality, we have had to ask but little of imagination, for *our crucial problem has been a lack of conventional means to render our lives believable.* This, my friends, is the crux of our solitude. (emphasis added; García Márquez 1982)

When it comes to conveying these "unbridled realities," the poverty of conventional representational strategies and styles is just as much an issue in ethnography as it is in the literary world of novelists like García Márquez. As he put it many years before, it is not the writing but the reality of Latin American and Caribbean social life and history itself that is "totally Rabelaisian" (García Márquez 1968: 53). In Latin America and the Caribbean, to paraphrase another of his remarks on this issue, surrealism runs through the streets, rendering prosaic literary strategies wholly inappropriate and ineffective.

Likewise, in Cuba, the magical (and often surreal) élan of power and historical memory thickens the air, so much so that even the revolutionary state, with all its hard-nosed emphasis on the demystifying realism of

Marxist-Leninist ideology, has found it difficult over the years to resist floating about within it. Indeed, politics and magic are (and have been for as long as anyone can remember) deeply entangled in the Cuban imagination. The question becomes not so much how to disentangle fact from fiction in the study of these political imaginaries as how to convey something of their lived veracity and meaning.

Political Authority and the Cultural Imagination

The difficulty that many have believing in the Comandante's resignation, not to mention his mortality, is, I would suggest, related to a much broader issue. Like other Caribbean leaders (see Derby 1999), the Comandante has been converted into a kind of fetish, an object of mystique whose powers seem to transcend natural laws and normal human limitations. Much of this is related to what is often imagined to be his uncanny ability to survive the most perilous of situations unscathed—he walked away from the attack on Batista's largest military garrison largely unharmed despite the fact that more than half of the fighters he organized for the assault were killed; he led a successful revolution against a corrupt dictator whose regime had been propped up by a world superpower (the United States); he crushed a CIA-backed foreign invasion in a matter of days; he has survived several hundred assassination attempts; and he brought the world the closest it has ever been to nuclear war without suffering any lasting political consequences. The revolutionary leader's capacity to transcend the boundaries of the "possible" was more recently confirmed when his personal physician, in an attempt to dispel rumors of his deteriorating health, reported that he was in such impeccable physical condition that he would live to be one hundred and forty years old (see Toscano Segovia 2004). And even though the danger of speaking openly about his eventual death has subsided in the last few years, the sense that he will somehow always remain a haunting presence is already stirring the public imaginary. "Even if he passed away today," one of La Mariquilla's neighbors told me, "they're not going to tell us about it. The state will make him a mummy so that we'll go on thinking he's still there."

As the imaginary center of state power on the island and a near-permanent fixture of the world political scene for nearly half a century, the Comandante has long been the screen for a bewildering array of moralizing political fantasies and desires. The mythologies that envelop this former head of state within a magical aura of heightened value and power, I propose, offer a promising vantage point from which to consider the relationship between political authority and the cultural imagination. Most of us are accustomed to thinking of politics as having little to do with the symbolic constructions and ideological fictions that characterize the cultural arena. Although the monarchs of earlier historical epochs may have been greatly invested in theatrical spectacles of power, modern politics is often uncritically assumed to be a wholly demystified arena of rational, utilitarian calculations and acts, an eminently practical, no-nonsense world entirely stripped of cultural embellishment. Power, however, does not operate within a cultural vacuum. Even though Weber may have promised us a world of government functionaries dwelling like so many zombies in a bureaucratic iron cage, power not only remains an inherently mysterious and opaque world, but it conjures up its own uniquely modern enchantments and cultural fantasies (Geertz 1977; Sanders and West 2003). What distinguishes modern politics from the political fashions of old, as Clifford Geertz noted many years ago, "[is] a certain view of the affinity between the sort of power that moves men and the sort that moves mountains, not the sense that there is one" (1977: 168). It is not somehow standing outside the social and cultural order in an intoxicated state of narcissistic exaltation that makes political authority appear numinous, but rather its "deep, intimate involvement . . . in the master fictions by which that order lives" (Geertz 1977: 171).

Like others, then, I take popular representations of the fetish powers of the Cuban state to be just as integral to the image of authority as the political figures themselves (Taussig 1992; Derby 1999: 96). Here I want to focus on a particular set of narratives and images that trace the Comandante's authority to a hidden world of magic, sorcery, and spirits. My central argument is that these tales give expression to a particular cultural understanding of power that is deeply rooted in the eccentricities of Cuban history. As I describe below, these metaphorical and magical constructions of power reflect a cultural ambivalence regarding the foundations of political authority. Rather than seeing power as a gift invested in political leaders and governmental bodies by the people, these narratives and images place the source of state power in a hidden world of mysterious, powerful forces. Yet they do so, I suggest, in very different ways with very different kinds of implications. Whereas some of these tales seem to envision the political process in terms of a model of power based on spiritual idioms of patronage, others appear to foreground a model of power based on magical idioms of command and domination.

The Comandante's Mystique

Despite rumors of the Comandante's deteriorating health and the fact that he has not publicly appeared for several years, Cubans have grown accustomed to seeing the Comandante as a permanent fixture of the national political landscape. Like some kind of monument in the flesh, this petrified image of the revolutionary leader reflects a timeless mythology of political indestructibility, often finding its most concrete expression in depictions of his superhuman body. In the popular imagination the Comandante, paradoxically, has a mortal yet invincible body, one that "condenses in itself all strengths, all talents, and defies the laws of nature by his super-male energy" (Lefort 1986: 300). I often heard people allude to this by referencing a mambo made popular by Beny Moré called "Siguaraya," comparing the song's imagery with depictions of the Comandante's political indestructibility. One of the song's most memorable lines is: "Siguaraya no, no. Without permission you are not going to knock it down" (*siguaraya que va, que va, sin permiso no va a tumbá*). The siguaraya is a strong, tough species of wild mahogany said to be very difficult to cut down. Given its extraordinary durability, the siguaraya is believed by many to possess magical properties. It is highly valued by local brujos, for example, who refer to it as either "path opener" (*abre camino*) or "path breaker" (*rompe camino*). The siguaraya can be ground into a powder and mixed with other magical substances to remove obstacles that prevent one from accomplishing some act or to prevent a rival or enemy from interfering in one's affairs.

Like the siguaraya, the Comandante's legendary durability is also magical. "He has governed here for more than forty-five years," a santero in Guanabacoa told me, "and do you know that almost every U.S. president and all those politicians who visited Cuba and shook his hand during that time have died? That's why he's the siguaraya; without his permission you can't knock him down." The Comandante's unyielding strength and masculinity is also suggested by one of his popular nicknames, *el caballo* (the horse), which, incidentally, some claim was given to him by Beny Moré. The colloquial usage of the term evokes the masculine qualities of a strong man (*caudillo*) who accumulates sociopolitical capital through a combination of machismo, chivalrous charm, and the sheer force of their personality.

In an introduction to a recent collection of the revolutionary leader's own personal writings, for instance, García Márquez describes the "magical" and "hypnotic" powers of his voice, his marathon speeches that "seemed to flow as long as the Amazon River," his photographic memory and voracious consumption of the written word, and his legendary image as "a drifting loner" and "a disorganized and unconventional insomniac, who may turn up for a visit at any hour and keep his host awake until dawn" (2005: 11–12). This image of a seemingly solitary and indestructible head of state who never sleeps (or at least not at night) recalls some of García Márquez's own fictional portraits (1975; 1984). This is perhaps why Arthur Miller's recollection of a dinner with the Comandante in the Palace of the Revolution seems so surreal:

> We had sat down at about 9:30. At 11:30 I began to wilt, and I recalled that [the Comandante], who was clearly gaining strength with every passing moment, enjoyed staying up all night because he slept during most of the day. I was hardly alone in my deepening exhaustion; clearly his retinue, having no doubt heard his stories and remarks numerous times before, were cranking up their eyelids. Now it was 12:30, and then inevitably it got to be 1:30, and [the Comandante] was filling with the energy of his special vitamin pills. . . . I saw that García Márquez was, as far as one could tell, in a deep doze sitting upright in his chair. [The Comandante] was now in full flight, borne aloft by a kind of manic enthusiasm for sheer performance itself. (2004: 15)

As the Comandante sinks deeper and deeper into the hypnotic power of his own manic oratory, the prolific giant of magical realist literature, whose novels have probed deep into the surreal and Rabelaisian excesses of power in Latin America and the Caribbean, is fast asleep in a chair at his side!

I myself remember a night when the state-run media cut into scheduled television programming to broadcast one of the Comandante's famed speeches. Everyone threw up their arms in protest, got chairs, and went to sit on the sidewalk. The streets were unusually full that evening when the lights suddenly went out—a blackout had hit. After that, everyone came outside. We passed at least four hours out there in the dark playing dominos, talking, and drinking. When the electricity returned, the TV turned on and—*voilà!*—there he was, still talking! Everyone threw up their arms in protest again and went back outside. In a similar case, a neighbor told me that she went to bed early one night after a televised speech by the Comandante cut into her favorite telenovela. When she woke up the next morning and turned on the television, he was still there behind the podium, "talking to the dead," as she put it.

"The dead?" I asked.

"Yes," she said, "because they're the only ones up at those hours."

The Comandante is also credited, as hinted in the previous chapter, with extraordinary sensory powers. Again, like the heads of state described in the novels of magical realist writers like Miguel Ángel Austurias (1963) and Gabriel García Márquez (1975), the Comandante has the uncanny power to be in more than one place at once, taking mystical possession over the body politic itself, extending his reach into everyday life and even the private thoughts and dreams of the slumbering masses at night.[2] Moreover, the Comandante has died many times over the years—in 1953, following the attack on the Moncada, in 1956, following his return to the island to wage guerrilla warfare, and several more times since his retreat from public life in 2006 (Booth 2009). Yet there were never any funerals. After every one of his many deaths, the Comandante has miraculously reappeared. As Vicente Botín, who lived in Havana for four years and worked as a correspondent for Televisión Español, writes:

> The unburied body of [the Comandante] walks the streets of Havana. There are those who are sure they have seen him brandishing his fist in the "forest of flags" facing the office of the U.S. Interests Section in Cuba, or in an animated chat with José Martí in Revolution Square. And it's not strange, because although the Cuban dictator is "dead," the state-run media gives assurance of his spectral capacity to appear. With the habitual evangelizing fervor of the Cuban press, the daily newspaper *Trabajadores* explains it as, "the kind of revelation of a modern communist Trinity between the people, the leader, and the revolutionary spirit." Thanks to this conjecture, [the Comandante] remains alive, attentive and vigilant of everything that occurs on the island. (Botín 2009)

It is, perhaps, this "spectral capacity" that explains why when Cubans mention anything sensitive about the Comandante, whether in public or private, they take care not to mention his name, preferring to use bodily gestures instead. There are many such gestures but the most common one is to tap one's shoulder with the index and middle fingers, a reference to the epaulettes that grace his iconic military uniform. Another consists of rubbing, in a downward motion, one's jaws and chin in reference to his beard. More recently, people began to rub their right shoulders inside of their shirts. The Comandante had a bad fall in October of 2004 that broke his knee and arm, one of the rare instances in which he has been publicly seen in a vulnerable physical condition (the other being the fainting spell he experienced during a 2001 speech). Whenever the Comandante appeared in public or on television afterwards, he was seen rubbing his shoulder, so people adopted this bodily habit to refer to him in sensitive public situations. This is mimicry, but it is not practiced in order to capture something of his power. Rather, Cubans use gestures in order to avoid not only being overheard, but the possibility of accidentally conjuring his presence. Using his name in the context of sensitive conservational topics, as Caridad put it, would be to invite a tremendous *salación* (misfortune or calamity). In the Cuban imagination, the names of people and things are believed to harbor magical power; giving voice to the name of a person, spirit, or force can function as an invocation. If a person or thing's presence is not desired, then Cubans will avoid mentioning its name out loud. Just as one does not mention the name of the Cuban *majá* (water snake) but rather a euphemism for it ("21," its number in the local Chinese lottery), one does not mention the Comandante's name in the context of a politically sensitive comment, complaint, or critique. Given his "spectral capacity" to appear as if out of nowhere, uttering his name out loud might be confused with an incantation.

Magic, Power, and the Historical Imagination

Tales of the Comandante's hidden powers and magic are not entirely unique in the Cuban popular imagination. They have their roots in popular chronicles of power that stretch far back into the colonial era. The subject of these popular rumors almost always concerns the secret powers that prominent members of society—landowners, judges, colonial governors, state functionaries, politicians, and heads of state—harness for material and political purposes.[3] By far the richest and most telling of these popular narratives, however, begin with the military dictatorship of General Gerardo Machado.

General Machado, who ruled the island with an iron fist between 1925 and 1933, embarked on an ambitious public works and modernization campaign. As opposition to the political corruption of his regime grew during his second term, Machado responded with increasingly repressive measures, including ordering police raids on the meeting places of his detractors and the torture and murder of student and oppositional leaders. Stories about his use of magical power center around his participation in a public ceremony just three years into his presidency. In celebration of the Sixth Pan-American Conference in 1928, Gerardo Machado hosted a state ceremony celebrating the inauguration of the newly reconstructed Park of Pan-American Fraternity in Havana. On the day of the ceremony, Machado planted a silk-cottonwood tree (*ceiba*) using soil taken from the twenty-one republics who participated in the conference. Because the ceiba is described in Ocha-Ifá mythic narratives as one of the places where the Afro-Creole saint Changó sought refuge from his enemies, some suggest that this masculine god of war, fire, and lightning and thunder ordered Machado to plant the tree to protect the dictator from his enemies (Lachatañeré 2004: 113–14). The park, according to Lydia Cabrera, has an "openly magical character":

> the soil (twenty-one) that they brought to plant it, the gold coins that they threw in the hole, the supposed work of the famous Sotomayor, a mayombero [brujo and spirit medium] friend of some influential politicians of that time, are very eloquent indications that "there's something" there and something very powerful, a very strong evil spell. (1983: 193–94)

One of Cabrera's informants told her that Fraternity Park was where some "prominent men" had buried their fetishes (*macutos*). They suggested that the fetishes had cast a spell on the nation, giving rise to a turbulent history of successive military coups, political assassinations, cronyism, and iron-fisted rule. "There will be neither calm nor order in this country," Cabrera's informant warned, "until they take it away from there and dismantle the nganga General Machado buried there twenty years ago. That prenda [nganga] is so strong and so offended that everything is in disorder . . . and it will cost a lot of blood" (Cabrera 1983: 193–94).

The figure who dominated Cuban politics during the tumultuous decades that followed Machado's fall from power—either behind the scenes or out in the open—was Fulgencio Batista. The leader of the military coup that removed Machado from power, Batista, a simple sergeant at the time, was the de facto leader of Cuba between 1933 and 1940 and president de jure between 1940 and 1944 and again, after yet another military coup, between 1952 and 1959. Batista's unusual rise to power and his enduring, influential behind-the-scenes presence in Cuba's prerevolutionary political culture became the subject of many rumors linking him to occult power. As mentioned earlier, one of these tales recounts how he came into possession of a renowned nganga that once belonged to a group of runaway slaves. The nganga facilitated the expansion of his powers and provided badly needed protection from his many enemies. Other stories claim that his sudden climb to the higher echelons of state power and his ability to so effectively manipulate national politics during that time was due to the fact that he was the "son" of Orúmbila, the owner of fate—or, alternatively, the "son" of Odúa, "king of kings"—regularly consulted the Ifá oracle, and personally financed large animal sacrifices and ceremonies attended by the most prominent santeros and babalaos of Guanabacoa (Lachatañeré 2004: 112–13; Díaz Fabelo 1974: 105–106). Moreover, some of these rumors would later be corroborated by reports published in the state-controlled press following the revolution:

After the triumph of the revolution, the prestigious journal *Bohemia* interviewed Chano Betongó, a known . . . brujo, who on every page insisted: "I was Batista's brujo." It is an ample report of five pages and is signed by Guillermo Villaronda, with some spectacular photos of Chano, a skinny black with dark sunglasses and a large Havana cigar. In his hands he holds . . . a plate on which he has placed a burning candle. The smoke traces strange forms on the bottom of the plate. . . . Chano read the signs; they said that Batista's *caminos* [destinies] were long and wide. But at the bottom of everything he saw "an immense sea, stirred up by a hurricane. A sea that began with a bank of gold and ended on the borders of the sky in a color more alive than blood." During his time in the country, rivers of blood did flow, in effect. . . . At the end of his days, desperate because the winds had changed, Batista made Chano sacrifice six young bulls, six pigs, and twelve hens. "But the smoke that remained in the plate was negative," Chano informed Batista. On January 1, 1959, while the beards [revolutionary fighters] occupied Havana, Chano consulted [his oracle] again: "I took a plate and moved it over the lit candle. Many black birds appeared in the smoke that flowed over the plate. They were birds fleeing ever so slowly. Birds that flew towards the horror. Toward where death reigns over sad islands." (my translation; quoted in Orozco and Bolívar 1998: 487–88)

If some of these tales regarding the hidden powers of the state suggest that the fetishes buried long ago by Machado and his cronies essentially placed a curse on national politics between 1933 and 1959, critics of the current regime believe that they continue to haunt the country into the present:

The spell that Machado cast on us is buried in the heart of Havana. It is planted beneath the ceiba. . . . It has all the iron implements. It contains the bones of the dead, soil from twenty-one countries and the cemetery, a lightning stone, and a prenda more Jewish than Moses. They worked it on Mondays, the day of the devil. To work it General Egregio's cronies looked for the most famous mayomberos [specialists in ritual work using nganga] in the country. Some of them had been slaves born in Africa. Others they already had nearby. Machado then prepared the extension of his powers. He carved out the mantle of cooperativism, reformed the electoral code to impede the legalization of new parties. Sick with pride and vanity, he needed six more years to complete his government work. The opposition grew. . . . Years of bloody reprisals did nothing to crush it. On August 12, 1933, boarding the plane on which he fled to Nassau, the general himself pronounced the prophetic curse, "After me, the chaos." . . . To General Egregio's sorcery we owe revolutionary messianism, pathological anti-Americanism, democratic disenchantment, the paralyzing demagogues, the cult of violence, intolerance even in baseball. All of that led to one inevitable result: [the Comandante's] revolution. Like the genie of the bottle of republican frustrations, he broke out. Machado condemned us to that. Machado's nganga . . . explains the miraculous survival of [the Comandante] at the Moncada, the shipwreck of Granma, the attempts against his life, North American aggression, the missile crisis, the staggering of the Special Period after the collapse of the Soviet Union [and] his providential luck . . . in having in Hugo Chávez another Soviet Union in his pocket (Cino 2005).

Despite its purportedly secular character, the political imaginary of the 1959 Cuban Revolution would also conjure up its own magical seductions and fantasies of power. A week after Chano glimpsed the image of Batista's departure in his prophetic smoke, the Comandante took the podium during his famous commencement speech. By then, the larger public had also begun to cloak the historic events taking place in an aura of mystique. Revolutionary forces had begun to converge on Havana on the first day of the year. For devotees of popular religions like Ocha-Ifá (Santería), this meant that the revolution was linked to the orichas/santos associated with that day on the liturgical calendar of the Catholic Church: Elegguá (El Niño de Atocha), owner of the crossroads and the one who "opens the roads" and controls destinies, and Odúa, creator of the world and "king of kings." According to Miguel Barnet, Ocha-Ifá devotees could be heard chanting Odúa's praises as they addressed the revolutionary leader at the podium (Barnet 1983: 158). The white doves that perched themselves on the Comandante's podium and shoulder were, to some, indubitable proof of his affinities with Obatalá, creator of human bodies and "owner of heads" (that is, intelligence). Regime loyalists at political rallies have also been heard singing songs that conflate the revolutionary leader and his discourse with the sacred power of this revered oricha—"watch out for the bourgeoisie," one song advises, "Obatalá is telling you" (Melgar 1996: 173). From Havana to Miami, both supporters and detractors have never since stopped speculating about which brujo, which priest-healer, or which oracle the Comandante turns to in his hour of need.

The association of Cuba's political leadership with the occult, then, is deeply rooted in the nation's politico-historical imagination. Popular perceptions linking the national leadership with hidden powers and magic are often fueled by the veiled meanings of a leader's specific character traits, the public symbols associated with their rule, the unusual circumstances that precipitated their rise to power, and/or their ability to emerge miraculously unscathed from a period of political turmoil. Ivor Miller has argued that Cuban political leaders deliberately manipulate public symbols in order to broaden their support both at home and abroad (Miller 2000). He takes this to be a particularly striking example of Caribbean duplicity or "double consciousness." Just as Africans and black Creoles hid their true religious practices behind a façade of Catholic saints during slavery, political leaders in the Caribbean make oblique references to local popular religions through the public deployment of European symbols. Thus they are able to both impress upon foreign interests their support of the status quo and persuade those at home that they are aligned with the common people by indicating their personal intimacy with "local secrets and esoteric power" (Miller 2005: 30).

While this is not necessarily an invalid approach, it perhaps too hastily ascribes to Caribbean political leaders an agency or intentionality not entirely of their own making. Although there is some evidence to suggest that Francois Duvalier ("Papa Doc"), the Haitian dictator and "president for life," self-consciously shrouded himself in an aura of vodoun mystique (Laguerre 1998), this is far from clear in the case of other Caribbean dictators (see Derby 1999, for example). I therefore find it more productive in the Cuban context to ask what meanings these narratives hold for those who tell them, a great number of whom are the leaders of cult houses, spirit mediums, and other religious devotees. While it seems clear that these narratives depict Afro-Creole religions and their magic as agents within the nation-state rather than its apolitical folkloric past (Matory 2005: 168), they also have much to say about the nature of power in general. What is most striking about the rumors that circulated about republican-era political leaders is that they coincided with an infamous public witch hunt that specifically targeted black devotees of Afro-Creole religions.[4] The black brujo was considered a social parasite, a vestige of African savagery that posed an obstacle to progress and modernity on the island. Rumors about politicians who commissioned the services of black brujos during this period, then, constitute a kind of subterranean history of power portraying the state as fundamentally hypocritical and inscrutable.

The sense that politics is a murky rather than a transparent world, one where nothing is as it seems, is, I suggest, at the very heart of these narratives. Fueled by popular anxieties concerning the inherent "opacity of power" (West and Sanders 2003: 2), these rumors and images reflect politically meaningful vernacular imaginaries that transform mysteriously powerful figures and events far removed from the contingencies of everyday life into tangible realities (compare Comaroff and Comaroff 1993). By interpreting national symbols and the behavior of public officials in terms of local cosmology and magic, they not only poeticize the relationship between people and spirits, but they significantly broaden the scope of their signifying economy and historical consciousness (see Hill 2003).

Yet, as the above examples suggest, rumors that link Cuban political leaders with Afro-Creole religion and magic suggest some very different visions of the nature of power. These rumors oscillate back and forth between what are ritually distinct popular idioms of power—one associated with the religious formation known as Ochá-Ifá (Santería), and the other typically referred to as Palo. As Stephan Palmié notes, ritually salient local distinctions between these two religious formations are conflated in the popular imagination with moralizing constructions of difference in which Ocha-Ifá is considered a morally sound and proper religion and Palo is cast as a morally dubious one, rife with "magic" and "sorcery" (2002). Yet, although Ocha-Ifá may hypothetically generate moral relationships based on a model of reciprocity among kin—initiates are described as the "children" of the santos—it more closely resembles forms of surplus extractions typical of relations of patronage. When practicers sing the praises of the santos and offer them animal sacrifices, the santos accumulate what is known as *aché* (spiritual energy and power). The santos need aché; they harness this divine energy or power to the task of maintaining order in the cosmos and human world. Yet the santos also redistribute aché. In exchange for their ritual labor and loyalty, the "children" of the santos receive aché from them in the form of spiritual protection and good health. In the ritual economy of Ocha-Ifá, then, "aché circulates through cycles of 'upward delivery' and 'downward distribution'" (Palmié 2004: 251). Palo, on the other hand, gives expression to more overt, magical idioms of command and domination. Those who dabble in the morally dubious world of Palo are brujos who steal, con, or extract spirits of the dead out of the grave, imprison them within fetishes like the nganga, and then force them to do their bidding. Palo thus conjures up a harrowing image of magical power and violence more reminiscent of slavery and wage labor than relations of patronage.

It is by projecting these moralizing constructions of occult power onto political figures and the state that Cubans "[rake] over the coals of events in search of the sense (and senselessness) of their sociality" (Taussig 1987: 394). Whether they give expression to a political cosmology based on relations of patronage or command, popular rumors regarding the hidden forces harnessed by state actors in the exercise of power deserve to be taken seriously. Popular images of the fetish powers of state are no less important to the political process than the political authorities themselves. As cultural constructions and understandings of power, they form an important part of the "master fictions" within which political authority is not only represented, but deeply and intimately involved (Geertz 1977).

Fables of Intimacy

The revolutionary Cuban state radically departs from the typical modern strategies of development, evincing a more postcolonial form of statecraft by attempting to co-opt cultural forces and social movements that were once marginalized by colonial governments (Whitehead 2002: 197). Like the *testimonio* writers described by Amy Fass Emery, this has produced "fables of intimacy" in which the revolutionary vanguard claims to speak for historically marginalized others not as their empathetic leaders but as "Selves intimately involved with the Others they represent" (Emery 1996: 20). Though likely tongue in cheek, the Comandante's claims over the years to be an aboriginal Indian and, following military campaigns in Angola, an expatriate African (during Nelson Mandela's visit to the island he remarked, "Look how far we slaves have come") have nonetheless reinforced his identification with historically marginalized groups, themselves synecdoches of the nation and revolutionary consciousness (Baloyra 1987: 271). These "fables of intimacy" have greatly contributed to popular perceptions of the Comandante's appeal to or possession of occult power.

Here, I find it useful to follow Lauren Derby's lead by examining the extent to which cultural understandings of power in Cuba can be traced to mimetic slippage, religious syncretism, the incongruity between an egalitarian ethos and the presence of unusual power, the political capital associated with access to secret knowledge and occult power, and patron-client networks (1999). First, similar to that which Derby notes regarding Rafael Trujillo's *muchachito*, the Comandante's possession of occult power via his spirit-guardians or *muertos* may be an example of mimetic association (1999:96). In the popular imagination, the Comandante's association with certain spirits is based on perceived affinities. So, for instance, he is sometimes linked with Elegguá, the spirit-child and trickster divinity of the Ocha-Ifá pantheon described as the one who "opens the roads" and controls destiny. No matter on which side of the political aisle one stands, few would contest the fact that the Comandante changed the course of Cuban history and, by extension, the destinies of millions of people. Moreover, the revolutionary leader's reputation for political astuteness and his almost miraculous ability to survive tricky international conflicts and standoffs with the U.S. government find resonance in Elegguá's status as a divine trickster. Also, the black and red colors associated with the 26th of July movement are those of Elegguá. A billboard depicting the letter Y, a heart, and the 26th of July colors could easily be read as, "I love Elegguá." The revolution's emphasis on programs for children are offered as further evidence of the Comandante's association with Elegguá (Miller 2000: 39–40). His photographic memory, his studiousness in those topics that interest him (for example, it is rumored that he possesses an encyclopedic knowledge of bovine reproduction and genetics), and his reputation as a historical visionary with special access to historical forces invisible to ordinary men all provoke perceptions that he possesses an almost superhuman intelligence (Fagen 1965: 281). Hence his affinities with Obatalá, the oricha most closely associated with human creativity and wisdom. Finally, his military prowess, legendary temper, and sexual charm also suggest affinities with Changó, the santo associated with fire, lightning and thunder, war, and masculine sexuality. Popular perceptions of the Comandante's secret affinities with Afro-Creole saints and, by extension, their implicit sanctioning of his authority suggest a cultural understanding of power that extends beyond the bounded, autonomous self, one generated in a relation to other entities rather than as an internal essence.

One of the most obvious influences on cultural understandings of power in Cuba can be traced to religious syncretism. African slaves and their descendants were forced to hide their true belief systems, cosmology, and ritual practices beneath a Christian façade. Catholic saints may have, at times, served as a kind of symbolic camouflage (though at other times, there may have been a coupling of affinities between the pantheons) enabling the devotees of black popular religions to practice their ritual activities while avoiding the risk of persecution by colonial authorities and the Catholic Church. Thus, the revolutionary leader's public persona may represent the visible face of messianic Christianity or saintly divinity (that is, El Niño de Atocha), while his spirit-guardians stand in as the invisible powers of subaltern cultural imaginaries. So here, syncretism becomes a way of reflecting on power, conceived of as a bifurcated whole between the visible and invisible, public tangibility and hidden presence.

This is especially relevant in the context of the socialist Cuban state, which places so much emphasis on moral incentives and the elimination of socioeconomic classes (and, by extension, all other forms of discrimination). That is, in those societies with a strong egalitarian ethos the exercise of authority and control by a single individual over others may be explained by their access to and possession of unusual power and a mastery of esoteric knowledge. Moreover, popular perceptions of that person's unique life experiences (for example, unusual birth, unexplained illness, and so forth) and, especially, their proximity to cultural others may be interpreted as having enabled privileged access to hidden power. One story, for instance, claims that the Comandante had strange fevers as a child that medical treatments failed to alleviate. Desperate, his mother consulted one of the Congolese household servants for help. The servant surmised that in order to overcome the illness, the young, would-be revolutionary leader would have to go through Palo initiation rites. The budding revolutionary then allegedly underwent a healing rite performed by a mayombero in eastern Cuba and was thereafter "marked" (*rayado*), or formally initiated. This episode recalls Victor Turner's discussion of the Bantu "cults of affliction" in which illness is often taken as a spiritual calling that leads one on the path to priesthood. In stories of the Comandante's nganga, we might say, the revolutionary leader becomes the high priest and medium of his own cult of affliction that encompasses the nation and its dead. A related story claims that the Comandante was baptized not by a Catholic priest but by a Haitian, leading some to believe that he was subject to a non-Christian rite (one associated with Haitian "voodoo," especially among some usually white members of the Miami exile community) (Orozco and Bolívar 1998: 486). The fact that the Comandante explained to Frei Betto that he was baptized by his teacher's husband, Luis Hibbert, who happened to be the Consul of Haiti in Santiago de Cuba, did nothing to stop the rumors (1985).

One of the most striking rumors concerning the Comandante's unusual power holds that he has his own personal nganga which he keeps hidden away somewhere, harnessing its magical power to matters of state and the task of fueling his political prowess. The nganga, people say, is fed with the sacrificial blood of imported bulls, and even though beef has not been made available in government rationing stores for years, the Comandante's nganga "never goes hungry." Given that Cubans frequently complain of being worn-out and weak because they work their fingers to the bone for meager government wages paid in pesos, are barely able to survive on paltry state allotments of food and basic goods, and generally lack the willpower to realize their own plans and dreams—"we're tired," people say, "and he just keeps on doing the same old thing; he's killing us"—this image of a stately nganga that never goes hungry is particularly suggestive. It creates the image of a leader who siphons the productive labor and vitality of his subjects off to feed his own ravenous appetite for power, a "Nietzchean vampire" who, like others before him, sucks up the people's will and dreams to bolster his own, leaving them weary, despondent, and without control over their own destinies.[5]

The religious beliefs and practices of the Comandante's mother have also been the subject of much speculation. The fact that she purportedly kept saints not included within the official canon of the Catholic Church—for example, the Virgen de la Caridad, San José, and San Lázaro—has only fueled the rumor mill (Orozco and Bolívar 1998: 486). Norberto Fuentes, for instance, once one of the Comandante's closest friends and collaborators, offers a curious literary version of these conjectures. In his ambiguously tongue in cheek autobiography of the Comandante, Norberto Fuentes assumes the voice of the revolutionary leader, weaving an extraordinary tale of inter-corporeal transfer between mother and son:

> That night . . . I learned the story. I learned that I was a son of the god Aggayú and about the whole process of initiating me into Santería from the womb. She knew I had an important destiny, she told me, and she sent for a Santería priest and it was he who specified my father was the god Aggayú. "I can tell by your left hand"—he told her—"because this is blood of your blood and through it I can see your son through you." Being a son of Aggayú complicated everything greatly because Aggayú, who is a top-tier warrior, hadn't had anyone who knew how to perform the saint-making ceremony for him in many years. The old Santería priests were the only ones who knew the ceremony, but all of them had died by the 1920s, taking their ceremonial secrets to the grave. So the saint wasn't one that could be made by its own initiates. In other words, and she took the liberty of using an example of modern medicine, you find the closest saint, which in this case was Changó, whose own Santería father is Aggayú, and you chant the ritual songs to Changó, like a kind of bypass. . . . So that was how . . . I made the saint through my mother. (Fuentes 2009)

This fantastic account of a corporeal "bypass" or transfer—that is, from the body of the mother and from the spirit-son of an oricha whose rites were lost to history to the body of the fetus—is perhaps nothing more than an intriguing literary footnote to the popular *chismes* (rumors/gossip) that circulate on the streets of both Havana and Miami. There is one little detail of this narrative, however, that merits special attention.

The santero "sees" the unborn revolutionary leader specifically through his mother's left hand. It is useful here to recall Robert Hertz's classic essay on religious polarity, which calls attention to the almost universal preeminence of the right hand over the left, as well as the polarized social values attributed to each of these body parts (1960). In many societies throughout the world the right hand is associated with socially desired values of cleanliness, strength, masculinity, lawfulness, and moral purity, whereas the left is associated, conversely, with filthiness, weakness, femininity, corruption, and evil. There are, of course, many exceptions to these value associations, but Hertz's general observation that moral values and cosmology are often mapped onto bodily spatiality and orientation (left/right, up/down, front/back, and so forth) still holds. The left hand is often also associated with morally dubious magic and sorcery. In Cuba, for example, Ochosi, the hunter/warrior oricha who helps his devotees find the shortest path to their highest destiny, is known as the "left-handed sorcerer." Similarly, the Comandante is sometimes erroneously described as being left-handed, and some Cuban exiles complete the association by referring to him contemptuously as *el Brujo Mayor* (the Senior Brujo). Fuentes' reference to the left hand of the leader's mother may be an example (and here I can only speculate) of his own imaginative literary sleight of hand, obliquely associating the leader with a set of morally dubious values and powers.

In April 2000, during the Elián González controversy, the London-based Cuban exile writer Guillermo Cabrera Infante put to print rumors that had been circulating in the streets of Miami for weeks. The most politically charged of them held that after learning of Elián's fate—that he had been rescued at sea, saved from sharks by dolphins who had encircled him, and had survived forty-eight hours in treacherous waters under a sweltering sun without any visible signs of burns, sores, or bruises—a group of babalaos hired as advisors to the Comandante allegedly declared that the boy was a "child" of the oricha Elegguá, and that if he remained in Miami the revolutionary leader would soon fall from power (Cabrera Infante 2000). According to Cabrera Infante, the Comandante's supposed embrace of the Ifá oracle, a rumor common on the island as well, was unsurprising given that he was facing the end of both his political and physical life. "After all," Cabrera Infante asserted, "other Cuban dictators, from . . . Machado to . . . Batista, also turned to acts of sorcery in their hours of need" (2000). Obviously, rumors of child sacrifice served the Miami exile community well, essentially fueling racist fears by recalling the hysteria surrounding the republican witchcraft scares, in which black brujos were supposedly kidnapping white children in order to sacrifice them to African gods— something that, of course, makes no sense at all within the Afro-Creole religious universe (Sahlins 2004; Palmié 2003).

Other links made to the Comandante's proximity to occult power are traced to the known religious lives of close confidants, the Cuban military campaigns in Angola during the 1970s, and the formal invitations extended to African leaders to visit the island. Celia Sánchez, for instance, one of the Comandante's closest confidants among the guerillas in the Sierra Maestra, believed to have been his lover, was a devotee and ritual "child" of Yemayá. A santero in Regla told me that Sánchez convinced the Comandante to "make saint" shortly after his arrival in Havana in January 1959. The ceremony, he claimed, took place in the house of a renowned santera somewhere along President's Avenue in Vedado, a heavily manicured thoroughfare containing numerous monuments to the likes of Salvador Allende, Simon Bolivar, and Calixto García. Similar links are made by referencing the Comandante's relationship with René Vallejo, his personal physician during the revolution, believed to have been a spirit medium, and Juan Almeida, a participant in the attack on the Moncada and a child of Changó.

Some claim that the Comandante went through the Ifá initiation ceremony known as *la mano de Orula* during the 1950s when Batista was still in power (Miller 2000: 36–37). When the revolutionary leader traveled to Africa in 1972 to meet with Sékou Touré, then president of Guinea Conakry, many became convinced that he had undergone ritual initiation, a belief reinforced by the fact that he appeared in public during this time wearing white, the customary dress of Ocha-Ifá (Santería) initiates, instead of his customary olive-green military fatigues. Some of Ivor Miller's informants told him that Touré was the Comandante's ritual godfather, and that when Cuba was in some sort of crisis he traveled to the island to perform ritual sacrifices with the revolutionary leader. Other stories posit more than just a diplomatic relationship between the Comandante and certain revered African leaders. Some say that in 1987, for example, oracular prophecies made by the babalaos had it that unless the Oni of Ife, the Yoruba king, traveled to Cuba and kissed the ground, the Comandante would die (Valdes

2001: 226). Later that year the Cuban leader hosted a visit to the island by Sijuwade Olobose II, the Yoruba "king of kings," who did in fact kiss the ground upon his arrival.

The Political Cosmology of the Revolution

Perhaps one of the strongest influences on Latin American and Caribbean cultural imaginaries that trace power to hidden sources is the "political cosmology" derived from patron-client networks (Derby 1999: 102). Patron-client networks are characterized by inherently unequal relationships between some person of status (or one who desires such status) and marginalized or underprivileged individuals or groups. These relationships presuppose a profound hierarchy of social status and authority in which oppressed groups cannot advance their own interests without the help of those in positions of influence. Patrons offer financial or other assistance in hard times and their clients in turn promise political support or loyalty. These networks provide the latter with a socioeconomic safety net and the former with an ever-expanding political support base. This model of power, Derby argues, suggests a model of personhood in which unusual power or status is traced to forces outside the subject and often to the occult world of spirits (Derby 1999: 102–103).

In Cuba, patron-client networks have spread across the social worlds of political elites and the leaders of local cult houses since at least the beginning of the twentieth century. Cuban politicians were courting the votes of Abakuá members, for example, throughout the republican period (Sosa 1982; Matibag 1996: 141). The most direct evidence we have of these networks, however, has been between political leaders and the babalaos, or Ifá divination priests. David Brown has documented several instances of this relationship between politicians and Ifá diviners (2003). The babalao Bernardo Rojas, for instance, who gave numerous masses in his Asociación Luz de San Francisco (created in 1936), was photographed there with one of his godchildren and patrons, the senator "El Chino" Ayón; the babalao may have offered the votes of his followers in exchange for financial support (Brown 2003: 84). The most striking example of these patron-client networks, however, directly implicates Carlos Prío Socarrás, president of Cuba between 1948 and 1952:

Tín [the babalao Quitín Lecón Lombillo], in an on-and-off fundraising effort with [Bernardo] Rojas, gathered building funds for a grand social and educational center (El Edificio Social y Centro Escolar) in Regla. . . . Tín secured over forty thousand pesos from his powerful godchild Carlos Prío Socarrás. . . . Like his predecessor, Ramón Grau San Martín, Prío, the last reform candidate of the Auténtico Party, presided over a "bloated," extremely corrupt, and "violent" administration, during which the term *gangsterismo* was coined in Cuba. Further research might discover that the history of Ifá's prosperity during this period was tied not only to social and political connections, but also to the patronage and cronyism economy of the Auténtico machine. A timely document, if not also a smoking gun, in this regard, may be the dramatic photograph of Tín receiving a whopping check for, it is believed, forty thousand pesos from Prío in the presidential Palace. (Brown 2003: 84–85)

Similarly, rumors circulate that the widow of one of prerevolutionary Cuba's most powerful santeros is still in possession of a multimillion dollar collection of gold and silver objects given to her husband in exchange for his ritual work by both Prío and Batista (Hanly 1995: 35).

Similar patron-client networks are rumored to exist between the Comandante and the island's babalaos. Some claim, for example, that the revolutionary leader has promoted regime-friendly babalaos as members of the state's internal security apparatus (Oppenheimer 1992), and as folkloric attractions geared to generate hard currency from visiting diplomats and foreign tourists (Tamayo 1998). Some of my informants speculated that the babalao Enrique Hernández Armenteros ("Enriquito") was the Comandante's favored "secret" advisor. The more recent state licensing of the Yoruba Cultural Association of Cuba (ACYC), an organization run by babalaos apparently sympathetic to the current regime, has only exacerbated rumors of the Comandante's patronage of the Ifá oracle. This association is jokingly referred to by some (and derided as such by others) as the "Ministry of Orula"—suggesting that the patron deity or oricha of Ifá divination and its priesthood have become so cozy with the political leadership on the island that they have been given their own government ministry.

These tales, I suggest, are not only significant because they reflect popular anxieties concerning the opacity of power, offering their own unique cultural readings of the inner workings and hidden meanings of political authority and behavior, but also because the state itself is intimately involved in creating and promoting these metaphorical and magical constructions of power. In recent years, as will be seen, revolutionary officialdom has made some rather incongruous attempts to harness popular imaginaries of power to the national agenda. It is to these entanglements that bring popular culture and the state together within a deeply promiscuous and ambiguous field of power that I now turn.

Conjuring the Past

CHAPTER 4

In Oliver Stone's documentary Comandante, *he asks the iconic Cuban leader how he manages to stay fit. The Comandante, dressed in his characteristic military fatigues and, ironically, sporting a new pair of Nike tennis shoes, decides to put on a demonstration. After checking his pulse, he makes a couple of speedy laps around his office. "I'm like a prisoner," he says, "and this is my cell." And, later, he adds, "I'm a dictator to myself, a slave to the people."*

A few weeks after the limpieza de casa at La Mariquilla's house, Arcaño invited us to a ritual "party for the dead" (*fiesta para los muertos*).[1] When we arrived, several men were removing the few pieces of furniture in Arcaño's living room to make space for the spirit-possession ceremony. Once some last-minute arrangements were settled—borrowing a few more instruments from neighbors and ensuring that there was an adequate supply of black market rum—the rites soon began.

After a couple hours of meticulous ritual work, however, the dead had still failed to make an appearance. The musicians, a ragtag ensemble of local initiates hastily recruited that morning, continued trading places at the large box drum, congas, and *guataca* (hoe blade). Losing his patience, Arcaño began pacing back and forth, occasionally entering the small, closet-like space apart from the main room of the house where he kept his spirit-doll (*kini kini*) and nganga. "Let's go, old man! [*¡Vamos viejo!*]" he shouted, "Get on with it! [*¡Dale!*]" (Figure 4.1). Finally, as a new singer took the lead,

4.1. From left to right: the nganga "Induatuá," the spirit-doll "Manuel," and the nganga "Tierra Tiembla."

the atmosphere of the room, which only moments before had bordered on a kind of dismal automatism, began to swell with fervor as the body of the brujo displayed the first signs of possession (convulsions, sudden outbursts, heavy breathing, and drooling, for example).

The lead singer quickly moved close to Arcaño, now standing in the middle of the room and rubbing his face. A few of the other musicians then gathered around him as the singer, raising his voice in a noticeably more aggressive register, intoned the first of a series of haunting refrains intended to hasten the arrival of the dead:

> Lead singer: I'm going, I'm going to the mountain!
> Chorus: Slave driver, release the dogs!
> Lead singer: He's not going to get me!
> Chorus: Let the dogs loose on the runaway slave![2]

What began as an ostensibly benign ceremony in honor of the dead had suddenly became charged with the violent imagery of a plantation overseer and his ravenous dogs, poised to chase down a slave in flight. The body of the brujo soon dropped to the floor, overtaken by the spirit of a nineteenth-century Congolese runaway slave frantically gasping for air—"the spirits of runaway slaves," one medium casually remarked, "are always out of breath;

they always come running in order to escape the overseer and his dogs."[3] Reluctant to emerge from his hiding place in the invisible bush, Arcaño's runaway slave spirit was forced into attendance by appealing to the terror- izing imagery of a colonial slave hunt. Facedown on the floor, he writhed about in one place with his arms firmly pressed against the length of his torso in a manner eerily reminiscent of the *boca bajo*, a disciplinary tactic that required a slave to lie facedown on the ground while receiving lashes. He soon recovered himself, stood up, and proceeded to give counsel to ev- eryone present in *bozal*, the broken Spanish once spoken by newly arrived African slaves.

It may be tempting, as my original field notes of that ritual episode sug- gest, to say that Arcaño and the other participants that day were collectively "remembering" slavery. The ritual simulation of a colonial slave hunt in Cuba might, then, resonate with the way in which, as Rosalind Shaw notes for the Temne of Sierra Leone, "the slave trade is forgotten as history but remembered as spirits" (2002: 9). But one question I raise here is whether it makes good ethnographic sense to gloss such phenomena in terms that foreground memory. After all, as David Berliner asks, "Can we really 're- member' something that we did not experience? Can someone 'remember' the slave trade?" (2005: 208).[4] Perhaps a more phenomenologically sensitive way to approach such ritual performances is to see them as constituting a kind of "vicarious memory" (Teski and Climo 1995). One might, therefore, examine the extent to which the "memories" of historical others become real for present generations through ritually stylized forms of social mime- sis. But then again, something altogether different could be at work here: what Michael Taussig points to in his discussion of "history as sorcery" (1987)—namely, the way that certain historical events are sometimes reified as magically empowered imagery capable of both causing misfortune and expanding people's power to act on the world.

The relevance of questions concerning the memory of slavery is, never- theless, especially acute given the various forms of institutionalized erasure that have tended to vaporize the slave past, reducing history's first system of globalization to a phantom. As Michel-Rolph Trouillot once remarked, "Slavery here is a ghost, both the past and the living presence; and the problem of historical representation is how to represent the ghost" (1995: 146–47). My purpose in this chapter, however, is not merely to ethno- graphically disentangle the meanings of such ritual evocations of slavery by demonstrating how, as essentially embodied forms of social praxis, they ingeniously defy those forces that conspire to silence such violent histories, but also to call attention to how recent efforts by scholars, nation-states, and international organizations attempting to undo this silence engender their own politics of memory which either ignore or seriously distort how local collectivities "represent the ghost." In Cuba, such issues are not only entangled in representations that draw parallels between black maroon resistance in the colonial period and the political ideology of the 1959 revolution, but also muddled by the cultural politics of post-Soviet Cuban society. Recent efforts to reinvigorate grassroots support for the revolution and bolster a culture of resistance in an era of material scarcity by harnessing the island's Afro-Creole religions to the ideological agendas of the state have produced some rather peculiar juxtapositions between ritual and revolutionary visions of the slave past.

Enshrining Resistance

A decade before his death, Joel James, esteemed writer and then director of the Casa del Caribe in Santiago de Cuba, made a stunning proposition regarding the material culture of ritual life on the island. In an article entitled, "La Brujería Cubana" (Cuban Witchcraft/Sorcery), James called on the Cuban revolutionary state to recognize the island's nganga, "veterans of thousands of battles on earth and in heaven," national cultural patrimony (James 1996: 114). Aware that even the suggestion that fetish objects like the nganga—which contain, among other things, purloined or otherwise illegally procured human remains—should be officially included in the nation's cultural heritage would be met with derision, if not outright scorn, James embellished his argument by appealing to revolutionary sensibilities. The "chain of nganga," or the ritual genealogies that link these sacred objects, which apparently stretch as far back as the mid-eighteenth century, he argued, parallel the development of Cuban nationality since colonial times.[5] The terms and conditions of the binding pacts made between the owners of ngangas and the dead, James continued, crystallize a whole "structure of relations" that have varied throughout Cuban history and generally reflect the development of social relations recounted in revolutionary historiography—that is, they mirror the long historical struggle that led the nation out of a recurring condition of subjugation (slavery, colonialism, and neocolonial rule) and into a state of true independence and equality with the 1959 revolution and subsequent socialist reforms. During the colonial era, according to James, the pacts between the owners of ngangas and the dead were made to help the individual endure the brutal conditions of slavery or the perils associated with marronage and, in the republic, as a means of defense against neocolonial forms of economic exploitation and racial discrimination. It was only after the 1959 revolution that such pacts came to facilitate "religious improvement and ascent to the transcendent" (1996: 123). The nganga, James argued, metaphorically condense not only the island's social history, but also its revolutionary ethos (1996: 114–24).

However much the ethnographic material I present below casts doubt on James' "ingenious" discovery of how the inexorable laws of the dialectic are at work inside the nganga, the timing of his proposition was nothing less than fortuitous. The United Nations Educational, Scientific and Cultural Organization's (UNESCO) "Slave Route Project" had been officially launched only two years before and its main priorities had been discussed by the specially appointed International Scientific Committee (ISC) in Matanzas, Cuba, in December 1995. James' proposition that the revolutionary state recognize the island's nganga national cultural patrimony was realized, if in a somewhat modified form, in what was among the first of the Slave Route Project's tangible achievements. On July 7, 1997, Cuban government and party officials, UNESCO representatives, a Cuban folklore group led by a prominent local spirit medium, local and foreign researchers from the Casa del Caribe, including James himself, and community members gathered together atop a mountain in El Cobre (Santiago de Cuba) for the unveiling of Cuban artist Alberto Lescay's "Monument to the Runaway Slave" (Figure 4.2). The site was chosen partly in honor of the royal slaves of El Cobre who between 1731 and 1800 fought Spanish troops until the Crown was forced to concede their freedom, making their struggle one of the first victorious slave rebellions in the Caribbean (Pérez Sarduy 2001). A towering, twenty-foot monument, Lescay's copper sculpture depicts a runaway slave standing in a giant nganga constructed from an iron cauldron recovered from a local sugar plantation and similar to the usually smaller ones used by Palo adepts all over the island. Standing inside the nganga, the runaway slave rises vertically towards the sky. He possesses a horse's head and his hand, extended above, reveals the form of a bird about to take flight, imagery that evokes local lore about the runaway slave's use of shape-shifting powers to elude slave hunters and slave-hunting militias.

Although for Lescay the sculpture was merely a symbol of the tenacity of African culture in Cuba, the monument has since taken on a spiritual

4.2. Alberto Lescay's "Monument to the Runaway Slave." Photo by Alberto Lescay, from UNESCO's *Slave Route Newsletter*, No. 1, September 2000.

significance for some local residents. Doudou Diène, who was present at the unveiling, foreshadowed the magical allure the monument would soon come to hold for some local religious devotees. "The most visible monuments in this place," Diène stated, "are the church of the Virgin of Charity and this monument to the runaway slave. Both monuments have a mystical meaning. I believe deeply that the runaway slaves are here now, inside us, to help us" (Casa del Caribe 1997). The 1995 display of excavated human remains in El Cobre, which some local residents believe to be those of a black maroon, and the presence of the Monument to the Runaway Slave appear to have prompted emergent forms of ritual praxis among local community members. The monument, for example, has not only become a ritual site for some local residents in recent years, but female spirit mediums (*espiritistas*) who once excluded such "crude," "unevolved," and "dark" spirit entities in the area have now begun incorporating runaway slave spirits into their "commissions" (*comisiones*), groupings of spirits that are consulted on a regular basis (Schmidt 2005: 185–91).[6] Moreover, during the annual Fiesta del Fuego festival, the monument is subject to ritual propitiations referred to as the "delivery of the *mpaka*" (*entrega de la mpaka*). This ceremony is attended by local and national representatives of government-licensed cultural institutions, their international guests, and community members. It involves the construction of an *mpaka*, a bull's horn stuffed with magically charged substances and sealed with a mirror and wax (it is commonly used as a clairvoyant device), prepared by a local *palero* and placed in the symbolic nganga of the monument to mark the beginning of the festival and bless its proceedings and participants (Gainza Chacón 2000).

If by engendering a whole structure of relations that have changed over time the nganga can be said to condense the island's social history, then the Monument to the Runaway Slave also performs its own particular kind of historical compression, one no less magical in its constitution than the fetish objects themselves. The Brazilian poet Thiago de Melo, one of the event's distinguished foreign guests, alluded to this in his comments the day the sculpture was unveiled: "The runaway slave is not only a sign of rebellion. . . . I learned that the runaway slave accompanies the very spirit of the Cuban people and all of those that seek its sovereign affirmation" (Casa del Caribe 1997). Thiago de Mello's comment not only reveals the ideological work that Lescay's monument is called upon to perform, but it does so by appealing to a familiar, romantic trope of revolutionary discourse as a whole—that is, the ideological identification between forms of slave resistance like marronage and the political culture of the 1959 revolution.

Shortly after the 1959 revolution, to cite a familiar example, Miguel Barnet's *Biography of a Runaway Slave* (1966), an oral history of maroon life based on interviews with the former runaway slave Esteban Montejo, provided a powerful image for revolutionary politics. As Matt Child notes, Barnet's retelling of the early experiences of Montejo, "a runaway who sought the solitary existence of life in the woods instead of the disciplined labor regime of the plantation, resonated and served as a metaphor for the Cuban political experience of the 1960s" (Childs 2004: 295). What appears to be unique about the use of this imagery in post-Soviet Cuba is its expansion to include not only revolutionary political culture but the historical experience of the nation as a whole. "More recently," as Pérez Sarduy and Stubbs note, "all of Cuba has been likened to a *palenque* (a maroon, or runaway slave, settlement)" (Pérez Sarduy and Stubbs 2000: 7). Joel James, for instance, provides what is perhaps the most striking example of this analogy. "Cubans," he writes, "are always in a cultural and social condition of marronage, of attack, of escape against . . . that which constrains their self-realization, and this disposition of guerrilla marronage [apalencamiento], these means of cultural defense, of defense against imposed death . . . which came about during slavery, were developed, redefined, and consolidated time and time again" (James 1999: 56). As a bastion of limitless resolve, resistance, and self-determination, Cuba is represented in statements such as these as a kind of "maroon" nation, vowing eternal flight from the global snares of neoliberal imperialism.

The Monument to the Runaway Slave reinforces such imagery. The monument is not only productive of an image of the slave's magic as a viable force of resistance and liberation, but it metaphorically extends that power to the revolutionary nation-state. The effect is that the political marronage of the Cuban state is made to not only appear genealogically linked to but sanctified by the magical forms of resistance employed by African slaves and their descendants on the island. Given that magic has often been maligned by the revolutionary vanguard as out of step with socialist modernity, it is patently ironic that the state is today extolling the virtues of ritually empowered forms of slave resistance, especially now that it finds itself "marooned" in a sea of global capitalism. The attempt by some revolutionary officials and scholars to assimilate these ritual poetics of history into the state's resistance against capitalist imperialism is productive of some rather peculiar metaphorics. Joel James, as mentioned earlier, is thus able to make the audacious claim in a posthumous publication that the Cuban nation itself is a "great nganga" (2006). These selective and domesticated objectifications of ritual imagery exemplify one of the emergent paradoxes of late-socialist Cuban society—that is, the revolutionary fetishization of Afro-Creole "fetishism." This much is obvious. What is less obvious, however, is the extent to which revolutionary appropriations might be finding their way back into the popular imagination.

Cosmologies of the Slave Trade

After writhing about on the floor for several minutes, the nineteenth-century runaway Congolese slave animating Arcaño's body that summer afternoon in 2004 soon arose and began demanding tobacco and rum. These were the only rewards worth risking recapture for. "Manuel," the pseud-onym by which he was known to everyone except Arcaño, the only one who knew his real name, walked with a noticeable limp no doubt caused by the shackles that were still attached to his ankle when he fled the plantation. He therefore needed to use a special cane to keep from falling. The runaway slave moved slowly around the room, followed closely by Arcaño's mother, who translated everything he said. He gave random bits of advice to various participants, stopping only to sip rum from a small gourd or take a long drag from the cigar given to him. These moments of silence were some-times filled by the musicians, who seized the opportunity to break into a quick song. Manuel tolerated these musical punctuations, but at one point he suddenly called for quiet after a teenage friend of Arcaño's son entered the house. As everyone present would soon learn, the teenager had recently had several brushes with the law for hustling (*jineteando*) foreign tourists and stealing from friends and neighbors.

Manuel grabbed the visibly frightened teenager by the arm, made him spread his legs, and proceeded to berate and question him for several min-utes in front of everyone. He said that a dark spirit of the dead (*muerto oscuro*) belonging to a "Jewish" nganga, the type used for black magic, had "stuck" itself to the boy, sent there by someone envious of the fact that he had family abroad in Hialeah.[7] Had the boy not been waiting to receive papers to go live there? Did he not suspect the jealousy and envy of some of his acquaintances as a result? Had he not suddenly resorted to hustling and stealing for no good apparent reason? Had he not grown so impatient that he had been trying to convince Arcaño's son to help him build an inner tube raft (*balsa*) and risk his life on the treacherous seas between Cuba and Miami?

Manuel then grabbed some white chalk and began drawing a magical signature (*firma*) on the floor behind the boy, pouring *aguardiente* (cane liquor) along its lines from a small clay pitcher (said to be the kind slaves drank water from). Standing behind the boy, Manuel placed the clay pitcher containing the remainder of the liquor on the floor and ignited the signa-ture, producing a very sudden and loud explosion. This miniature explo-sion was intended to cast off the malevolent spirit attached to the boy and send it back to its owner. The dark spirit, which in this case was not the spirit of an actual slave, but rather the spirit of the recently dead who had nevertheless been forced or contracted into magical servitude by an act of predatory sorcery, was almost certainly "tied" by "shackles and chains" to the "Jewish" nganga from which it was sent. To what extent the ironies of this impromptu dispossession in socialist Cuba (specifically, the spirit of a nineteenth-century runaway slave liberating a young boy from the predations of a ghost enslaved by a fellow comrade) were apparent to anyone else is a matter about which I can only speculate.

Anthropologists and historians have long noted that a variety of local cosmologies throughout Africa and the Americas link magic and witchcraft with the forced or contracted deployment of persons or spirits in a phantom-like "second universe" where they perform various kinds of labor for their living proprietors, imagery that clearly resonates with the history of the transatlantic slave trade and the labor regime of plantation slavery (Austen 1993: 92; MacGaffey 1986: 62; Shaw 2002; Matory 2007; McCalister 2002: 103; Palmié 2002: 174). One particularly dramatic example of this comes from west Central Africa, where witches are said to steal people's souls and then transport them across the Atlantic to be put to work in U.S. factories (MacGaffey 1986: 62). In Haiti, zombies are figures magically dispossessed of their own volition; their souls are captured and imprisoned in bottles, thereafter commanded by whip-yielding sorcerers (McCalister 2002: 103). The class of spirits known as *Exú* in Brazil, referred to as "slaves" or "people of the roads" and associated with the illicit activities of urban street life, are placed under the command of sorcerers through the use of spells and imprecations (Brazeal 2007; Hayes 2007: 284). To what extent slavery was incorporated into preexisting magical idioms as opposed to actually being productive of them remains a matter of speculation. Nevertheless, such ritual images and practices are read by some scholars as mute indictments of the deleterious effects of conquest, colonialism, slavery, and neocolonial rule, as well as local idioms for the contemporary work of transnational or global capitalism (Shaw 1997; Comaroff and Comaroff 1993; Taussig 1997).

During her fieldwork in Cuba in the 1940s and '50s, the Cuban ethnographer Lydia Cabrera came across a similar set of phantasmagoric images evoking the labor regime of plantation slavery, military command, and wage labor in the fetish objects known as nganga or *prendas* (literally, "jewel"), earthenware pots or tripod iron cauldrons resembling those once used to boil sugarcane. Her informants described the spirit forces of the various plant substances and animal remains used in the construction of these fetishes as "slave gangs" (*cuadrillas de esclavos*), "workforce" (*dotación*), and "subalterns" (*subalternos*). The plants and animals that made up this slave or subaltern workforce were supervised by the dead (*fumbi*), referred to as the "overseer" (*mayoral*), the "general of the forces" (*general de las fuerzas*), and the "boss" (*jefe*). The entire assamblage of spirit forces and entities, however, was in turn subject to the command of its living "owner." Occasionally, however, this subaltern ghost world was said to "rebel" (*reviran*) (see Cabrera 1983: 131).

As Stephan Palmié so cogently argues, the nganga magically condense and redeploy a particular set of historical experiences linked to slavery, marronage, and wage labor (Palmié 2002: 159–200). The owner of an nganga "is a mystical entrepreneur commanding a labor force by contract or capture" (Palmié 2002: 168). This phantom labor force is recruited from among the dead interred in local cemeteries; they are either contracted, conned, or stolen and then relocated and imprisoned within the nganga. There they are subject to the authoritative command of their owners and work on commission—that is, they receive "payment" in the form of blood sacrifice only after they have successfully completed some task.

Ritual evocations of slavery are further reinforced in the procedures for activating these fetish objects. The nganga, as Fernando Ortiz noted, are sometimes insulted, spit on, or flogged as a way of forcing them to work or carry out a given task (Ortiz 1958: 851). Cabrera also noted, for instance, that when the dead took possession of her informants they began a set of rites described as "moving around the sugar mill," the purpose of which was to clear ritual space of any impurities or "twisted intentions" (Cabrera 1979: 142). Images of military reconnaissance are also salient. The owners of nganga sometimes acquire the character of "generals" in command of spirit forces who act as scouts, spies, or sentries in charge of maintaining the perimeters of ritual space or certain circumscribed areas of urban space (Brown 1989: 376). The presence of such imagery is likely related to the historical experience of marronage and the defensive strategies intended to protect runaway slaves from recapture by slave hunters and more organized slave-hunting militias. There is also evidence to suggest that the ritual salience of such military metaphors may be associated with or otherwise reinforced by the ritual activities of maroon communities in the eastern regions of Cuba during the struggles against Spanish colonial rule in the latter half of the nineteenth century, regardless of the still-unsettled question of whether or not, or under what conditions, they actually supported the insurgents (Palmié 2002: 185–88; Thompson 1983: 125; Roa 1950).

Sugar's Ghosts

The spirits comprised of slaves and maroons are often referred to as "*boza-les*," a word used in the colonial era to denote those African slaves who were "just off the boat," able only to speak broken, rudimentary Spanish and entirely unfamiliar with social life in the colony. The spirits of these bozales are described as "crude," "brutish," and "uncivilized" but, at the same time, empowered by extraordinary gifts of clairvoyance and magical prowess. The spirits of the bozales are thus subject to a familiar series of paradoxical attributions of power that have their roots in colonialism. Although their coarse, brutish, and backward nature is in keeping with their status as slaves or maroons, it also bolsters their reputation as gifted sorcerers possessing secret, esoteric power and knowledge.

When I first met Arcaño he had been a practicing brujo and spirit medium for over thirty years and had long since developed a working relationship with a nineteenth-century runaway slave known to others only by his pseudonym "Manuel." One afternoon when Arcaño was "mounted" (possessed), the spirit of the runaway slave called for me. "Where's the worldly pants [foreign man], the white man [*mundele*]? My horse [Arcaño] tells me you want to know my history. Is that true or false?"

"True," I said.

"I'll share my history with you but you have to treat it with respect. You can't just go around telling everyone without caution." As Arcaño's mother stood there translating the speech of this bozal, an often incomprehensible blur of arcane words and fragmented syntax, Manuel took a knife to his mouth and proceeded to cut his tongue until drops of blood fell from his lip into a plate on his lap:

> I was born in Mozambique and taken from my people when I was eighteen years old. They took me to a sugar plantation in Baracoa, El Central Australia, where I labored for many years in the refinery. They called me Manuel Noche Oscuro [Manuel Dark Night]. That's because I would always wander off in the bush at night and get lost. You see I was a rebel, a maroon. When I set off for the mountain I was still in shackles. That's why my left leg is dead. I spent the rest of my life on the mountain. I lived to be one hundred and fifteen years old. My secret is buried beneath the silk cottonwood tree [*ceiba*]. What more do you want with me, mundele?

"I was still in shackles," he had said, as blood dripped to his lap below. What some colonial authorities once characterized as an affliction—the tendency for some slaves to resist their enslavement by running off into the surrounding woods and mountains—is described here as a natural-born propensity to rebel by wandering in the bush, seeking its transformative power. The "bush," for many black Cubans faced with the violence of slavery, referred not only to extra-social space or those out-of-the-way places where the spirits dwelled, but also to those spaces promising freedom and escape from the tortures and dehumanizing conditions of plantation life. In this sense, historical experiences linked to slavery spilled over into local cosmology, filling undomesticated magical spaces like the bush with a corpus of urgent existential meanings.

When Arcaño was just a boy he too would often wander off into the bush (*el monte*) at night and get lost, hypnotized by its fantastic forms, cacophony of sounds, mysterious odors, and shadowy figures. His mother's worried calls could not break the feverish hold these nightly sojourns had on him. She and others would go looking for him, and finally he would emerge out of the darkness limping and complaining of sharp pains in his leg. The doctors at the polyclinic who examined him were never able to detect anything out of the ordinary. They assured his mother that her son was in perfectly good health. But the nightly wanderings and phantom aches and pains continued. Arcaño's mother, a spirit medium herself, decided to organize a spiritual mass (*misa espiritual*) to find out if her son's mysterious behavior might be the result of some invisible agent. What Arcaño eventually learned from those sessions was that he was experiencing the vicarious wanderings and sufferings of a nineteenth-century runaway slave who had been a great sorcerer in his lifetime. Because unregulated contact with the dead is fraught with danger, it must be ritually managed in order to ensure that the dead person's living host is not harmed.

Wuicho, a rumba singer and brujo in Central Havana, had a comparable set of experiences. One night when just nine years old he was laying in his bed in his family's small apartment in an urban *solar* when there suddenly appeared before him "the image of a very dark-skinned black man, of very rough features, eyes wide-open, *guano* hat, looking at me fixedly and with great seriousness but without intending to harm me." Afterwards, he would sometimes tremble with chills or experience strong palpitations, "like something had seized me without allowing me to speak." Wuicho's mother began taking him to "spiritual schools" (spiritist centers), "because the doctors knew nothing about sorcery." At these "schools" the strange sensations passed through him with even more intensity. It was then that the first spirit of the dead "mounted" Wuicho. "It was all very fast and strange," he explained, "when you start to feel in your body all of the sensations that a person felt in their life and much more the symptoms that person felt in their last days like gasping for air." This particular spirit, the same one who had first appeared to him as a little boy, was "Joaquín," the spirit of a runaway slave who shared affinities with Sarabanda, a nature spirit associated with iron and, by extension, iron objects such as machetes, as well as all that they are used for, such as cutting cane and as weapons in slave uprisings.

Wuicho later recalled his encounter with another runaway slave spirit. One day he went walking alone through the cane fields of Camagüey and got lost. He arrived at an abandoned sugar mill and had the strange sense of having been there before. Yet, since this was his first trip there that was impossible. He remembered a dream he had had in which the spirit of a runaway slave appeared to him, and wondered if the dream and his mysterious sense of déjà vu were linked. Wuicho began asking the locals if this had in fact been a place where slaves once labored and, to his surprise, their descriptions matched what the runaway slave had conveyed in his dream. The spirit in question was "Francisco," an African-born runaway slave who had arrived in Camagüey via Haiti, a terribly "impulsive" and "brutish" character who nonetheless "had a great knowledge of sorcery." Wuicho would soon develop a relationship with Francisco's elder sister, "María Caridad," a very "refined" woman who not only knew much about the world of the whites since she had been a domestic slave, but was also particularly skilled at preparing magical powders. Her brother would occasionally "come out of the bush and she took care of him by giving him food and affection."

On one level, stories about slave spirits can be read as mute indictments of the brutality and terror associated with life on the island's sugar estates. One female medium, for example, spoke of her protector spirit "Mariaregla," an African-born female slave who worked on the Mercedes sugar estate. Mariaregla had been pregnant with twins but lost them due to a miscarriage induced by a brutal lashing from the plantation overseer, the pain of which still occasionally manifests itself in the belly of her living host. When "mounted" by Manuel, Arcaño's body, the spirit's "horse," limped and had to use a ritually adorned cane to keep from losing its balance, while the spirit inside frequently complained about the pain caused by those shackles cutting into his flesh. There were also moments when the old maroon spirit begged for the shackles to be removed, only to be reminded that they were already gone. What these examples illustrate is the extent to which spirit possession lays bare the affective power of history as a more tangible presence in the sensible body (Hale 1997: 393; Stoller 1994).

Yet the experiences of mediums like Arcaño and Wuicho reveal much more. The feverish meanderings of a child in the bush at night or the dreamlike sense of "having been there before" when confronted with the unfamiliar ruins of a sugar mill recall what René Devisch has described as a kind of initiation "leading to a rebirth into alterity or the elsewhere. . . . [The] sorcerer's highly developed capacities of passion, scent or sight allow him passage to this alterity which he enjoys, sensing it rather than conceptualising it" (Devisch 1999: 66). It is through this highly sensual experience of solitarily wandering and losing oneself amongst the night shadows of the bush and the ghostly remains of abandoned sugar estates that the brujo, in a sense, becomes his own other. Like the phantom limb described by Maurice Merleau-Ponty (1962), the past manifests itself here as a spectral presence in the body of the brujo, expressing the proximate alterity of history through sensorial rather than conceptual or textual registers. The phenomenology of the brujo's experience and ritual praxis is fundamental to this. By submitting to these visitations and cultivating one's spiritual sensibilities and gifts of clairvoyance, mediums "incorporate" themselves into a whole chain of spirits that reach far back into the slave past. They thus mend the historical ruptures and silences that keep present generations alienated from such violent histories.

Conjuring the Slave Past

As the above examples illustrate, the "embodied history" of slavery has not become so internalized as second nature that it has been forgotten as such (Bourdieu 1990: 56). Spirit mediums are clearly aware that imagery recalling the historical experience of slavery is at the heart of their ritual work. Yet it is also clear that mediums like Arcaño employ this imagery in ways that do not so much memorialize the slave past as harness its magical capacities to specific ritual tasks in the present. The embodiment of slave spirits, for example, constitutes only one dimension of the medium's ritual dreamworld—the other being sorcery. This aspect of the brujo's profession often involves forays into local cemeteries in search of spirits, which they either purchase, steal, or con out of the grave, and then subject to magical enslavement in their nganga or those of others.

The question that hangs like a shadow over this subject—that is, whether or not the often macabre stories describing sorcerers who harvest human bones from local cemeteries under the cover of darkness are merely Orientalizing fictions or bona fide ritual praxis—was settled for me early one summer morning. I accompanied Arcaño and an unlicensed taxi driver who had commissioned his magic to a local cemetery in order to "catch the dead" (*coger un muerto*). El Gordo (the fat man), as the taxi driver was known, had asked Arcaño to ensorcell (*embrujar*) the lover of his estranged wife. Despite repeated warnings from Arcaño that such acts of predatory sorcery were unpredictable and risky since they could always turn away from their intended victim and "stick" (*pegar*) to the caster instead, afflicting them with all kinds of misfortune and cosmic retribution, El Gordo did not sway. He was convinced that sorcery (*brujería*) was the only thing that could break the powerful seductive hold El Tipo (the lover), as he was called, exerted over his wife. El Tipo was a high-ranking military official not only in a position to take bribes and thus supplement his meager government salary, but also with access to coveted consumer goods confiscated from foreign tourists at the José Martí National Airport. El Gordo thus believed that his estranged wife had left him not because he had failed as a husband, but because she had been seduced by the material comforts El Tipo could offer her. El Gordo's story reflects a typical source of anxiety of many Cubans in the post-Soviet era—the pervasive doubt about the possibility of altruistic love and social beneficence in an age of scarce resources and opportunities (Hernández-Reguant 2002: 385).

We arrived at the cemetery not under the cover of darkness, but in the full daylight of early morning. Arcaño approached an older white man who was sitting outside the gate and they soon began trading phrases in what appeared to be a kind of impromptu test of each other's ritual knowledge and prowess. It turned out that the old man was a grave digger and a brujo, an apparently common combination among those who feel they need to protect themselves from the occupational hazards of working so closely with the dead. We followed the old man inside to an older grave that had recently been dug up to make room for others. Human remains, in the form of small fragments, were scattered about. Arcaño worked quickly. He first drew the signature of the whirlwind on the sidewalk in front of the grave, then placed a piece of paper with El Tipo's name, his photograph, and a piece of bone from the cadaver in its center, a way of luring the dead out of the grave since "they always go looking for what is theirs [*siempre andan buscando por lo suyo*]." He then lit a white candle in the center and began chanting, blowing black market rum on the signature and into the pit of the grave. After pouring more rum onto the spiraling line of the signature, the "road" or "path" (*camino*) along which the dead would soon travel, he placed the rum bottle near the bottom, where the signature began, and lit it. The flame quickly moved out from the direction of the grave and into the bottle, creating a small explosion. Arcaño hurriedly capped the bottle. The dead had been tricked out of the grave. Forced out of the ground in search of "what is theirs," the dead are "caught" by directing them into and imprisoning them within containing devices such as rum bottles. Arcaño then began singing while he ripped the piece of paper with El Tipo's name on it into five pieces and tied them around four candles using corn husks. He placed the four pieces in a square on top of the signature and then blew *chamba*, a ritual drink containing magically imbued substances, onto the signature and into the grave. When he was done he forcefully threw the four pieces into the four corners of the pit. Finally, he grabbed a handful of soil from the grave, which he placed inside a plastic bag along with the photo, the rum, the *chamba*, and the remaining piece of paper. As we left Arcaño told El Gordo to give the grave digger/mayombero ten pesos, about forty U.S. cents, enough for a pack of cigarettes.

Although in this particular instance the purpose was only to "catch" the dead and send him off on a kind of "freelance" mission, similar ritual procedures are employed to uproot the dead from the cemetery and transport them to the nganga, where they are kept to perform various kinds of mystical labor for their owners.[8] Although it would appear that much older brujos trace the construction of the first nganga to Africa in narratives that have nothing to do with forced servitude (González García 2000: 114–15), my informants directly linked the creation of the first nganga on the island to slavery.[9] Arcaño, for example, explicitly traced the mythical first nganga to marronage. A slave by the name of Congocorama, he told me, escaped from his owners and ran off into the surrounding bush (*el monte*), where he "captured the mystical powers of nature." The first nganga, then, according to Arcaño's narrative, was nature itself. But because Congocorama was always on the move, he constructed an *mpaka*, which he stuffed with magically imbued substances, including human remains, and sealed with a mirror using candle wax. Wuicho, on the other hand, described how a dramatic episode of violent slave revolt brought these fetish objects into existence:

> The first . . . nganga, Luwanba, was mounted in Camagüey. A black Congo slave in a moment of rage killed the slave driver. He was tired of his abuse and so he took his machete from him and severed his head. There's a song that says, "*mambele mayoral . . . mambele, mambele mayoral . . . mambele*"; he killed the slave driver with his own machete and used his head to serve his own needs. How? He used the head of the slave driver in his nganga. . . . They got the skulls of the slave drivers, of the whites, so it would be a representation of what they were like in those times.

Here, the hierarchy of power associated with plantation slavery is recast as a mystical chain of command in which the slave-sorcerer becomes the "owner" of a phantom labor force controlled by the spirit of the abusive overseer he first slays in an act of violent resistance and then magically resurrects and contracts for work in his nganga. Whether real or imagined, such narratives suggest that the ritual mimesis of the "spectacular terror" associated with plantation slavery might find one of its most stunning examples in Cuba (compare Brown 2003). It is certainly possible that the ritual use of mutilated remains and/or body parts may have constituted ingenious attempts to capture some of the power associated with the spectacular violence and disciplinary regime of plantation slavery, such as public displays of the severed heads of rebel slaves, by imitating them in ritual praxis.[10]

However, it is striking and even peculiar that anything even remotely resembling Arcaño's and Wuicho's narratives does not appear anywhere in the fairly extensive literature on the nganga until fairly recently. Joel James is the only Cuban scholar that to my knowledge has ever alluded to how such original acts of resistance against slavery may have figured in the magical constitution of the nganga, and these assertions come only in his later publications in the late 1990s. The imagery expressed in the narratives of brujos like Arcaño and Wuicho would appear to at least partially support the assertions of revolutionary scholars like James, who, for example, derided the Cuban social sciences for ignoring the "fact" that the earliest nganga on the island contained the remains of slave traders, owners, and overseers (James 1996: 124).

Yet the literature on the nganga before the Special Period contains no such references to the ritual use of the remains of these colonial agents. In fact, the only reference to the ritual use of the remains of prominent white social actors comes from one of Lydia Cabrera's informants in the 1940s and '50s. This informant suggested that the skulls of white elites in the postcolonial era were among the most highly valued human remains for ritual use in the nganga. He mentioned an acquaintance, for instance, who was in possession of the remains of "a great *mundele*," or white person, "a little bone" for which this person "paid dearly" (Cabrera 1983: 132). This informant went on to explain that the skulls of white cadavers were highly prized not only for their "intelligence," but also for greatly expanding the social field of power in which the nganga was able to maneuver and act:

> Before, the sorcery of the black man did not always catch up with the white man. He needed to put a little piece of the white man in the pot. Today, they put the two brains [skulls] together. . . . Now they are equals according to that constitution [the constitution of the republic that notionally promoted liberal values such as racial equality through legal provisions]. And the Prenda kills the white man just as it does the black man. [You] will understand that if I ask [the spirit of] a white man to knock down another white man, that it shake him hard for me, he'll play the fool; the [spirit of the] white man will not go. . . . And the black man does the same thing as the white when he does not want to harm another like himself. . . . There are mayomberos who have nothing more than mundele, and their nganga never catch mundele. (Cabrera 1983: 132–33).

The phenomenology of Cuban race relations during the republic reverberates here in the structure of mystical relations embodied by the nganga. Since the spirit of a person would never cooperate in a mystical attack on another of his own race, it was necessary to expand the field of power largely circumscribed by race by placing the remains of both white and black cadavers in the nganga, "now equals according to that constitution." Yet the remains of powerful priest-healers, spirit mediums, and sorcerers of color were also highly prized, even as earlier as the latter half of the nineteenth century. The corpse of the famous Andrés Facundo Cristo de los Dolores Petit, for example, was rumored to have been relocated from the old colonial cemetery in Guanabacoa to the Espada Cemetery in Havana in order to "protect them from enemies who coveted his skull" (Cabrera 1977: 2). The contemporary salience of ritual discourse and imagery linking the nganga's historical origins to dramatic, romanticized visions of slave resistance, such as beheading an overseer and making a fetish of their skull, appears, then, to be a more recent development.

Another striking image recalling slavery conjured up in some spirit-possession ceremonies is the plantation bell. "We sing a song here," Arcaño noted, "*me esta llamando, me esta llamando, me esta llamando la campana de la bereta* [it's calling me; it's calling me; the *bereta* bell is calling me]." This song references an imagined dialogue between a runaway slave and the slave hunter who goes off with his dogs to hunt him down. "[The runaway slave] hears the slave hunter ringing the *bereta* bells," Arcaño continued, "which were used to wake up slaves and call them to work." Somewhere in the mountains the slave hunter releases the dogs, but the other slaves who are accompanying the slave hunter trick him by saying that they had seen the maroon running off in the other direction. "The bell marking the rhythm of the endless tasks," Moreno Fraginals wrote, "was like a sacred and profane symbol of the sugar mill. Just as a church without a bell tower was inconceivable, so with mills and coffee plantations" (Moreno Fraginals 1976: 148–49). The bells of the island's sugar mills punctuated the everyday rhythms of slave life; they served as a system of communication for everything from waking slaves up for predawn work to announcing the death of one of their number. In Arcaño's narrative the plantation bell takes on additional meaning. As the slave driver goes out looking for the runaway slave, he deliberately rings the plantation bell, a habitual form of hypnotizing aural terror intended to lure the runaway back. Like the spirit-hunting dogs mentioned at the beginning of this chapter, the haunting sounds of the plantation bells that once echoed throughout the cane fields and surrounding areas of the sugar estates are today invoked in ritual song to frighten the spirits of runaway slaves out of their hiding places and press them into ritual service.

The ritual mimesis of slavery is then at the heart of the mystical relations of command that bring together the nganga and the brujo. This imagery is further reinforced, for instance, by the dense materiality and semantic complexity of the nganga. The vertically arranged sticks that line the perimeter of these ritual fetishes, as David Brown perceptively noted, not only evoke images of the Cuban bush or wilderness, but may also serve as material metaphors for the *palenque* (fortified maroon settlements) built by runaway slaves on the island (Brown 1989: 373–74). Yet the imagery evoked in narratives like Wuicho's suggest a different interpretation; that is, the nganga do not appear to constitute symbolic palenques as much as they do microcosmic slave plantations. The vertical alignment of sticks might just as well recall the palisades that were sometimes built on the grounds of sugar estates to better control and monitor the movements of slaves, preventing them from fleeing to the surrounding hills and blocking the access of agitators who might incite the slaves to rebel (see Singleton 2001).

And what about the central place that dirt occupies in the nganga? What might the magical use of soil have to do with colonial slave hunts and their use of specially trained dogs for tracking down runaway slaves?[11] Dirt is a crucial ingredient in all nganga. Arcaño's nganga, "Tiembla Tierra" ("Shakes Earth"), for example, is stuffed with soil taken from within and around twenty-one different places: the bush, savannah, a hill, a palm tree, a silk cottonwood tree, a river, a beach, an anthill, a crossroads, his house, a Catholic church, a polyclinic, a hospital, a police station, a court tribunal, a prison, a cemetery, the seven tombs (siete tumba), a funeral home, and the slave quarters of the plantation in Baracoa where Manuel once labored in the sugar refinery. What is so striking about Arcaño's nganga, however, is that it not only compresses salient features of the local rural and urban landscape, but that this magical cartography also condenses a more global or transnational geography. Arcaño claims that his nganga contains soil taken from at least seven locations abroad—Ethiopia, Nigeria, Angola, Haiti, the Canary Islands, Hialeah, and New York. To some extent, the inclusion of these soils represents a spatial compression of the migratory circuits that define both Cuban history and the more recent diaspora that began with the 1959 revolution. The nganga then turn out to be much more than just microcosmic plantations or symbolic runaway slave settlements. Rather, they are stunning magical constructions encompassing a more global space-time compression in which salient geographies of the present are transposed within a cosmological structure that mirrors the historical landscape of power associated with the institution of slavery.

The soil collected and packed tightly into the nganga serves as a kind of olfactory map providing the dead with a sense of location or orientation, enabling them to navigate unfamiliar terrain, literally allowing them to smell their way to their destination. The centrality of imagery associated with olfaction betrays some rather striking genealogical links to colonial slave hunts on the island. Professional slave hunters, for instance, were often accompanied by "infernal dogs who paralyzed the runaway slave with fright. With their infallible sense of smell, these dogs would follow the scent to the mountains, the forest, and the hills and invariably discover and attack them" (Cabrera 1979: 43). The spirit of the dead residing in an nganga was sometimes referred to as a "dog" (el perro) by my informants. Some explain such imagery in ways that clearly recall the whole economy of chase and capture associated with colonial slave hunts on the island:

> Why do we call it a dog? Because the spirit of the dead [muerto], like a dog, follows the scent of the signatures [firmas, which are ideographic signs written in chalk or talcum powder] . . . and also because he follows the commands of the other spirit, the overseer. He's there to serve the other. And when I draw signatures and say, "Go see what such-and-such is doing," he goes tied by a chain. Because, look, if I order him to go to, I don't know, Pepe Cojo's house, Pepe Cojo could have the same thing as me and he could, through the mirror of the mpaka, capture the image of the dead. He could wind up imprisoned in the mirror.

In some ways, then, sorcery operates like a magical slave hunt; like the runaway slaves who were always in danger of being caught by slave hunters and their "infernal" dogs, the spirit "dogs" that are the dead are always at risk of being caught by rival sorcerers and imprisoned in their nganga. The "dogs," then, have to be magically tied to the nganga by invisible "chains" (cadena), not unlike a slave, who was sometimes literally shackled to the sugar plantation.[12]

The Specter of Revolt

The nganga and the brujos who work them are a great source of imagery for expressing local ideas and perceptions about social predation and the circulation of power in the post-Soviet present. This imagery, for example, sometimes directly implicates political culture. Rumors of various Cuban generals, politicians, and presidents who commission the magic of brujos or employ their own nganga for explicitly political ends are fairly well documented in literature (for example, Cabrera 1983: 193–94; Orozco and Bolívar 1998: 487–88; Miller 2000: 47; Miller 2004). This imagery not only feeds the political imaginary, but also provides a particularly rich idiom for moral commentary concerning social predation in an era of economic austerity. The links between sorcery and the deteriorating socioeconomic and moral conditions of the Special Period are perhaps most succinctly expressed in the song "El Tren" by the enormously popular Cuban *timba* group Los Van Van. After alluding to the moral derailment of social relations in the post-Soviet present by declaring that, "No one cares about anyone else; The care for others is over [*Nadie quiere a nadie; Se acabó el querer*]," the singer exclaims, "With me, no! With the *nganga*! [*Conmigo, no! Con la nganga!*]," warning his foes that messing with him would constitute a direct assault on his nganga, an offense with potentially dangerous consequences.

What popular cultural expressions such as these suggest is that the corrosion of socialist values that many link to the material scarcity and deprivation of the present has made it increasingly necessary to defend oneself against nefarious acts of social predation by seeking magical forms of protection. The nganga are one of the most valued resources for this kind of magical defense in contemporary Cuban society, and one that continues to be expressed in terms that emphasize both mystical subjugation and retaliation.

I would like to close this chapter with a brief example that vividly illustrates the extent to which ritual work provides such a powerful idiom through which to both express and address the moral derailment of social relations in post-Soviet Cuba. The moral repercussions associated with reckless acts of social predation are clear in the case of one brujo with a particularly infamous local reputation for alcohol abuse and morally dubious ritual activities. Salazar had been a gifted brujo, but in recent years he began spending much of his time and money consuming black market rum. He was also said to have become increasingly envious of one of his neighbors—an occasional drinking buddy—who had recently been befriended by a Spanish tourist. One day the two had an argument over money after spending much of the afternoon drinking at a local outdoor bar. Salazar felt that his friend was obligated to pay the bill since he was the one getting rich by hustling the Spanish tourist, another very common form of social predation in the post-Soviet present, but his friend insisted that they split the cost. Infuriated by what he perceived as a selfish unwillingness in his neighbor to share the gains earned from hustling, Salazar later told *his padrino* (ritual godfather) that he planned to get even by preparing some malevolent magic (*trabajo malo*) for his friend; that is, Salazar would attempt to ensorcell his neighbor. His padrino warned him not to do it because it would end badly for him, but Salazar ignored his advice:

> One morning he woke up fast and the first thing he did was construct a model hearse (*carretón*) and paint it black. He then made a doll using black cloth and stuffed it with the bones of a cadaver, soil from a nearby hospital, funeral home, cemetery, and the back patio of his friend's house. He placed the doll in the model hearse and waited until midnight. At midnight he placed a candle on the four street corners surrounding the man's house and with a rope pulled the hearse around the block, encircling the house. When he returned he left the hearse on the sidewalk leading to his friend's house and placed the doll in his nganga.

The following day Salazar's friend was drinking in a local outdoor bar and got into a fight with someone. Things took a turn for the worse when the friends of the man he was fighting with ganged up on him. They ended up stabbing him to death with a knife. Tormented by what had happened, Salazar's drinking got worse until finally, one day, in a drunken stupor, he poured *chispa de tren* over his nganga and lit it with a match, severely burning the object he felt was responsible for his woes. Later that very same day, he slipped on the sidewalk, hit his head on the concrete, and died. Salazar's alcoholism and reckless use of magical power had caused him to lose control of his nganga. The spirit of the dead residing there revolted, gaining the upper hand and turning on its owner in a dramatic act of mystical retaliation. This story resonates with what would eventually happen to the taxi driver mentioned in the previous section of this chapter. When I last saw him, El Gordo was getting around on a rusty old Chinese bicycle. He had lost his car, his primary source of income, had been forced to sell his furniture and television, and had abandoned his hopes of traveling to the United States due to his financial problems. The aggressive magic and sorcery that he had asked Arcaño to perform to get his wife back had instead "turned around" and "stuck" (*se le viró y pegó*) to him instead. In the end, El Gordo had only managed to ensorcell himself. It would seem, then, that the spirits of the dead—that come to acquire something of the character of slaves as residents of nganga—do indeed sometimes revolt.

Tying the Yuma to the Stick

CHAPTER 5

10 July 2004: El Gordo, the taxi driver, took us to visit Arcaño today. Arcaño's neighborhood is what Cubans call a llega y pon *(literally, "arrive and put down," but better translated as "shantytown"). Actually, it was a shantytown that had been partially transformed into more permanent housing. The result was a confusing jumble of simple, freshly painted concrete bungalows that stood up straight and weathered, wooden shacks that leaned at dramatic angles. Arcaño, out of rum and cigarettes, sent one of the local boys down to the* bodega *(government rationing store), and then led us down the narrow passage* (pasillo) *that led to his house, which he had recently covered in stucco with money he had managed to save from his only source of income, performing ritual services for his many clients.*

About forty minutes later a young, dark-skinned black woman approached and gently knocked on the door. Although she possessed a commanding, robust stature, Yaima, a thirty-two-year-old dancer at the infamous Tropicana nightclub in Havana, was timid and hesitated to explain the reason for her unannounced visit. "Now, tell me and don't worry," Arcaño told her in his deep, gruff voice, acquired from years of ritual singing, chain-smoking, and the daily consumption of the cheap black market rum that Cubans call "train spark" (chispa de tren), *"we're all family here." After a few aborted attempts at small talk, Yaima, visibly nervous and wringing her hands, explained that she had come after hearing stories of the power and efficacy of Arcaño's ritual work. The year before she had been the lover of a Spanish tourist. When he left, the Spaniard had promised to return within a few months and the two had made plans to resume their love affair. The Spaniard did indeed make another trip to Cuba, but two weeks after his arrival he still had not made any effort to contact the young dancer. Concerned that he had lost his desire to be with her, Yaima asked for Arcaño's help in bringing the Spaniard back.*

Arcaño, who was apparently accustomed to such requests, as would soon become clear, agreed to help. He instructed her to bring him a white dove, a piece of firebush (palo paramí), *a branch of wild tobacco* (guaraguao), *a marigold* (maravilla), *and the flower of a butter daisy* (boton de oro).[1] *He explained that with these materials and the name of the Spaniard he would bring him back to her.*

A week after Arcaño performed his magic, the Spaniard called Yaima twice from Havana but still did not express any intentions of meeting with her. Arcaño decided that stronger magic was needed; they would have to "sweeten" (*endulzar*) and "soften" his heart (*ablandar el corazón*) using a magically charged powder. He told her that she would in fact see her lover again, and that when she did she would have to secretly release the powder in his presence. The powder was prepared using cinnamon, firebush, wild tobacco, muskweed (*yamao*), a small branch from an almond tree, a spiderweb, and a piece of *nfumbi*, or spirit of the dead. Arcaño explained that some of these materials were things that the oricha Ochún liked and often used to seduce her lovers.[2] He instructed Yaima to take a bath infused with white flowers, chalk, and perfume before she met up with the Spaniard. A couple of days after their reunion, Yaima and the Spanish tourist resumed their love affair.

Returning from Arcaño's house after first meeting Yaima, La Mariquilla was more concerned that I might suspect her of doing ritual work on me than she was shocked to learn, as I was, that the national economy is not only subject to but perhaps somewhat dependent on such magical manipulations of foreign tourist desire:

> Look, I know what you're thinking. I don't do those things. But those things do happen a lot today. I don't like it, but the people do them. What happened is, after the socialist camp fell, a tremendous arroz con mango formed here. Now, with money [hard currency], everyone moves! Everybody wants to meet a tourist. They do a little ritual work [*trabajo*] so they will come. That's how it is. But those things are dan-

gerous. That's why I don't get involved with that stuff. One does his little work [*trabajito*] and everything is good; they are drinking beer, eating steak, and going to the discotheque, and the next day they lose everything. The magic turns on them.

It is striking here that the revolutionary state has revived prerevolutionary institutions such as the world-renowned Tropicana cabaret and nightclub, attempting to capitalize on the magical allure of republican decadence in the form of a fetish, the tropical female body. At the Tropicana, for instance, foreign tourists can now experience, or perhaps relive, the opulent capitalist decadence associated with the nation's republican past. Alluring showgirls wearing glittery headdresses and little else—the predecessors of whom paraded before international gangsters and jet-setters before the revolution—now shake (*menearse*) themselves for curious and nostalgic tourists who pay in the hard currency upon which the socialist economy now depends. No less conspicuous, however, is that a quasi-informal economy based on the magical manipulation of foreign desire has also risen in unison with state efforts to revive the tourist industry.

State economic strategies that mimic something of the tropical hedonism associated with the republic spill out into an informal tourism sector where street hustlers, or *jineteros*, compete with one another as objects of tourist attention and longing. "Spellbound by the magic of an alien value form [foreign currency]," Palmié notes, "Cuba nowadays lives less on the sugar that it still officially sells than off the *caramelos* (lit. 'sweets,' but more adequately translated as 'favors') that its populace finds willing to (or unable not to) make available to powerfully effective foreign demand" (Palmié 2002: 273). As Yaima's story illustrates, local efforts to tap into this global economy of desire entail harnessing the occult powers of orichas like Ochún Yeye-Moro, the "perfumed whore" and patron saint of many courtesans and prostitutes in the 1940s and '50s (see Benítez Rojo 1996: 15; Cabrera 1980: 310–18), herself a refraction of the infamous nineteenth-century *mulatta* who used her sexuality to trap white men of means in dependent relationships.

This chapter focuses on a so-far unexplored dimension of the literature on the Special Period—namely, the ritual management of desire via the use of love magic in the tourist-driven economy of Havana.[3] Tracing ethnographically some of the ways in which love magic is both talked about and practiced, I focus on how the distortions of a dollarized tourist economy have come to be perceived as magically controlled and controllable. Despite the revolutionary state's disparaging view of such local social actors as jineteros, the national economy, I argue, is not only subject to but to some extent dependent on the magical manipulation of desire and the fantasies of both foreign tourists and the Cuban masses.

Occult Economies

"Money is transcendent!" La Mariquilla exclaimed in dismay. Ildamis's daughter had just stopped by and asked me to exchange one of my dollars for her twenty-six pesos. It never occurred to me that this mundane, seemingly innocent request may have actually been an act of predation—the sorcery of money. That money and objects are "transcendent," that they can be transformed into mystical agents conveying secret desires and hidden intentions, was brought home to me that night in Guanabacoa. "You should never have done that," La Mariquilla admonished, "she is envious and that money could be ensorcelled [*embrujado*]." In the hustle economy of post-Soviet Cuba, where the magical power of sorcery circulates alongside the equally magical, affective power and lure of hard currency, the desire to meet, befriend, and maintain intimate relationships with foreign tourists has not only become a major means of local economic survival, but also a strategy for transnational migration. Romances between locals and visiting foreigners hold out the prospect (or promise) of a coveted immigration visa, a ticket out of the country to better opportunities abroad. Rather than leave this process to chance, some attempt to enhance the value of their emotional and erotic labor by turning to the seductive power of love magic. Ildamis's daughter may not only have been eager to swap the faded images of Cienfuegos, Maceo, and Martí that grace the massively devalued Cuban peso for the once-forbidden, emerald images of Washington, Lincoln, and Franklin. Her request to exchange money, La Mariquilla and her family feared, might also have been a covert attempt to "tie" (*amarrar*) me down, to magically seduce me into beginning a prolonged, romantic contact with her.[4]

Challenging the widespread view that magical epistemologies and practices reflect the irrational superstitions of backward, "primitive" societies, a number of recent ethnographic studies have demonstrated that magic, witchcraft, and sorcery have not only developed in conjunction with but constitute meaningful responses to modern economic, social, and political conditions (for example, see Taussig 1980; Apter 1993; Geschiere 1997; Comaroff and Comaroff 1999). In a highly influential article, Jean and John Comaroff, for example, focus on the alarming rise in what they call "occult economies" in South Africa (1999). This term refers to the real or imagined deployment of magical means for material ends (ritual murder, theft of body parts, production of zombies, pyramid schemes, and other financial scams). The Comaroffs trace the alleged rise in the magical production of wealth to the ideological confrontation of rural South Africa with the alien ideas of millenial capitalism and the neoliberalism. As Brian Brazeal notes:

> The central tenets of this "occult economies school" are that impover- ished people in post-colonies become aware of increased capital flows in their countries and vast sums of money concentrated in the hands of some of their compatriots. Since this money is not being earned through traditional channels like agriculture, industry and extrac- tion, they conclude that earning money depends on the manipulation of occult forces. So they accuse the rich of manipulating occult, evil forces for their benefit, or they themselves undertake various forms of black magic for their own enrichment. Magic produces value without labor, land or capital. As Mauss put it, magic is "pure production *ex nihilo*." (2007)

Brazeal, however, notes that although certain local actors may harness morally dubious occult forces to economic strategies, more often than not they are merely trying to subsist rather than get rich. Their appeals to occult forces are part of a precarious balancing act that mediates between the con- tradictory pressures of economic necessity, on the one hand, and religious and social obligations on the other. The use of magic for material ends is, then, a more nuanced practice, a morally ambiguous way of participating in a morally ambiguous economy. Although some ritual economies may mimic "the productivity of capital with alienated labor," morally dubious wealth gained through paid ritual work can be laundered or whitewashed, then allowed to recirculate within a broader system of social relations that stress reciprocity.

Likewise, love magic targeting foreign tourists in post-Soviet Cuba is hardly a get-rich-quick scheme. It is simply one strategy to make ends meet in the new culture of *resolver*. "Wealth" generated through ritual work that violates morally acceptable constraints can be and is, in fact, domesticated.

La Mariquilla, for example, placed all morally suspect monies beneath her Elegguá, saying that after a few days of resting there the bills could be used to buy a little tobacco, rum, and candy for the spirit guardian of the house. The money, in other words, could not be employed for personal use; it would have to be spent on Elegguá. Yet the ritual domestication of new wealth can also function as a smokescreen for conspicuous consumption. Seduced by the magical allure of global capitalism and a consumer lifestyle, some seek in popular religions like Ocha-Ifá a less stigmatized arena for what Cubans call "speculation"—that is, a kind of ideological contestation based on ostentatious spending, the consumption of luxury items, and the hedonistic ethos of living for the moment (Holbraad 2004).

The social permutations and distortions that have come about as a result of the introduction of hard currency into the national economy and due to the pervasive presence of foreign tourists from mostly wealthier nations fuel perceptions of an economy both mystically managed and manageable. Although the state publicly shuns incipient capitalist values, singling out the jinetero as the primary culprit for the moral corruption that threatens socialist modernity from within, both official and extra-official strategies attempting to tap into global economic flows are tied at the hip. The intimacy between local magic targeting foreigners and the state's flirtation with capitalist economic models, therefore, cannot be adequately explained by appealing to the binary categories that mark scholarly discourse on domination. Moreover, as I describe below, magical idioms of power are not merely expressions of the work of global capitalism in another register, but rather, as Vidal and Whitehead note, "part of an original and independent postcolonial political condition" (2004: 77). In contemporary Cuba, love magic constitutes a unique political imaginary, both an interpretation of and attempt to influence the circulation of power in society.

Between Fact and Fantasy

Love magic exists somewhere in the borderland between fact and fantasy, intentional act and salacious rumor, the desiring subject and the love object itself. It is a common subject of local, neighborhood *chisme* (gossip and rumor) or *radio bemba* (word of mouth). It is in this context that all unofficial and informal circulation of news and sociopolitical commentary takes place. In a society where all news media are subject to state ownership and serve as the formal organs of state propaganda, radio bemba provides a medium through which citizens chronicle both local minutiae and the public secrets of the nation-state, narrowing the gap between "official" news and people's lived experience (Miller 2000). It is both a trade in dirty secrets and an informal social palaver, where "stray facts, manic theories, and well-told lies" characterize popular discourse on the morality of power.

I remember something Lucita, one of La Mariquilla's neighbors, used to always say. Whenever I asked how everything was going, her favorite response was always, "I'm in the fight," or the daily struggle to make ends meet, "looking for a foreign sugar daddy [*estoy en la lucha buscando un pepe*]." Although Cubans frequently joke about such matters in this manner, Lucita's response calls attention to the very real desire (and perhaps necessity) among some Cubans to pursue relationships with foreigners either for temporary monetary gain or the long-term benefits of marriage and migration. The bulk of the state's resources are now invested in reviving the island's tourist industry. As economic deprivations worsened throughout the 1990s and the number of foreign tourists from Europe and North America increased, the country experienced a sharp rise in illicit economic activities. This ranged from an expanding black market to what is referred to in popular speech as *jineterismo*; that is, the hustling and courtesan-like entrepreneurialism that takes place within the island's tourist zones. Although many, including some Cubans, use the term to refer exclusively to prostitution, the purveyors of this new form of hustling, the jineteros, actually engage in a broad range of economic activities ranging from the selling of various goods and services to providing both friendly and romantic company and, in some cases, sex to tourists. In return they may receive money, consumer goods, a nice meal in a hotel restaurant, or an invitation to a local discotheque for a night of free drinks and entertainment. In exchange for providing romantic companionship and sexual favors, they may also receive marriage proposals and invitations to leave the country and live abroad.

Hustling and black market transactions have raised concerns about the potential for moral decay and corruption of both socialist and cultural values; jineterismo, for example, is derided by the revolutionary Cuban state as reflecting decadent capitalist values that promote individualism, accumulation, and consumption. The Special Period has also witnessed the reappearance of the racialized images of sexuality that first emerged during the colonial era and were later reinforced by rampant prostitution in the republic that gave Cuba its infamous epithet: "the brothel of the Caribbean."

In both the popular and revolutionary imaginations, the illicit economic activities of jineterismo, which may or may not involve commodified sexual exchanges with foreigners, are more often than not associated with women, and, more precisely, women of color. The resemblance of the figure of the jinetera to the seductive mulatta of bygone eras, the erotic image of which was produced primarily through the prism of white male desire, is uncanny. The predatory eroticism of the colonial and neocolonial-era mulatta was a fantasy that transformed white men of means into the victims of black and mulatta women and freed them from the guilt of sexual attraction, oppression, and rape (Helg 1995: 17,018). Her supposed salacious appetite for sexual liaison was held to be responsible for disrupting the orderly social boundaries of race and class that defined civil society.

Likewise, the erotic agency of the black or honey-colored jinetera of post-Soviet Cuba is not only a fantasy that frees male sex tourists from the guilt of sexual exploitation, but she is also a local scapegoat for the anxieties about capitalist entrepreneurialism and globalization that plague the Special Period. By flirting with capitalist values, the jinetera threatens to open tropical socialism to global capitalist penetration through morally dubious forms of intimacy with foreign tourists. Since she alone is to blame, the jinetera frees the rest of society from the guilt that has accompanied liberal economic reforms and an increasing reliance on foreign tourist dollars. Like her colonial and neocolonial predecessors, the jinetera has become a "symbolic container" for all of the assorted unease, contradictions, and competing values associated with the *apertura*, or "opening," that followed changes in Cuba's post-Cold War policy (Kutzinski 1993: 7–11).

A comparable stock of racialized sexual imagery characterizes popular discourse on love magic. Almost invariably, women, and especially women of color, are said to resort to the use of magical charms, powders, baths, perfumes, and incantations to manipulate the amorous sentiments of desirable men of means. The association of love magic with women of color, so common in ethnographic literature on this subject (for example, see Ortiz 2001; Cabrera 1980; and Lachatañeré 2004), was immortalized in Guillermo Rodríguez Fife's popular composition "Bilongo," in which the singer confesses his love for the beautiful "*negra* Tomasa." His love for her is so unusually strong that he accuses her of casting a spell on him (*esa negra linda que me echó bilongo*) by introducing magical substances into his coffee and food. Love magic continues to be associated with black and mulatta women in the popular imagination. Yet, during my stay on the island, something had changed. Whereas most believe love magic itself has essentially remained the same, the mystical erotic manipulations of local black and mulatta women were now said to increasingly prey on male tourists.

These suspicions are not just typical of local discourse, but have begun to capture the social imaginary of foreign tourists as well. Stephan Palmié, for example, recounts how a German tourist once contacted him after going to Cuba and spending a night with a woman there. The tourist wanted to know whether or not a garlic clove he had found on the windowsill of her house the following morning might have been an ingredient in some kind of magical operation to bind him to the woman (Palmié 2002: 286–87). The gender conceptions and racial imagery that underpin these stories about male victimization by magically empowered women in the Special Period have clearly been reinforced by popular discourse on jineterismo. The literal meaning of *jineterismo* is "horseback riding," implying that the female jinetera figuratively "rides" both the new economy and male tourists through hustling and/or sex trade (Fernandez 1999: 81). In the popular imagination, jineterismo and love magic are implicitly linked; both cast black and mulatta women as the purveyors of a new entrepreneurial spirit and a mercenary sexuality that preys on male tourists and thus represents a threat to local machismo, socialist values, and the metaphysical boundaries of the nation-state.

Ochún, Love Magic, and Cosmopolitanism

The use of magic by Cubans in long-distance love affairs is not entirely new. One of Lydia Cabrera's informants, for instance, told her the story of their godmother, who commissioned the magic of a local brujo after her Galician lover left her and returned to Spain (the date is unspecified, but most likely it occurred sometime during the 1940s or '50s):

> The sorcerer that my godmother went to consult in Regla passed three eggs over her body. He made two dolls. One represented her and was stored away. The other . . . he tied . . . to a *garabato* [hooked stick] of wild sugarcane with twenty-one knots. In a little play boat he also placed pome fruit and small bags. She didn't know what they had inside. He placed the doll in the boat and said that it would go looking for the man. He ordered her to take the boat to the Malecón,

to the Castillo de la Punta, and there she put it in the water. There were waves, and she saw the little boat fighting with the surge and it went along rowing, straight ahead, and far away into the sea until she lost sight of it. After a few months the Galician returned very much in love! (Cabrera 1979: 199)

More than just a curious entry in a long compendium of magical recipes and formulas, this brief ethnographic anecdote suggests that the cosmopolitan nature of Cuban love magic reaches much further into the past.

Specific examples like this one, however, are few and far between in ethnographic literature on this subject. Where mention of such practices does occur, it usually consists almost exclusively of a vast inventory of magical materials and methods that are extracted from their personal and sociocultural context. Nonetheless, there are a few ethnographic particulars that shed some light on the general contours of these practices in Cuban society, both past and present. While most Cuban ethnographers usually make some reference to love magic, no systematic account of its varieties exist. The occasional ethnographic forays into the subject by Fernando Ortiz, Rómulo Lachatañeré, and Lydia Cabrera, however, along with what I was able gather, together paint at least a general picture. All magical operations are usually subsumed under the rubric *trabajo*, meaning "work." Love magic, in particular, straddles what is in effect a morally thin line between those trabajos designed to "attract" (*atraer*), "subdue" (*amansar*), "soften the heart" (*ablandar el corazon*), "seduce" (*seducir*), or "captivate" (*cautivar*), on the one hand, and those intended to "conquer" (*conquistar*), "dominate" (*dominar*), "bind" (*ligar*), or "tie (*amarrar*) on the other.[5] The difference is essentially between magical procedures that work to arouse desire in the other and more aggressive efforts that aim to mystically circumscribe their sexual potency or behavior. Although both types are considered morally dubious in the popular imagination, the latter is more clearly associated with mercenary sociality or predatory sorcery.

Although a number of organic substances and aphrodisiacs make up the magical arsenal of these practices (and their materiality is no doubt central to their efficacy and tangibility), the basic guiding strategy of most forms of love magic is the blurring of corporeal boundaries between the desiring subject and the desired love object. Reflecting the desire for anonymous access to the body of the other, love magic, following Ioan Couliano, is perhaps one of the most fundamental strategies for intersubjective transference (1987). The more immediate and concrete focus of love magic, then, is on the ritual management of bodily, sensory, and eroticized exchanges between the desired and those who would like to arouse desire in them. Many trabajos, for example, involve placing bodily substances such as saliva, pubic hair, or genital secretions in the food or drink of the other. The consumption of these substances, whose fetish powers derive from their status as carnal synecdoches of the person, grants one access to the other's body or, more precisely, their desires vis-à-vis the heart.

The deliberate blurring of corporeal boundaries is further reinforced by the sensorial primacy rituals attach to smell. Perhaps because of their ethereal quality, odors are often associated with the liminal transgressions of love magic and the subliminal experience of desire and dream (see Howes 2003: 276; Gell 1977). In Cuba, many of these practices deploy pungent and/or sweet-smelling botanicals such as muskweed, cinnamon, almond tree blooms, orange blossoms, and roses. Love charms are made in the form of powders, scented baths, and perfumes that are either placed on or rubbed into the bodies of the authors of such acts or else released discreetly in the presence of the other. "When I was in my glory, and even more so later as an old man," Lydia Cabrera's informant Calazán recalled, "a little splinter of cinnamon in my mouth to sweeten my words always made a woman fall in love" (Cabrera 1983: 364). Cinnamon powder, Cabrera found, was also mixed with makeup by "flirtatious women" and then rubbed into their bodies, "because cinnamon attracts men like flies to honey" (1983: 365). There are trabajos, of course, which focus on other sensory organs, such as the eye—for example, the eyes of the *majá* (water snake) are among the ingredients included in an amulet whose purpose is to "hypnotize" a lover; photographs and proxy dolls depicting the two parties are "stuck" together using magnets and honey and then tied in a magical act of binding. Transmission through food consumption, olfaction, and bodily absorption, however, were the most common means of delivery in those cases of love magic I was able to document.

Although there is evidence that men also commission trabajos for love matters—for example, the efficacy of men's love magic is often said to be made possible through the supernatural agency of Changó, and women's through Ochún—some of the earliest accounts of these practices directly associate them with women. Fernando Ortiz, for instance, suggested that love magic did not interest the "stronger" sex, but instead belonged to the domain of women, who were interested in guaranteeing the romantic or sexual fidelity of men (cited in Lachatañeré 2004: 232).[6] La Mariquilla seconded this opinion, once commenting that women use love magic "because we are weaker than men and suffer more in matters of love."

Though sometimes embraced by women, these social clichés may in fact be rooted in male anxieties concerning the female body and sexuality that are traceable to the colonial period. Gender demographics in Cuba's slave economy during the nineteenth century, as Vera Martínez-Alier's study makes clear, were uneven; whereas men significantly outnumbered women in the white Cuban community, women significantly outnumbered men in the free black population (1974). Because the relatively small number of white women belonged to the elite classes of wealthy families and colonial officials, poor, white Spanish immigrants often took black and mulatta women as lovers and, in some cases, spouses. Sexual liaisons across the color line not only fueled masculine anxieties by upsetting the colonial metaphysics of blood (that is, the racial purity and sanctity of the white female body) upon which the orderliness of the slave economy depended, but also contributed to black male unease by undermining their role as the patriarchal guardians of black and mulatta women (Martínez-Alier 1974: 118). Although one might expect black males to have been more invested in mystical romantic coercion (and perhaps they were), given their tenuous hold on black female sexuality, women were nevertheless overwhelmingly associated with the morally dubious practices attributed to love magic.

Two related masculine attitudes may have conspired to produce this association in the popular imagination by the turn of the twentieth century: first, the mythical status of black and mulatta women as sexual mercenaries and harlots, an idea which freed white men from the shame of racial miscegenation and the transcendental moral stains it impressed upon the body politic; second, the lack of honor they experienced as a result may have fueled masculine unease across the racial divide and motivated their attempts to instill guilt in women vis-à-vis their alleged promiscuity, on the one hand, and their attempts to manage their own romantic and sexual labor on the other. Perceptions of male victimization by "loose" black and mulatta women could then have easily generated fantasies about the latter's predations through love magic. If so, it would not have been the black and mulatta female's status as the weaker sex so much as her actual exercise of power in relation to erotic predation that reinforced these associations in the male imagination. Whereas men are feminized in this discourse by the female's attempt to circumscribe male desire, women assume the male role of sexual aggressor.[7]

These associations are often reinforced in the state-run media. Take, for example, the Cuban telenovela *Al compás del son*, which chronicles the story of a wealthy, white family and the daughter's love affair with a mulatto *tres* player during Machado's rule between 1925 and 1933. The mother of the girl disapproves and repeatedly prays to the Virgin de la Caridad del Cobre (who for her is the Virgin Mary) to make her daughter and a prominent government official fall in love and marry. Meanwhile, a poor mulatta who is also in love with the mulatto resorts to love magic using honey, perfume, sunflowers, and the image of the Virgin de la Caridad del Cobre (who for her is Ochún) to make the musician fall for her. Although both racial classes are ritually invested in these neocolonial economies of desire, both desiring subjects are women. Racial fantasies are, nonetheless, reinscribed in this revolutionary soap opera. The mother, for instance, appeals to supernatural assistance only to protect her class interests. The mulatta, on the other hand, who is ultimately held responsible for destroying the relationship after she tells the daughter a lie about the musician (thus becoming the purveyor of a malicious rumor), is depicted as being actually involved in mystical forms of sexual predation.

The fact that women apparently embrace these fantasies may reflect an entirely different kind of gender maneuvering—namely, female sentiments vis-à-vis the moral foundations of power, and the perception that they suffer more in matters of the heart.[8] The racial cartographies and essentialized masculine values associated with relations of command (typical of colonial authority), the successive military dictatorships of the republican era, and the several decades of rule by the revolutionary elite are symbolically undermined by tales of Afro-Cuban women's mystical romantic agency. Take, for instance, the racialized erotic imagery associated with Ochún and especially her privileged status as the supernatural fulcrum of black and mulatta women's magic. First, there are the depictions of her as a sensual, cosmopolitan mulatta, a figure that was soon converted into a national fetish and screen for Creole fantasies:

Ochún, oricha of the river, love, and all things sweet, found out that those who were sent to Cuba were lonely and sad, so she decided to go there to dance, comfort, and keep them company. However, she worried about the long voyage from Africa to Cuba. Full of apprehension, she went to visit her sister Yemayá, oricha of the sea, and told her, "Yemayá, I have to cross the sea to go to Cuba and be with my children but I am afraid of the long trip." Yemayá comforted her, "Don't be afraid, Ochún, I will take care of you. I will take you to the bottom of the ocean and we will cross it without hazards." Appeased, Ochún said, "You have reassured me, but tell me Yemayá, you who reach all the way to Cuba and visit its shores and beaches, how is Cuba and how are the Cubans?" Yemayá told Ochún, "Cuba is very much like Africa. There are many coconut and palm trees, it is never cold, and it has peaceful rivers and long tropical nights. However, all the Cubans are not black as the people here, some are white and others are mulattoes." Ochún, still apprehensive, told Yemayá, "I am worried since I am not used to people different from us. I would like you to grant me two wishes. As we make our way to Cuba I want the waves of the ocean to straighten my hair just a little bit and its foams to lighten my skin just a little. Thus, when I arrive in Cuba I will neither be black nor white. I will be accepted by all Cubans, blacks, whites, and mulattoes. All of them will be my children." With her queenly and maternal demeanor Yemayá granted Ochún her two wishes, and this is why Cubans were graced with a mother who resembles them all (paraphrased from Sandoval 1983: 620).

Given the fetish power of her image as the sultry, supernatural mulatta, the owner of love, it is not surprising that Ochún would also become the mystical agent most commonly associated with feminine varieties of love magic. Indeed, one of her avatars, Ochún Yeyé-Moró, clearly embodies many of the features attributed to this mulatta seductress in the colonial imagination (compare Murphy 2001: 95).

During the republican era, when tourist casinos and dapper social clubs became the Dionysian playground of wealthy North American gangsters and elites, this same Ochún became the patron saint of many prostitutes, courtesans, and brothels. In the popular imagination she is known for her charm or flattery (*zalamería*), playful romanticism, and seductiveness. Ochún Yeyé-Moró, as Arcaño put it, "is a whore, but here whoreness is sacred [*es una puta pero su putería es sagrada*]." Courtesans and prostitutes solicited her supernatural assistance in their trade by filling basins with river water, then adding five roses of varying colors, five grains of roasted corn, five grams of Guinea pepper, five drops of honey, four spoonfuls of Valencia rice, incense or cologne, and Florida water. After covering the basin with a yellow handkerchief and leaving it overnight beneath her bed, the stage of her erotic arts, a prostitute would then use the liquid to wash the floors of the house, which was believed to ward off harmful magical substances and attract clients (Cabrera 1980: 318). There was also the so-called prostitute's powder—a love charm prepared using "talisman powders" such as the hairs of a dog in heat, the shell of a brooding dove, deer antler shavings, incense, white precipitate, valerian powder, cinnamon powder, chalk, musk wood, and five corals. The powder was blown and/or spread at the entrance of the house or rubbed into the woman's body "when in business" (Cabrera 1980: 310–11).

Just as Ochún had been the favored patron saint of prostitutes and courtesans before the 1959 revolution, the jinetera of the post-Soviet era is also typically depicted as a devotee of this oricha. The jinetera is said to carry around her amulets and special powders in order to "sweeten" and awaken desire in male tourists, gaining the magical upper hand in this changing economy of desire. Her flirtation with capitalist values, pornographic subversion of "the moral imaginary sustaining revolutionary governance" (compare Hernandez-Reguant 2006), cosmopolitan fantasies, and romantic mystical coercion of foreign tourists have transformed her into the screen onto which revolutionary anxiety is projected in post-Soviet Cuba. Her body is one of the most privileged sensual terrains upon which the moral cartographies of the Special Period are increasingly being mapped.

Magic, Tourism, and the Global Economy of Desire

The jinetera's alleged embrace of the new spirit of entrepreneurialism embodied in hustling activities and morally dubious solicitations of foreign tourists makes her the most stereotyped representative of the new culture of resolver.[9] There are direct continuities, as Stephan Palmié notes, between the global inequalities of international tourism and the hegemonic power of colonial and postcolonial economies (2002). Just as colonial economic arrangements fueled the development of Caribbean societies and solidified their dependence on foreign capital, contemporary tourist economies are dependent on a single source of hard currency that appropriates local human and natural resources in order to satisfy the momentary pleasure demands of foreign consumers.

These arrangements are not just driven by rational self-interest, but by specific economies of desire. The consumption habits and pleasure demands of wealthy Europeans gave rise to a whole system of commodified slave labor in the Caribbean and made possible a global structure of imperial power which racialized consumption. Black bodies were inextricably linked to the colonial economy of desire, a fact that explains the constant slippage between economic and sexual matters in colonial discourse. These bodies were in effect screens for the gendered, racial unease that haunted the colonial imagination. Likewise, sex tourism reflects a desire to satisfy fantasies of control over self and others in a sexual, racialized, and gendered context. So it is not just the erotic allure of exotic bodies that matters here; rather, it is the transformative work that exotic bodies perform in the valorization of identity that deserves attention (Palmié 2002: 271–76). Given the extent of local economic deprivations, the buying power of tourists is so great that racial fantasies casting tropical women of color as lusty nymphomaniacs that are always "hot for it" are willingly and routinely acted out for male sex tourists (O'Connell Davidson 1996: 46).

We are dealing here with what Denise Brennan has called an "economy of desire based on difference" (2004:22). What she describes concerning the Dominican Republic is equally applicable to Cuba. Sex tourists, for instance, tend to be motivated by gender and racial fantasies whose potential realization is imagined to lie in usually underdeveloped nations. Discontent with gender and race relations in their home countries sometimes fuels their eroticization of cultural gender and racial differences. Not unlike the state-run tourist industry, sex workers attempt to capitalize on the imaginations of foreign travelers, even if their fantasies are based on gender and racial stereotypes. According to Brennan, they are often consumed by an economic fantasy in which "[they] dream of European men 'rescuing' them from a lifetime of poverty and foreclosed opportunities" (2004: 20). During my fieldwork, for instance, women involved in these kinds of relationships often contrasted what they believed was the general politeness and respect of foreign tourists to the *guapería*, or machismo, that they believed to be typical of Cuban men. Cuban men described women, however, as being "lucky" with tourists. Sex tourists, on the other hand, warn others like them not to fall in love (Palmié 2002:284), alerting them to the dangers of falling for those "feminine," "polite," "classy" women who, "unlike their American counterparts . . . are completely comfortable being women and do not feel compelled to compete with men."[10]

The almost exclusive focus on commercial transaction in much of the literature on sex tourism in Cuba and elsewhere, however, has often helped sustain the myth of the sex worker as victim. Popular imagery associated with the jinetera, by contrast, explicitly acknowledges her erotic agency and the way in which she undermines sexual objectification:

> the *jinetera* is not just a depersonalized object of tourist desire, and her sexuality is not a mere object of commercial exchange. Rather, popular discourse inverts this imagery by casting [the *jinetero or -tera*] . . . as an agent who literally "whips the money" out of his or (more often) her victim whose desire she has aroused for strictly mercenary reasons, impassioning him (*apasionarle*) literally to *buy* into his own fantasy of sexual domination. It is, thus, the tourist's personhood that is reduced to an objectified source of hard cash. (Palmié 2002: 282–83)

The implication is that the jinetera does not simply attempt to satisfy the terms of a sexual exchange but "seduce[s] the stranger into potentially unwilled forms of emotional experience" (Palmié 2002: 284; Cabezas 2004; Fosado 2004). Yet the erotic agency of the jinetera also happens to be the source of her undoing in the popular imagination. In a society where old-fashioned machismo still defines the modus vivendi of public life, one of the side effects of this imagery is the jinetera's association with symbolic masculinity (as sexual predator), *interés* (material interests), and even mystical predation via love magic.

Love Magic as Political Discourse

This calls attention to the tendency in both popular discourse and the literature on sex tourism to eschew the emotional economy of transnational romantic and sexual relations (see Constable 2003; Fosado 2003). The fact that feelings of emotional attachment, affection, and even love sometimes figure prominently in transnational romantic encounters is simply unthinkable for some, a structural impossibility for others. This premise is even played out in popular media. The Cuban teleplay *Pompas de jabón* (Soap Bubbles), for instance, depicts a young Cuban woman who feigns love for a wealthy, much older, French tourist. The silence in popular discourse regarding the emotional economy of jineterismo in post-Soviet Cuba has very tangible racializing effects. The rise in the number of interracial romantic relationships between foreigners and black and mulatta women during the Special Period, as Ariana Hernandez-Reguant notes, "became the talk of the town, subject of scorn in jokes, plays and novels, and revealing, above all, a status quo of segregated intimacy" (2006). Many white Cubans routinely express their doubts about racially mixed, romantic encounters between locals and tourists, dismissing them out of hand as illegitimate or counterfeit and stigmatizing them by associating them with interés and the mercenary sociality associated with jineterismo (Hernandez-Reguant 2006).

Yet the use of love magic by women in the Special Period often undermines these caricatures and presents a more nuanced picture, one inextricably entangled with the murky interpersonal dynamics of the increasingly cosmopolitan spaces of Havana's tourist zones. What emerges is the sense that, in some instances at least, love magic resembles what de Certeau has called an "antidiscipline" or "tactic;" that is, the use of love magic by women as a mystical subversion of the local and global economies of desire that encourage their subordination (1984). Take, for instance, the story of Elcita, the older sister of one of Caridad's schoolmates:

> I know this jinetera named Elcita that was with this Italian tourist. Things were all right between them but the foreigner's family didn't like the fact that he was going [andando] with a black girl. The first time he came here everything was good. But after he left he never came back. So, Elcita went to see this sorcerer I know. He made some kini kini and a powder out of I don't know what. Later, Elcita wrote a letter and mailed it to Italy with the powder inside. A few months later, the Italian came back here to see her. They were in love and wanted to get married. Elcita wanted to go live with him in Italy. When he returned she took him to meet the sorcerer. He didn't know anything about the magic. The sorcerer performed a purification rite [despojo] with seven strong herbs for Elcita because she was the one the Italian's family had problems with. The sorcerer was concerned that they had their own magic. They never got married because of his family but the Italian still visits her at times.

As this story and many others like it suggest, love magic is sometimes an attempt to magically counteract both the fleeting or episodic character of romantic encounters between locals and tourists and the global dynamics of racial marginalization and exclusion.

The use of magic to stop the flow of people or thwart the exit of lovers "to other countries across the seas," for example, has been common since at least the time of Lydia Cabrera's ethnographic field research in 1940s and '50s (Cabrera 1979: 199; 1980: 305–306). This is no less the case in the tourist-driven economy of post-Soviet Cuba. Elcita's use of love magic is not so much mystical predation as it is a defensive act; she is in love and turns to magic in order to circumvent abandonment and her rejection as a *negra* by her lover's family. Here, the magical realism of popular culture subverts the magical power of neocolonial imaginaries that serve to mystify power relations (see Taussig 1987; de Certeau 1984: 17–18). Elcita's sorcerer suspects that her lover's Italian family may be deploying their own mystical arsenal to defend their racial fantasies from being jeopardized by interracial intimacy. The mystical power of love magic, then, is only matched by the equally mystifying effects of racial hegemony.

This is not just a problem that Cubans potentially face with their lover's or spouse's family abroad. Perceptions of racial profiling in the tourist zones of Havana function to prevent unregulated contact between locals and foreign tourists. In those sections of the city with a high concentration of tourists, police frequently stop black Cubans and ask them for their *carnet* (national ID card). Furthermore, Cubans, until recently, were not allowed in certain tourist hot spots (for example, hotels, theaters, and beaches) unless they were accompanied by a tourist. A policeman who stopped (and eventually detained) a black friend of mine along the Malecón one night, for example, told me that it was done for "our protection"—meaning, to protect foreigners from local hustlers. Most black Cubans, however, call attention to the fact that white Cubans are hardly ever stopped and that this really reflects a deeply rooted racist association of blackness with criminality. The National Revolutionary Police (PNR), as one acquaintance speculated, assume that tourists feel safer and spend more money the less "black" an area looks. This is what many black Cubans refer to as the "tourist apartheid" of the Special Period (see Schwartz 1997). Not a few of them carry special protective charms (*resguardo*) to evade police harassment. The need for mystical assistance is even more acute in matters related to travel and immigration. The stigma that immigration policies both at home and abroad attach to transborder marriages, especially if the couple is interracial, prompt many to seek extra help. It is perfectly normal for a Cuban to carry special magical powders and talismans prepared for them by some brujo or priest-healer on the day of their visa interview, which they then deposit somewhere on the grounds of the immigration office.

The pervasive conviction among many of my acquaintances in Cuba that women are more vulnerable in their romantic relationships with men, that they "suffer more in matters of love," was a common explanation for the association of women and love magic during my fieldwork. The tourist's mobility, as well as their ability to conceal much more of their personal life than can their romantic interest on the island, is a source of much anxiety for those locals involved in transnational romantic relationships. Juanita, for example, a thirty-year-old mulatta and waitress in a Vedado restaurant, told me she had initially resorted to hustling tourists in order to support herself and her mother, who was unable to work due to medical problems. Juanita told me about her various foreign "boyfriends" (*novios*), as she called them. When I asked if she had ever fallen in love with any of them, she said, "yeah, I was in love with a Spaniard. We used to do everything together but the problem was that he never told me he was married until later." Juanita continued her relationship with the Spaniard nonetheless, hoping that he would eventually leave his wife, but he never did. With very few available means to seek redress for male sexual predation, objectification, or abuse, Cuban women sometimes feel that the mystical power of love magic is the only recourse. The use of love magic in these kinds of situations constitutes what might be described as mercenary acts of retribution directly linked to the gendered violence of both local machismo and the predations of sex tourists.

Stories abound in published literature and on the streets, for example, about women's appeal to magic as a way to circumscribe male sexual prowess or adulterous wanderings, evade abandonment, or provide escape from an abusive lover or spouse (for example, see Lachatañeré 2004: 133–34). Arcaño was enlisted by the mother of a woman trapped in an abusive marriage with a German. The woman's daughter, the mother explained, had married a German tourist and left the island to live with him in Germany, where they were raising a child together. The man, it turned out, was a drunk, and he had begun to beat his Cuban wife. Although she was desperate to leave him and return with her child to Cuba, the husband would not let her go. So, the mother, greatly concerned about the health and well-being of her daughter and granddaughter, asked Arcaño to help her do something about the situation. He had the mother bring an unsealed letter addressed to her son-in-law, into which he placed a powder to "incapacitate" the man and cause him to release his wife and daughter. After the letter was left for a week or so in Arcaño's nganga, he gave it to the mother, who then mailed it to Germany.

Sometimes, however, abuse by a foreign spouse is said to be retribution for the predations of the jinetera. The moral trappings of mystical sexual predation are expressed, for example, in the following story about Ildamis, La Mariquilla's neighbor:

> Ildamis was a jinetera but she didn't have any luck getting a foreigner. So, one day she went to a sorcerer [brujero] and paid him to help her get an Italian she had met in Havana. The sorcerer took the money and performed a trabajo to change the woman's luck and attract the foreigner. But the magic didn't stick to him. Instead, the magic came back and stuck to her. Then things were worse. But Ildamis didn't believe it was the sorcery. She walked around telling everyone that it was the evil eye of her neighbors that was ruining her luck with foreigners.

Accusation and counteraccusation constitute a whole economy of blame in post-Soviet Cuba. Those stories that I encountered dealing with this particular theme, which not coincidentally sometimes border on the fantastic, point directly to the moral ambiguity of hustling and mystical sexual predation. In other words, they form a popular discourse that warns of the moral repercussions of using others as mere means to an end:

> There was this black jinetera who married an Italian. Things didn't work out for them in Italy because the man figured out she had been hustling him the whole time. He told her that he knew she had never loved him and demanded that she pay him back the money he spent marrying her and bringing her to Italy. The woman ended up selling one of her kidneys to pay him back.

Another of these stories similarly describes a black jinetera who married an Italian and moved to Italy. She woke up one morning with her eyes covered in bandages. The man, it turned out, had drugged her and paid a surgeon to remove her eyes, which he then sold to a friend whose blind son was in need of a "transplant." These stories are deliberately sensational. They attempt to seize the imagination and force one to consider the horrific consequences of the social predation embodied in jineterismo when it is reversed, in this case eroding one's personhood through metaphorical cannibalization or consumption in the underground European organ trade.

Magic, Money, and the Revolutionary Economy of Desire

During my fieldwork, men frequently voiced complaints about women's "luck" when it came to meeting foreign tourists and their shallow, materialistic desire for expensive consumer goods. Such male frustrations are finding expression in recent popular music and literature on the island. Timba music—the percussion-driven salsa that distinguishes Cuba's variety of this international genre—and reggaeton—dance music that combines reggae, dancehall, and hip-hop with local genres popular among Cuba's youth—both of which are largely the product of male artistic labor, serve as informal social chronicles of the Special Period. As Ariana Hernández-Reguant notes, they describe fleeting sexual encounters with little or no emotional commitment between Cuban men and women, and express doubt about the possibility of altruistic love in an era of scarce resources and opportunities (2002: 385). They give voice to the aggravation, hopelessness, and anger of many Cuban men who are financially unable to satisfy the growing consumer demands of their female counterparts and have grown accustomed to seeing foreign men fulfill this role. For example, in the popular timba song "Leave it to Me," by Los Van Van, the singer expresses his grief over recent romantic trends between Cubans: "for a little bit of money, and a few drops of warmth, you left me for a Spaniard." In Charanga Habanera's song "El Tembla," women are told to go find themselves a *papirriqui con guaniquiqui*, or "a sugar daddy with lots of money" (Hernández-Reguant 2002: 244). Reggaeton songs popular on the street frequently ridicule the jinetera and her fascination with consumer goods, her reluctance to suffer the hardships of economic deprivation like everyone else, and her interest in finding a *pepe* or "sugar daddy." In his "dirty realist" novel (2000), Cuban author Pedro Juan Gutierréz describes the jinetera as, "hypnotized by Yankees and dollars" (see Whitfield 2002).

Just as the imagined lack of female honor in the nineteenth century undermined black men's role as the patriarchal guardians of black and mulatta women (see Martínez-Alier 1974), the jinetera's alleged promiscuity, materialism, and fascination with the yuma is represented as a threat to local machismo and men's patriarchal status as the *papi* (daddy) of the nation's

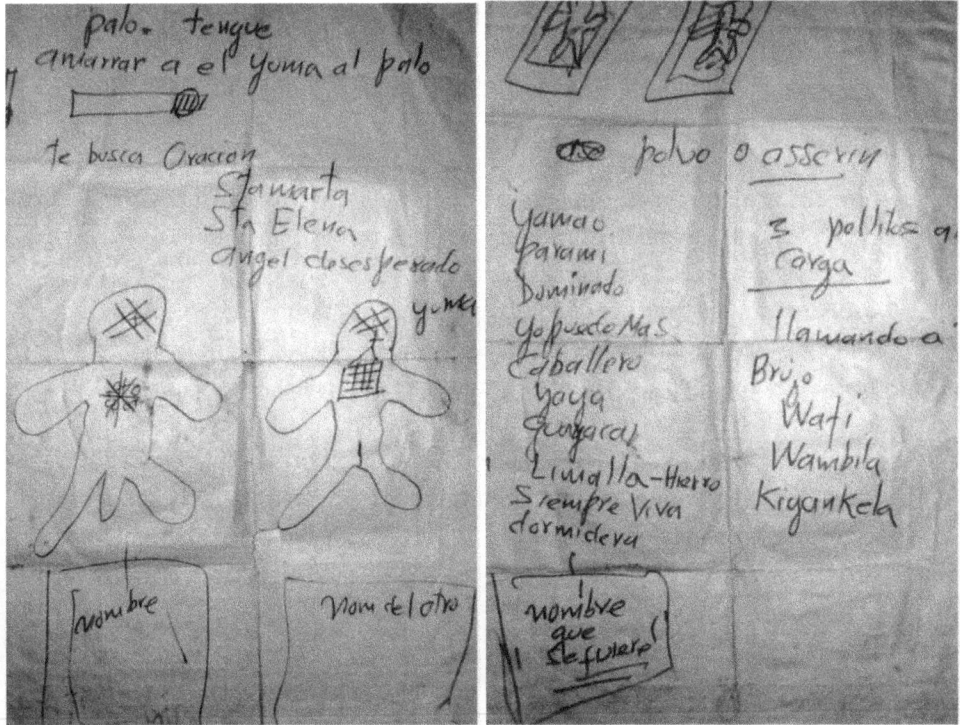

5.1a. and 5.1b. A magical plan to "tie the *yuma* [foreigner] to the stick."

women. A struggling economy coupled with both the influx of foreign tourists wielding disposable wealth and perceptions of women as "spellbound" by the yuma and the lure of hard currency have had an emasculating effect on the Cuban male imaginary. It is not surprising, then, that some of the most aggressive magic targeting tourists I encountered originated from Cuban males.

29 January 2005: Today I asked Wuicho, a rumba singer and brujo, if he had ever heard of special magic to attract foreign tourists. He stared at me for a few seconds without saying a word. Then he turned around and started rummaging through a stack of papers on the desk behind him. He pulled out two pages and showed them to me. They were plans for a trabajo *called, "tying the yuma to the stick" (Figures 5.1a and 5.1b). A younger acquaintance had dropped them off one afternoon, wanting him to review the plan and make sure that everything was right before going through with it. This young man wanted to magically tie a foreign women he had recently met. But Wuicho just shrugged the whole thing off. "I don't like it when people do that [ensorcell foreigners]," he said, "because it always ends in blood. It's more or less the same magic that you would use to 'tie' two Cubans together but it's more dangerous."*

Stories warning about the potential threat of such acts of social predation—even more dangerous, we are told, when it involves foreign tourists—may be read as expressions of moral ambivalence regarding both the new hustler economy and the seductive lure of capitalist consumption, lifestyles, values, and desires that tourism has reintroduced on the island. Yet, by turning the revolution into a tourist attraction, the state has fueled perceptions that it too is spellbound by the magical allure of hard currency, secretly harnessing the ritual work and erotic labors of the populace to drive these transformations in the revolutionary economy of desire. The state itself, then, might be seen as employing its own magic to "tie the yuma to the stick."

The Cult of the Profane

CHAPTER 6

La Mariquilla often described her misfortunes in supernatural terms. Indeed, the entire family, she said, seemed to be cursed by a terrible *osogbo*, a kind of cosmic bad luck. In addition to an accident related to a kitchen fire that had left her scarred for life, both her son and niece had been hit by cars. Although her son survived, her niece did not. La Mariquilla's nephew was also struck by a car one day while playing in the street. Later, he was disfigured by a fall from a tree. The family had always wondered if these misfortunes were the lingering effects of past acts of ritual work that might still be casting a negative influence on the house and its inhabitants. La Mariquilla and her sister recalled a deceased santera who had been in love with their father. It was believed that, consumed by her unrequited sexual passions and desires, the santera had sent some bad sorcery (*echó un trabajo malo*) to the house. The sorcery may well have been intended for La Mariquilla's mother, but such sorcery can miss its intended target and instead "stick" (*pergarse*) to the spiritually "weaker" members of the house. These are members of the household who do not enjoy the kinds of mystical protection that may come about naturally at birth (that is, through a natural affinity with a guardian saint who watches over them), by participating in limpiezas and accumulating protective charms, or through formal initiation rites referred to as "making saint," in which the saint is seated in one's head. The recurrence of such tragic incidents always aroused family suspicions that some lingering influence of the late santera's trabajo was working evil.

This idea was reinforced by the iron ball that La Mariquilla's son and her nephew discovered while playing in the house's back patio. The iron ball was similar to those used to restrict the movements of recaptured runaway slaves when attached to their shackles and chains. Given her now-deceased father's close association with Arcaño, La Mariquilla and her family often wondered if the ball was a remain of some ritual work. Although opinions differed, the concern was that perhaps her father had shackled a spirit of the dead to the back patio, and that it might be rebelling against its confinement and abandonment by bringing down all sorts of calamities and afflictions on the family.

La Mariquilla decided that it was time to get to the bottom of all this. She commissioned the services of a group of three *espiritistas*, or spirit-mediums. The mediums, an elderly black man and woman accompanied by an Italian-born man in his fifties, arrived at the house, recited their orations, and then began "feeling" the place. Occasionally, one or the other would stop to ask a question, but it was the white medium who spoke the most. La Mariquilla asked him if the family's problems might have something to do with the deceased santera's love magic and the buried iron ball. He did not hesitate in responding, "I don't think so but you should continue with the limpiezas every now and then to be sure." Yet he was sure about one thing: "Yours are not the slaves [*lo tuyo no son los esclavos*]." The medium's remark had a double meaning. Not only did La Mariquilla's troubles have nothing to do with the spirits of slaves, but they were not among her spirit companions at all. In other words, Palo was not La Mariquilla's spiritual calling. The medium continued:

"What you've got is not a slave but a Creole woman, a mulatta, an Ochún, an Ochún Yeye Moro. You like the street, right? You like music, rumba, parties; you like to shake your booty (*menearse*), right? And when you fall in love you fall hard, right?" he asked.

"Yes, they've told me that before. It's true, it's true. What happened was that . . . they say that after the accident it was Ochún that helped me, that I would have to make saint. But you know things are hard. One has to work hard for this, save for many years, and that's not easy," La Mariquilla responded.

"Well," the medium said, "she is calling on you. You are one of her children. You will have to go to the pilgrimage to El Rincón and, if you have the means, make saint but, meanwhile, you need to make yourself a *cajón* [spirit-possession ceremony]. She will send you some of her children there."

La Mariquilla had been making the annual pilgrimage to El Rincón every year after her accident. There, she prayed to San Lázaro to bless her with good health. Although La Mariquilla was familiar with the cajón ceremonies, it had been years since she had participated in one. I began accompanying La Mariquilla and her family to these spirit-possession ceremonies. As I would soon learn, the spirits and mediums associated with the cajón bring to life a marvelously prosaic world of Creole spirits and an entirely unique poetics of Cuban history.

My focus in this chapter is on the "spirits who like rumba," as a Cuban friend once described them, and the kitschy theater of spirit-possession staged in their honor in late-socialist Cuba.[1] I am referring to a little-known Cuban spirit-possession ceremony called the *rumba del cajón al muerto*, or "box-drum rumba for the dead."[2] The cajón ceremonies, which are privately arranged, financed, and hosted by individual families or households, exist independently of the various popular religions practiced on the island. They are deliberately hybrid, drawing from an assortment of ritual idioms borrowed from Kardecian Spiritism, Afro-Creole religions, and folk Catholicism. They combine the secular rhythmic styles of Cuban rumba with spirituals in praise of various classes or "commissions" of the dead—"wild" Indians (*indios bravos*), "black nations" (*negros de nacion*), clairvoyant Moro gypsies, Chinese mystics, sailors versed in the secrets of the seas, personal spirit affinities, and family spirits of the dead. Apart from their practical focus on healing and resolving everyday problems, the cajón ceremonies, I suggest, celebrate a bewildering entanglement of bodies, racial geographies, cosmological domains, and historical fields. Through the central metaphor of spiritual "labor," these ceremonies express hybrid religious imaginaries of belonging that stress the transnational roots of the Cuban nation. It is the particular way in which these ceremonies fuse the sacred and the secular, the spiritual and the material, history and cosmology, and especially spirit-possession and the state, that I wish to examine here.

The Lusty Mulatta and the Elderly Black Brujo

27 December 2004: "You've been calling on all those negras *[black women] and forgetting about me," the dead brujo fumed, prompting laughter among the twenty or so women who had gathered to participate in this ceremony honoring the Creole spirits of the dead. Carelessly waving a machete and tilting his head upwards to pour copious amounts of cane liquor seemingly straight into his throat, the dead brujo, moving and speaking through the body of a young black woman, berated the singer for ignoring him. The body before Wuicho, the singer, was that of his sister, but the force animating her was their deceased uncle, an alcoholic who had died tragically in front of his nganga. "He was a drunk," Wuicho explained to me later, "but he was really knowledgeable about sorcery. Unfortunately, he used all that knowledge to do bad things and soon enough all of that ends." The belligerent dead brujo then turned to the women in the small apartment in Bahía, an eastern suburb of Havana, to boast of his masculinity and magical prowess in an almost incomprehensible slur, swinging his machete and snarling at the crowd. It was not the first time that night that Wuicho's sister had been "mounted" (possessed). Earlier that evening, María Candela ("Hot" María), a sassy, seductive, proud mulatta, had also taken hold of her body. Without the least bit of reticence, María Candela paraded the undulating curves of her (or rather her host's) body before us as the rest of the women sang her praises. She shared all the sensual allure of the renowned and stereotypical nineteenth-century Cuban mulatta, the honey-colored seductress who used her predatory sexuality to lure upper-class white men into relations of dependency.*

Despite the fact that they had their own personal identities and histories, the two Creole spirits of the dead that walked before us that night in Bahía recall two familiar national icons that have their roots in the colonial and postcolonial imagination. The tantalizing eroticism of the mulatta, for instance, a nineteenth-century image produced primarily through the prism of white male desire, was constructed through contradictory discourses that promoted "the symbolic privileging of a socially underprivileged group defined by its mixed race, gender, and its imputed licentious sexuality" (Kutzinski 1993: 7). The image of the mulatta arose during the nineteenth century, when Cuba was experiencing great economic growth, due to an expanding sugar industry, momentous increases in the importation of African slaves, racial miscegenation, growing resentment of Spanish control, and ideological censorship. As Vera Kutzinski notes, the mulatta eventually became a symbolic reservoir for "the multifarious anxieties, contradictions, and imperfections in the Cuban body politic," as well as for all those thorny questions about "how race, gender, and sexuality inflect . . . power relations" (1993: 7–11). By the end of the nineteenth century the body of the mulatta essentially constituted a national fetish and screen for the anxieties and desires that consumed the emerging Cuban nation.

Her symbolic counterpart, the elderly black brujo, did not fully enter the nationalist imagination until the turn of the twentieth century, after Cuba had finally wrenched itself free from Spanish colonialism. Coinciding with the witchcraft scares of the republican era, the postcolonial vilification of the elderly black brujo effectively victimized him. Unlike the lustful mulatta, he was incapable of fathering biracial offspring. Rather, he represented a mystical danger to the emerging nation, threatening to infect and even eviscerate youthful white women with his dark arts and thus jeopardizing the country's future, which was inevitably presumed to rely on the sanctity of the white female body (compare Martinez-Alier 1974). Whereas the figure of the mulatta represented a colonial history of miscegenation, illegitimacy (in the form of mixed-raced children being born out of wedlock), and sexual disease, the elderly black brujo's body, as Stephan Palmié notes, represented the lingering effects of African savagery, slavery, and subaltern forms of knowledge like magic which were considered to be out of step with modernity and progress (Palmié 2002: 222). While the mulatta threatened to disrupt the social order and boundaries of colonial society, the elderly black brujo represented a sociocultural anachronism. He was the socially irresponsible purveyor of a magical epistemology deemed incommensurate with the scientific rationality upon which this newly independent nation would construct its place in the modern world.

The "spirits who like rumba" are national caricatures. Rather than attempting to deconstruct these sexist, racialized images of the nation's past (and present), spirit mediums in the cajón ceremonies embrace them. Here, the complex play of reflections and mutual appropriations between magic and national politics is performed in dramatic interactions with the dead. As moral artifacts of the colonial and postcolonial imagination, these profane, historical images are refracted through local cosmology and brought to life in the very flesh of spirit mediums. Despite the revolutionary state's efforts to break with these racial ghosts and the carnal desires and fears they embody, such imagery has resurfaced in the public domain of post-

Soviet Cuba. The reemergence of imagery rooted in colonial and postcolonial fantasies may, I suggest, reflect efforts on behalf of the revolutionary state to tap into the magical capacities and dreamworlds of local cosmologies, on the one hand, and to exploit the global economy of desire that drives tourist demand for local exotica on the other.

In contrast to the Monument to the Runaway Slave, which implicitly links revolutionary political resolve to slave resistance, the mulatta performs a very different kind of ideological labor in Special Period Cuba. Paraded around like some kind of fetish through the tourist zones of Havana, she condenses all the sensual allure of tropical socialism, the privileged symbol of racial democracy and national unity. Likewise, the black brujo, spirit medium, or priest-healer has also been typecast in this theater of state power to fulfill a certain economic and ideological agenda. Not only is he called on by the state to satisfy tourist demand for local exotica, but he is also expected to ensure relations between the cult of the *monte*—the spirit world—and the cult of the revolution are not led astray.

The Cult of the Profane

25 December 2003: Wuicho was not home. He had already left to attend a cajón a few blocks away in an old, run-down, colonial-era solar, or tenement house. His wife told us where to find him and we set off. By the time we arrived it was already dark and there were several people outside smoking cigarettes. We asked for Wuicho and one of them offered to take us inside. We followed our guide through the dark corridor of the tenement house and passed the open doors of several tenants. Music and the sound of chattering neighbors and barking dogs filled the hall as we walked around women cooking on propane camping stoves, dodged the maze of clotheslines, and began ascending a very steep, narrow, and crumbling staircase. When we reached the top I could already hear a group of people reciting prayers. As we entered the small room, where around twenty-five people, mostly women, had gathered, we were immediately doused with perfume by an elderly mulatta woman and told to "get in line." Copious amounts of these "spiritual" perfumes—like those sold by the state featuring kitsch images of Ma' Pancha, a santera, and Ta' Francisco, an elderly black brujo standing over an nganga—would rain down on us throughout the night.

As the group mumbled the words of several orations, we took our place in line to wash with the specially prepared herbal water that sat on the altar against the wall. The altar consisted of a table covered by a white cloth. Like the bóveda espiritual *(spiritual altar) that many Cubans keep in their homes, which functions as a portal for communication with deceased family members, the cajón al muerto altar contains seven glasses of water, one of which usually contains a miniature wooden crucifix. Around these glasses of water were placed white lilies* (azucena)*, sunflowers,* príncipe *flowers, cigars, candles, aguardiente, a bottle of perfume called Siete Potencias (the seven powers, referring to the orichas), chalk, and scattered flower petals. On occasion, photographs of loved ones and other images and objects are included—for instance, paintings of Congolese brujos and miniature ngangas called* prendas de palo espiritual *(ngangas that do not include human remains), mermaids, magically charged commercial baby dolls, statues of Catholic saints, and ceramic portraits or statues of North American Sioux Indians with feathered headdresses. Because these ceremonies are personally arranged by certain households, who often must spend several months of the year saving to fund them, the kinds of images and objects placed on the altar vary considerably from one cajón ceremony to another.*

Once the initial prayers were completed, the musicians, led by Wuicho, began performing. Their instruments were simple: a clave, three ideophones made from plywood and painted in orange and brown, the metal head of a farming hoe, which was tapped with a medal rod, a cowbell, and a chékere. As people trickled in and out throughout the night, some just stopping by long enough to wash their face, neck, and hands with the herbal water, the musicians performed without rest and the participants swayed back and forth. The first set of songs they performed were replete with references to Catholic saints. It was not until they began a set of songs called "Bush Songs" (cantos de manigua)*, associated with the Congolese dead, that the first spirit arrived in the body of a middle-aged mulatta woman. The song began with a Congolese man describing his arrival by a mountain path and his discovery of a human skull while weeding his garden. As things heated up, Wuicho began singing praises to* madre agua *(mother water), a Congolese* mpungu *(spirit) associated with the Virgin of Regla. "I was in the river getting sand," the chorus repeated as Wuicho continued feeding the room's energy. It was at this point that the atmosphere in the small room became more intense, with Wuicho straining to sing over the clamor of the rhythm section. A few minutes later, the first spirit of the dead arrived, a Congolese runaway slave.*

The musicians took a break while the Congolese introduced himself, giving an unusually long name: Francisco of Seven Rays and a Whirlwind of Four

Winds (Francisco de Siete Rayos y Remolino Cuatro Viento). Out of breath, Francisco asked for water and afterwards began greeting everyone individually and mumbling in bozal. He grabbed everyone in the room in turn by their hands and jerked them downwards in a movement intended to rid the body of "bad currents." The forceful jerking motion, which jolts the body from hands to feet, knocked several off balance, causing them to stumble forward. This greeting/corporeal purification rite took several minutes. As someone passed the bottle of perfume around yet again (this happened repeatedly throughout the night), Francisco offered everyone advice without bothering with formalities or inviting the participants to share their concerns or worries. Since he was speaking in bozal, several people were simultaneously translating his words into Spanish, which created an almost incomprehensible murmur in the room. Wuicho stood in as my impromptu translator.

The dead Francisco told a pregnant woman to keep her husband off the streets. Another woman learned that she would soon be struck with some illness, but a few offerings of flowers to Saint Lazarus would ensure that her suffering would only be momentary. The white woman who had brought her teenage, mulatta daughters with her was told that she would have to make special offerings of prayers and flowers if she wanted her husband to return to her. The girls, frightened by this dramatic display of otherworldly communication, and perhaps by the subject of the exchange as well, huddled in a corner and cried as their mother consoled them. Wuicho was warned to take special care with his money and I was told that I needed magical protection from "those blancos [whites] at the university." The ceremony lasted several more hours, during which time many more dead came and went.

Visceral Histories

In Cuba's somewhat "crowded" Afro-Creole religious landscape, where ritual formations are distinguished not merely by reference to their transatlantic origins, but also by laying claim to specialized forms of magical and spiritual labor, the cajón represents something of an anomaly. Although friends and most of the acquaintances I met during the performance of these rituals reject the term, Cuban scholars tend to classify these ceremonies as a form of "crossed spiritism" (for example, James 1999). To understand what they mean by this term and how these ceremonies are arranged, financed, and executed requires some ethnographic elucidation. Because I never had the opportunity to follow one person or household throughout the entire process by which they learned it was necessary to host a cajón al muerto, I will have to piece together a few ethnographic vignettes in order to make some sense of how this event comes about.

While in Matanzas in December 2003, I had the opportunity to visit the temple house (*casa templo*) of Xiomara, a local white santera. Since my visit was unannounced, we only managed a brief introduction before Xiomara, who along with her assistant had been busy preparing a healing ceremony for one of her ritual godchildren (*ahijados*), asked us to wait while she completed her ritual duties. Xiomara and her assistant were getting ready to perform what she called "food for the shadow" (*una comida a la sombra*), a rite whose purpose is to provide spiritual fortification by ritually "feeding" one's shadow. Her ritual godchild, a black Cuban woman in her thirties, had been suffering from insomnia, which left her body drained of energy (*cuerpo flojo*). Xiomara, relying on coconut-shell divination (*dilogún*) and her own powers of clairvoyance, surmised that unregulated contact with an *eggun* (ancestor spirit) had breached her shadow and, as a result, "bad currents" were circulating throughout the woman's body. The shadow, Xiomara explained, provides spiritual fortification by protecting one from harmful magical substances, malevolent spirits, and even well-intentioned but otherwise unknown or unrecognized spirit beings. A weakened shadow exposes one to a bewildering array of potentially debilitating forces; strengthening or "fortifying" the shadow would be the first necessary step on the woman's road to recovery.

Xiomara decided the best way to strengthen the woman's shadow was to "feed" it. On Xiomara's back patio, the woman was made to stand erect in front of a burning candle, facing the rays of the morning sun. Behind her an assistant traced her shadow in chalk on the concrete below. Another burning candle and a plate of food consisting of roasted corn kernels, raw black beans, and pieces of raw coconut were placed within the head region of the shadow. Once placed within the chalked enclosure, the food is purportedly being consumed by the shadow. Xiomara then spiritually "cleansed" the woman with a branch of white lilies, which are associated with the dead in Cuba, while naming all of the eggun that accompanied her. She then removed a white dove from a cage nearby, sprinkled chalk over it, sprayed it with perfume, and brushed the woman's body with the bird while singing in *lucumí*, the ritual language initially spoken by Yoruba slaves and their descendants in Cuba. She then plucked some of its feathers, dropping them on the plate within the shadow, and twisted its head off with her hands, allowing the blood to trickle down onto the plate of food and flowers below. After this, the woman's back was brushed with the dove's twitching carcass and the backs of her heels were marked with its blood.

Xiomara then performed coconut-shell divination once more, revealing that the woman's recently deceased mother had been attempting, without success, to communicate with her. Since she did not know how to recognize her mother as an eggun or muerto, the contact had weakened her by breaching her shadow and dangerously exposing the woman to unseen but nonetheless tangible and harmful magical substances and wandering dead. The ritual feeding of her shadow would provide temporary fortification, Xiomara explained, but she would have to attend a spiritual mass (*misa espiritual*) conducted by an experienced *muertero* (one who works with the dead) in order to resolve the complications that arose through the unrecognized human-dead contact with her deceased mother. The significance of Xiomara's recommendation should not be overlooked. Not only does it reveal the informal system of referral that exists between various popular religious or ritual formations on the island, but also the ritual labor and expertise to which each lay claim. Her suggestion that the woman attend a spiritual mass—which devotees also do prior to undergoing formal ritual initiation in Ocha-Ifá in order to determine the identity of the often numerous spiritual guardians or affinities they have and which dead accompany them—indicates that the dead occupy their own distinct spiritual terrain and therefore require their own specific ritual techniques and know-how, to be sought outside of Ocha-Ifá. This is ritual labor more commonly associated with Kardecian Spiritism and Palo.

The spiritual labor of the muertero or espiritista is almost wholly confined to individual consultations and the *misa espiritual*, a séance-like session in which the clairvoyant channels communication between the living and the dead. It is in the so-called spiritual mass that individuals discover their *córdon espiritual* (spiritual cord), or the group of spirits that they have some affinity with and who accompany them throughout life. These spirits include one's guardian spirit (present at birth), family spirits, and others with whom the person may not share any prior biological, social, or historical connection. In the third case there are hidden affinities that await discovery. So, for example, in addition to identifying one's guardian spirit and the deceased family members who "hang around" (*andar*) a person, the espiritista may "see" spirits in close proximity to the person though they are in effect total strangers from distant epochs and/or lands.

The spiritual mass is responsible, then, for the articulation of imaginative, personal mappings of an individual's known and unknown links with the past, as identified through the medium of spirits of diverse ethnic/racial, gender, class, and religious backgrounds. Moreover, it is often in the spiritual mass that an individual learns of the needs and desires of their particular spirit affinities, how to communicate with them and contribute to their spiritual evolution (which I describe below), and, in turn, how to receive their blessings and protection. Yet the spiritual mass also has its ritual limits; its purpose is to provide a medium through which human beings and the spirits/dead can communicate with one another. The spirit medium or spiritist who presides over the mass acts as an intermediary between the visible world of human beings and the invisible world of spirits. Their ritual labor is limited to acting as a kind of spiritual translator. The spirits and the dead, however, are not always comfortable with this kind of mediated interaction. Some of them require, even demand, a more direct and visceral relationship with their living descendants and/or associates. They want to be able to revisit the sensual comforts and pleasures of having a physical body, which death has taken from them. Stripped of their corporeal existence, some spirits want to vicariously drink rum, smoke cigars, talk, feel the pulsating rhythms of drums, and touch and dance with the living, but they are unable to do so without a living host, someone willing to lend their body to a spirit who desires to revisit the gratifications of material/corporeal existence. In short, such spirits want to celebrate physical life. Because the spiritual mass requires the presence of a third party (an experienced medium), does not employ percussive instruments, and generally lacks a festive atmosphere, these spirits' demands have to be satisfied through other ritual means.

Most of the cajón ceremonies that I attended had only been arranged after an individual learned during a spiritual mass that the spirit affinities or dead that "walk by their side" had requested one. Given its more directly visceral character (involving ritual possession or spiritual embodiment), its emphasis on the sensual, corporeal dimensions of sociality, and the fact that it enables the spiritual development of both spirits and human beings, the cajón al muerto provides a particularly acute ethnographic example of the ritual realignment and reordering of sensory exchanges between the body, the living world, and the group (Devisch 1993). In the cajón al muerto ritual performance does not so much concern the formal manipulation and mediation of elaborate symbolic systems and their meanings as it does the intersubjective relations of intimacy and belonging between persons, existential dimensions, and temporal horizons. Ritual here is primarily concerned with mending tears in the social fabric and reestablishing proper sensory exchanges between particular participants and between the living and the dead, the present and the past. This is what I take to be the significance of the healing ceremony described above ("food for the shadow"), which is further elaborated in the cajón al muerto. Moreover, given its explicit emphasis on the past and the transatlantic origins of the nation (via images of spirits and the dead from distant epochs and lands), the cajón al muerto not only reconfigures sensory exchanges between people and spirits/muertos, but it also reflects an attempt to influence the circulation of power in society through the imaginative registers of subaltern knowledge, popular memory, and ritual embodiment.

The cajón al muerto is one of the most popular, practical, and comparatively inexpensive ways to honor and celebrate one's dead ancestors. Ocha-Ifá ceremonies, for example, are often very costly, requiring the purchase of several animals for sacrifice as well as musicians who specialize in songs for the orichas and *batá* drum ensembles. During my stay in Havana, for instance, a cajón al muerto could typically be arranged for around six hundred pesos (twenty-four U.S. dollars), the bulk of which, around three hundred and fifty pesos, goes to the musicians. This is nonetheless a sizeable amount of money for most Cubans, the equivalent of three months' salary for most of my friends and informants. Those who host a cajón al muerto, then, often must save for several months and resort to black market transactions. The social atmosphere at these ceremonies is also considerably less aggressive and imbued with less machismo than in other ritual arenas. Finally, it is the ritual conveniences that these ceremonies afford and their spiritual efficacy that participants find appealing. A cajón ceremony allows participants to celebrate not just one class of dead, but all of them. This reinforces the idea expressed by many spirit mediums that the dead are what unite Cuba's diverse ritual landscape and, perhaps, the nation itself.

Transatlantic Cosmologies

The ritual preparations for and performance of the cajón al muerto are deceptively simple, for the implicit ritual threads and cosmologies invoked are anything but straightforward. Because they are not officially attached to any particular cult house or religious formation, characterized by the absence of officiating priests or an otherwise discernible hierarchy of ritual authority, and deploy a secular musical genre (rumba) with sacred intentions, these ceremonies resist categorization and easy definition. As mentioned above, most Cuban scholars characterize these kinds of ritual performance vaguely as "crossed spiritism;" that is, they define them as essentially Spiritist ritual formations or nodes representing the intersection or overlapping presence of various spiritual beliefs and ritual idioms. It is for this reason, I am convinced, that scholars both on and off the island have failed to mention, let alone dedicate their critical attention to, this ceremony. The cajón al muerto is implicitly shunned as ritual kitsch or the apparently random and tasteless appropriation of images and styles belonging to various religious formations (see Bettelheim 2005). The cajón, I suggest, should be taken seriously as a ritual pastiche of preexisting, hybrid religious formations. This decentralized, rhizomic assemblage of heterogeneous ideas and practices associated with human-dead interaction reveals much about the way in which Cuban citizens remember and rework imagery associated with the past and nationalist imaginaries of belonging. It is the cajón's rather brazen disregard for conventional cosmological and ritual distinctions that make it perhaps Cuba's most vivid example of what Raquel Romberg calls "creolization with an attitude" (2005). Like other "Creole" expressions, the cajón undermines the search for unitary origins, authenticity, and, to some extent, order through strategic forms of ritual mimesis and piracy (Balutansky and Sourieau 1998; Taussig 1987; Romberg 2005).

The cajón appears to be loosely held together by a kind of "meta-cosmology" derived from Kardecian Spiritism. It was this belief system, following Stephan Palmié, that provided the cosmological "glue" necessary to integrate heterogeneous ideas about the dead from disparate religious traditions that were forced into proximity with one another by transatlantic slavery, colonialism, and postcolonial migration (2002). As such, the mpungu, slave and Maroon spirits, the eggun, orichas, the spirits of gypsies, Indians, nuns, monks, mariners, deceased priest-healers, family members, personal spirit guardians, and so on could be considered together as occupying various stages of spiritual evolution (Palmié 2002: 192). Although Palo Monte, Ocha-Ifá, folk Catholicism, and Kardecian Spiritism all bear features which reveal their mutual influence on one another (for example, cross-associations and comparisons between their respective saints, deities, and spirits; ritual idioms of purity; an informal referral system that establishes loose networks between them, and so forth), they are kept strictly separate in ritual contexts, ensuring that each maintains a hold over its own particular ritual niche. The cajón, however, breaks with this implicit ritual logic by bringing together the threads of various transatlantic cosmologies and ideas about the dead in a single performative context. As a ceremonial commemoration of the dead, the cajón provides a ritual mapping of the diverse ethnic/racial and subaltern geographies that comprise the nation's transatlantic roots.

Allan Kardec, the nom de plume of Hippolyte Leon Denizard Rivail, the intellectual "father" of Spiritism, was born in Lyon, France, in 1804. Rivail's investigations into "table-turning" and "spirit-rapping" eventually led him to codify the doctrine that today provides the philosophical foundation of Spiritist beliefs and mediumship around the world. He published his first book on the subject in 1857 under the pseudonym Allan Kardec, allegedly his Druid name in a previous life. During the nineteenth century, Kardec's doctrine was embraced by the educated middle classes of Europe and the United States as a rational explanation of Christian revelation. Kardec's books were soon translated into Portuguese and Spanish and sold across the globe, notably in Latin America and Asia (for example, in the Philippines). There, Kardec's doctrinal Spiritism mingled with other syncretic religions to spawn even more complex hybrid formations such as Vietnamese Caodaism, Brazilian Umbanda, and the subject of this chapter, the Cuban cajón al muerto spirit-possession ceremonies.

Kardecian Spiritism most likely entered Cuba through multiple international channels. It may have been introduced directly from France and/or Spain (Mason 2002: 88; Argüelles and Hodge 1991: 177), through the migratory circuits connecting Haiti, Cuba, and New Orleans (Miller 1995: 225), from the transatlantic routes that linked Cuba with Bahia, Brazil, during the latter half of the nineteenth century, by Americans during the U.S. occupation of Cuba between 1898 and 1902, or later by West Indian migrant laborers in the first few decades of the twentieth century (Wirtz 2003: 34, 342). Beginning around 1865, spiritist centers began popping up all over the island. The spread of these centers across the eastern regions of the island, in particular, was so alarming that it caught the attention of colonial authorities and those sympathetic to Spanish control. During the 1870s, for instance, Enrique José Varona spoke of a "spiritual epidemic" in the eastern regions of Cuba, where Spiritism had been embraced by insurgents as a source of progressive ideas in their struggles against Spain and the Catholic Church (Agrüelles and Hodge 1991: 177–78). Similar to the situation Raquel Romberg describes in Puerto Rico, the Creole Cuban elite embraced cosmopolitan, global discourses like Kardecian Spiritism in order to fashion "new progressive national and civic identities against Spanish hegemony" (2003). While it may be tempting to suggest that Spiritism moved downward from the upper, educated classes to the lower classes, this is far from clear. There is even some evidence that the opposite was the case (see Roman 2000).

This brings us to what is perhaps most unusual about the cajón—namely, its ingenious appropriation of the normally secular rhythmic styles of Cuban rumba. Rumba is a percussion-driven popular dance music historically associated with marginal black neighborhoods and the illicit diversions of the street. As Alejo Carpentier once remarked, the word itself "has passed into the language of Cubans as a synonym for noisy partying, licentious dancing, and cavorting with loose women." The cajón ceremonies are said to be performed for the "spirits who like rumba." These spirits constitute a kind of "underworld" class of the dead. Unlike the enlightened, evolved spirits of status, these spirits are still closely associated with the carnal desires and imperfections of the material world. Despite their unevolved status, these spiritual underlings nevertheless posses their own unique powers and magical capacities that the living can harness to practical matters of everyday concern. In exchange for the opportunity to come party among the living, briefly enjoying a little rum, tobacco, and dance, these "spirits who like rumba" help the living resolve a host of everyday problems, misfortunes, and existential predicaments with which they are perhaps all too familiar.

More than likely, it was not until sometime during the twentieth century that the possession ceremony known as the cajón al muerto came into existence. The Spiritist notion of a shifting hierarchy of spirits within which all souls progress through recurring cycles of reincarnation may have provided the cosmological infrastructure that enabled the integration of seemingly incommensurable ideas about the dead from among various popular religious formations. Spiritism places the dead along a vertical continuum between "spirit" and "matter," providing a ranking of spirits according to the amount of "light" (*luz*) they radiate, or, in other terms, the degree of spiritual purity they embody. It is perhaps because of this continuum that Wuicho, for instance, made such a clear-cut distinction between "spirit" and "dead" (muerto):

> A lot of people say that the eggun, the muertos, and nfumbe are all the same. In a certain way of speaking that could be. But they are not the same. Right now, someone dies. What remains in the tomb is the dead. But the spirit separates from the cadaver. That's what we call eggun or the spirit. What remains of the person is the muerto.

The dead, then, are directly associated with the material world. Their material and, by extension, unevolved status indicates their proximity to the world of the living and the material struggles that characterize it. Put somewhat differently, the lower-ranking spirits of the dead have yet to completely detach themselves from their former lives. Higher-ranking entities have progressed beyond this darker "material" realm towards ethereal spiritual purity or "light."

Those forces that took over the bodies of participants in the cajón al muerto ceremonies that I witnessed belonged to the lower ranks of the dead, as opposed to those spirits who have reached higher evolutionary levels, such as Catholic saints and the orichas of Ocha-Ifá. It is, perhaps, their primitive spiritual status as well as their proximity to the world of the living that makes them both so fraught with danger and so necessary for providing the kind of practical assistance requested of them by devotees. Despite their low-ranking status in the spiritual world, the dead are what many described to me as the spiritual nexus or substrate of all Cuban popular religions. In an interesting reversal of conventional religious mythology (and history), Wuicho argued that without the dead and the cajón al muerto ceremony to honor them, Ocha-Ifá and Palo Monte would not exist. This reflects, of course, an old philosophical truism linking spirituality with mortality or death.

Although the eggun (muertos) form a category of spirits in Ocha-Ifá and are honored at the start of all ritual performances, the santero's ritual labor focuses on the regal orichas (deities). The orichas were also once spirits of the dead, but many explain their royal status in the spirit world in Spiritist terms. The orichas are "evolved" spirits who radiate more "light" (that is, purity). The orichas, not the dead, "own the heads" of their devotees and "mount" them in spirit-possession ceremonies, which are considered a form of human-divine exchange. Many devotees and scholars suggest that there is an implicit ranking of orichas that roughly follows the spirit-matter continuum of Spiritism, with some orichas placed closer to the material world than others. One can discern within the Ocha-Ifá cosmology an implicit vertical continuum of spiritual purity extending from Obatalá (the sculptor of human bodies and owner of intelligence) and Orula (owner of Ifá divination), for example, down to the so-called warrior orichas (Elegguá, Oggún, Ochosi, and Ósun). The latter group, following David Brown, is more closely linked to the human world and its material struggles, *la calle* (the street), hard labor (on the plantation), violence (drunken brawls and revolution), and social unpredictability (precipitous changes, sudden attacks) (2003: 172–73). Moreover, these varying degrees of purity among the orichas also resonate with popular Cuban distinctions between the unpredictability, danger, and contaminating influence of the street (*la calle*) and the order, safety, and cleanliness of the house (*la casa*). So, for instance, in the homes of many Cuban devotees of Ocha-Ifá, ritual objects dedicated to Obatalá and other "evolved" oricha are elevated and often located inside glass cabinets. Elegguá, in contrast, is found on the floor by the front door, indicating not only his liminal status as the messenger between devotees and the other orichas, but also his ambiguous position in the threshold between *la casa* and *la calle* (see Brown 2003: 173).

That the dead who borrow the bodies of the living in the cajón al muerto are more closely associated with the material domain was reinforced by Wuicho's response to my question as to whether the orichas show up at cajón al muerto ceremonies. After all, the orichas are referenced in song during these ritual performances, though of course I knew that they did not mount participants. Rather, my question was an attempt to access the implicit notions that give these ceremonies coherence for participants. "Do you really think Changó is going to show up in a cajón?" he asked. "No, because the santo [oricha] may be a muerto but it's a senior muerto, a muerto that has already passed through many levels of existence." In comparison to the royal orichas, then, the eggun/muertos are more clearly associated with the material realm in Ocha-Ifá. As a category of spirits in Ocha-Ifá, the dead are normally associated with danger and sickness unless properly honored. If the dead are not appeased, they will seek retribution on the living. The crudest or most unevolved eggun, as the late *babalao* (Ifá divination priest) Lázaro Marquetti explained, are those spirits of the dead who have been neglected by their families and therefore are destined to wander around pestering others or picking through trash in the street. A second class of the dead, the *araé*, are family spirits who seek some kind of assistance or attention from the living. The healing rituals designed to placate a harassing spirit of the dead, as indicated in the "food for the shadow" ceremony described above, reveal how ritual expertise and labor are divided up among popular religions on the island.

Since the dead belong to an unevolved class of spirits, they are considered dark, impulsive, and even dangerous. This is ritual terrain more commonly associated with Palo Monte and Spiritism. The dead are at the center of Palo Monte ritual practice, which is an assemblage of magical and ritual practices historically associated with Bantu-speaking slaves and their descendants in Cuba. Here, relations between the living and the dead are contractual; the dead carry out the demands of the living in exchange for some kind of symbolic payment. The two parties enter into a pact or agreement, but the terms are necessarily unequal. Ideally, the dead are tricked into a dependent relationship with the living. The living take advantage of their unevolved status and proximity to the material realm by magically subjugating them and controlling their ghostly labor. If this relationship of domination is not ritually managed, however, the dead will seek moral retribution, which in extreme cases can lead to sickness and even death. Palo Monte, then, is characterized by a mercenary relationship; the dead have to be "captured" and then subjugated in order for the mayombero's magical labor to be efficacious, a ritual logic clearly associated with slavery. These are the exploitative means by which one comes to exert dominion over some particular spirit of the dead, extracting their mystical labor to achieve some real-world effect.

Like the implicit hierarchy of spirits in Ocha-Ifá that appears to follow the spirit-matter continuum associated with Kardecian Spiritism, Palo Monte exhibits a vertical scale of spirit beings—ranging from the lowest ranks, which are occupied by brutish slave and maroon spirits, to the upper echelons, which are occupied by the mpungu (Madre Agua, Siete Rayos, Cholambembe, and so forth). In popular discourse, however, *all* Palo Monte spirit entities and the dead in general are considered less spiritually pure and evolved than the orichas of Ocha-Ifá. So, for example, the most highly evolved Palo Monte nfumbi is often considered to be less refined than the lowest-ranking oricha. This implicit "hierarchy of hierarchies" appeals to the same basic principles of the spirit-matter continuum of Kardecian Spiritism. Palo Monte is described in popular discourse as crude, uncivilized, and therefore "dark" in comparison to the more advanced, refined, and spiritually pure or "light" Ocha-Ifá. This implicit logic of determining spiritual purity also translates into the temporal order of successive ritual initiations; a person can, for instance, become "marked" (initiated) in Palo Monte and then at some later date "make saint" (go through ritual initiation into Santería), but not the other way around. These implicit rules governing the temporality of ritual entrance into these popular religions, however, does not preclude one's participation in all of them simultaneously. For example, as long as a person becomes "sworn" in one of the Abakuá societies and "marked" in Palo Monte before making saint in Ocha-Ifá, it is possible for them to maintain a lifelong involvement in all three.

The Spiritist cosmological "glue" enabling the integration of disparate images of the dead provides, I suggest, yet another example of the ways in which popular moralizing constructions of difference and the historical imagination find their way into local cosmologies. In Cuba, as mentioned in the previous chapter, popular discourse explains the internal differentiation of black popular religions by reference to a moral dichotomy of magic/sorcery and religion; that is, Palo Monte versus Ocha-Ifá. Scholars often attempt to explain these moralizing constructions of difference by reference to the geo-cultural origins or "source cultures" of these two ritual societies—the former being traced to Bantu-speaking peoples of the Congo and southern Africa and the latter to Yoruba-speaking peoples of southwestern Nigeria. Moreover, this scholarly consensus on the geo-cultural origins of black popular religions on the island has found its way back into the popular discourse, supplementing and reinforcing local representations. So, for example, it was not uncommon during my fieldwork to hear people describe Palo as "primitive" in comparison to the more "civilized" Ocha-Ifá. Moreover, Palo Monte is often described as more "syncretic" and, by extension, spiritually corrupt or dubious. Ocha-Ifá, on the other hand, is generally believed to represent a more direct line of transmission, making it more spiritually "pure." This may be related to the relative longevity of these ritual formations in Cuba. The sporadic importation of smaller numbers of Bantu-speaking slaves on the island significantly predates the comparatively large-scale importation of Yoruba slaves in the nineteenth century. I can only speculate about the role that Kardecian Spiritism may have played in provoking, influencing, and/or reinforcing these popular moral distinctions between Palo and Ocha-Ifá. But, considering the central importance of idioms of purity in Spiritist cosmology, not to mention the rather obvious influence of evolution on Alan Kardec's thinking, it would not seem to be much of a stretch to suggest that Spiritism was a contributing factor. This suggests that the ritual idioms of purity so prominent in Ocha-Ifá may have had multiple transatlantic origins (see Matory 2005).

Spirit Possession and the State

So what does this "cult of the profane" have to do with politics? During the 1940s and '50s, Lydia Cabrera came across spirit mediums who not only channeled famous and "elevated" spirits such as Martí's, but did so in order to influence the political process:

> One speaks with the goddess Oshún or with Obatalá the same as with the Apostle Martí or with Dr. Bruno Juan Zayas, hero and famous disembodied doctor; and thanks to the incredible abundance of mediums the souls of the deceased can . . . converse with their relatives and friends, smoke cigars, the brand they liked when they were alive, give their opinion about things going on today and intervene, unofficially, in all matters. Those "that are really elevated" are so political that they come from the other world in order to support a candidate with the same passionate interest of the living, and in the same tone of apocalyptic fury that the deafening oratory of the flesh and blood politicians of the earthly realm adopt in Cuba demanding votes for the party of their liking. (1983: 30)

Although some Cubans place little Cuban flags and photographs of national icons such as Antonio Maceo or Ernesto "Che" Guevara on their *bóvedas* (altars), I never witnessed a single spirit-possession ceremony in which figures of such monumental status took control of the bodies of mediums. A priest-healer in Vedado, however, insisted that there were spirit mediums who channeled the spirits of famous people, not only José Martí and Antonio Maceo, the iconic black independence fighter, but also Beny Moré, perhaps Cuba's most famous popular singer and the descendant of a Congolese slave, Celia Sánchez, a close confidant and rumored lover of the Comandante, and even Abraham Lincoln!

When I read Cabrera's quote and described what my Vedado acquaintance had said in response, however, my friends in Guanabacoa not only aggressively rebuffed these assertions as fabrications, but became visibly riled in the process. They found even the suggestion that it was possible to channel the spirits of such national icons insulting. My attempts to draw them into a more orderly discussion of the matter were fruitless. "If it's possible to be mounted by an Indian or a nineteenth-century runaway slave," I asked, "then why wouldn't it be possible to call on the spirit of José Martí?" The logic of my questioning was to no avail, for most were too incensed to even consider it. Others would preface their response by reminding me that they had been participating in these ceremonies for decades and had never seen or heard of such things. It was, in their minds, unimaginable.

This episode provides a particularly vivid example of what R. G. Collingwood calls the "historical imagination," or the various ways in which we emphasize and value certain aspects of the past in order to justify our particular worldview or render it plausible. Historical consciousness is motivated not by an objective and transparent desire to know the past, but by a practical desire to make sense of the present through the selective appropriation of the past. What is important here, following Stephan Palmié, is not splitting hairs over the truth of competing versions of the past, but rather ascertaining what makes certain claims on the past negotiable and others unthinkable (Palmié 2002). The spirits of celebrated national icons such as Maceo or Martí do not enter the historical imaginary of the cajón. These ceremonies celebrate history from below; their spiritual labor is directed toward the subaltern dead. Just as Changó would never demean himself by showing up at the more "material" cajón ceremony, so too are the "elevated" spirits of the famous dead foreign to it. Lower-class muertos, so to speak, such as the unevolved Indians or Congolese slaves, however, remain close to the living and derive their power from their proximity to the material world.

Yet many Cubans, including those same informants who doubted the channeling of spirits of national icons, do not hesitate to compare invocations of the dead in popular ritual performances with state ceremonies that summon the fallen heroes of the revolution. Like the santeros who begin their ceremonies by reciting the names of ancestors, every March 13th the Comandante participated in a state ceremony in front of the University of Havana in which he named the martyrs of the revolution (Miller 2000: 40). Some suggest that the ubiquitous busts of José Martí—painted white, placed atop a dais, and often surrounded by bouquets of flowers—which can be found even in the most remote corners of the country, are like miniature spiritist bóvedas that revolutionary officials use to summon the father of Cuban nationalism. Even the location of the heart of the revolutionary state's political machinery, the Plaza de Revolución, with its mammoth white marble statue of Martí and lines of royal palm trees that symbolize the nation, has been described as, "an enormous civic bóveda to the spirit of José Martí" (Miller 2000: 41).

Like the María Lionza cult of Venezuela, the Cuban cajón is something akin to a "dream factory built from the bottom up" (Sánchez 2001). Yet, unlike the former, the cajón has so far not broadened the scope of its signifying economy by systematically incorporating the iconography and historical figures upon which the state relies for its own legitimating history. One may see an occasional Cuban flag or photograph of some national figure placed on a bóveda, but, so far, the ancestors of the revolutionary state have not descended during this ceremony to mount local spirit mediums in dramatic displays of national fervor. The revolutionary leadership's monopoly on political discourse may explain the absence of such monumental spirits in ritual arenas like the cajón. Performed for "the spirits who like rumba," the cajón essentially remains a cult for the subaltern dead rather than some local expression of revolutionary monumentality in another register.[3]

Nevertheless, there does exist a symbiosis here between spirit possession and national politics. Although the "spirits who like rumba" have their own personal histories, they are caricatures, prototypical colonial and neocolonial images of otherness transformed into national icons. Converted into national fetishes and screens for the anxieties, contradictions, and desires that consumed the emerging nation, all of these figures live on as salient images in the Cuban popular imagination. Moreover, these images have resurfaced in public culture as well, especially in the tourist zones of Havana. Appealing to tourist longings for the old, prerevolutionary Cuba, the state's manufactured trinkets, rum bottles, and refrigerator magnets featuring brujos and their ngangas, íreme masquerades, divination priests, and seductive mulattas are sold at the stores that line Obispo, the thoroughfare that links Old Havana to Central Havana. Not only has the state revived the infamous Tropicana Nightclub, which features cabaret performances by scantily clad women of color, but tourists can also encounter state-licensed, clairvoyant black mediums in the streets who will read their destiny in cards and go on so-called Ocha-Turs that bring them to the temple houses of Afro-Creole priest-healers, diviners, and paleros. Rather than attempting to deflect the exoticizing gaze of foreign tourists, the state-run tourist industry willingly caters to these colonial and neocolonial fantasies.

Likewise, rather than offering up counterimages of the brutish yet magically empowered runaway slave, the bewitchingly erotic mulatta, or the violent, predatory, elderly black brujo, spirit mediums embrace these stereotypes, attributing to them their own unique magical capacities and putting them to novel use. The promiscuity between the popular imagination, on the one hand, and officialdom, on the other, is apparent in the circulation of these subaltern images between ritual arenas and the tourist zones, between the bodies of spirit mediums and the body politic. The intimacy between the two appears to be fueled more by the state's "commitment to realigning politics and domesticity" than by some popular fascination with power on high.[4] In the cajón ceremonies, spirit mediums do not channel the exalted spirits on which the revolutionary state relies for its legitimization. Rather, the state attempts to harness the subaltern images of popular culture to both the tourist economy and the task of reinvigorating grassroots support for the revolution. Local mediums thus see their spirits and imagery refracted through officialdom. In doing this, the state clearly seeks to "disarm alterity" by appropriating for itself images normally associated with subaltern culture and power.[5]

Songs of Enchantment

During my ethnographic research I collected dozens of songs performed at the cajón al muerto ceremonies from xeroxed pamphlets, studio-produced CDs, and my own original recordings. The full name of these spirit-possession ceremonies, rumba de cajón al muerto, reflects their rootedness in the secular musical genre known as rumba, which is historically associated with inner-city, lower-class black neighborhoods. The rumba de cajón al muerto may be related to the style of rumba known as *yambú*, which typically deploys box drums. This custom most likely began with the arrival of the first slaves in Cuba, before which animal-skin drums did not exist in Cuba. During the nineteenth century, when slaves and free Creoles were prohibited from playing drums—which were frequently confiscated in police raids—by colonial authorities, many returned to playing on box drums and makeshift instruments. Musicians at that time began using codfish boxes to provide the rhythmic foundation for their songs (Daniel 1991: 2). These ceremonies, as one Matanzas resident put it, are performed "for the spirits who like rumba," an explanation that reinforces the contention that these ceremonies privilege the more profane, "material" muertos; that is, the nation's subaltern dead. The rumba, a secular musical style, in this context is transformed into a sanctifying musical expression by changing the lyrical content of the songs in honor of the spirit "commissions." The rumba de cajón al muerto, then, is a celebration of the nation from below; it reimagines a secular popular music genre associated with the lower, phenotypically "darker" classes as a spiritual device for communicating with and honoring the spiritually "dark," lower-class muertos.

Although these ceremonies mention the enlightened spirits of Catholic saints (for example, the Virgin Mary, Saint Lazarus, Saint Manuel, and so forth), local patron saints (the Virgin of Regla and La Caridad del Cobre), and Ocha-Ifá orichas, their purpose is to attract the less-evolved dead. It is these "crude," unrefined spirits of the dead that respond to the rhythms of the spiritual rumba de cajón and show up to enjoy cigars, rum, and dancing. The vast majority of the dead that are summoned in the cajón ceremonies are associated with the border zones of Cuban history and nation-building. One of the most salient geographic zones mentioned in the songs, the ocean, elicits numerous images historically associated with Cuba—for example, its status as an island, as a backwater way station of the Spanish colonial empire, and later as a central node in the transatlantic slave trade. The songs associated with this vast body of water and witness to the great traffic in wealth and human lives pay homage to seafaring mariners, mermaids, and an African woman whose mysterious voice rises from the ocean's depths. The set of songs referred to as *cantos de manigua* tell the stories of Congolese maroons crossing back and forth between their hiding places in the mountains and the domestic spaces of towns and, one could easily infer, sugar plantations. Songs about clairvoyant gypsy women conjure up memories of these groups' mobility across nation-state borders. Finally, the "wild Indians," the vanquished of Cuban history, are also summoned; the most common image being that of the Indian Christ carrying a wooden cross on his back.

The four most prevalent iconic historical figures mentioned in these songs—the sailor, the gypsy woman, the Congolese runaway slave, and the Indian—are all associated with mystical labor and subaltern knowledge. These songs are, in fact, replete with references to labor; either that of the participants and musicians or that of the dead they reference. The *marinero* (mariner), for example, who risks his life transporting people and goods across large bodies of water, is linked with the mysteries of the sea and, by extension, the mpungu Cholambembe (or Chola) and the oricha Yemayá, who some say is the messenger of Olokun, the oricha associated with the unknown mysteries and treasures of the ocean's depths. In one song, the singer pleads with the marinero to lend his boat for mystical "navigation." He pleads with God to keep him from the grave "among the sounding lines of the sea," and to give him the strength and courage to escape from the abyss. Later, the purpose of this mystical navigation is revealed; the speaker in the song is searching for sand from the bottom of the sea. This sacred sand is what he calls his "chamalongo," referring to the Palo Monte system of divination. The song goes on to make another important reference—"all come from faraway lands." This explicit recognition of the nation's trans-atlantic origins was further reinforced by a female participant in another cajón al muerto, who said, "everyone here in Cuba came from distant lands . . . the Spanish, Africans, Chinese, Gypsies . . . even the Indians who were here first came from other lands."

In another song, "Sister Rita," a gypsy, is called on to open her "sanctuary" and share the mysteries of her "prodigious cards," a reference to her clairvoyant powers as a reader of fate and fortune. The Congolese runaway slave is glimpsed in the bush (maleza) "working material" with his clay pot (cazuela de barro) and mpaka (a gourd or bull horn stuffed with medicines and sealed with a mirror through which the mayombero "sees" things from a distance). In the cajón al muerto, at least one song is dedicated to the Indians. This song typically describes a cross-bearing Indian who is both "good" and bravo, meaning "brave," "fierce," and/or "wild." This imagery, suggestive of the Indian Christ, may be a reference to Hatuey, a sixteenth-century Taino chieftain (cacique) considered by some to be the island's first national hero due to his resistance to Spanish conquest. The Spanish burned Hatuey alive at the stake in Yara, in eastern Cuba. Today, there is a cult organized around his image, and pilgrims travel to the site of his execution in search of the supernatural "light" associated with it, said to provide both physical and spiritual vitality or force.

That the mystical labor of the Congolese is associated with undomesticated space and the material world, especially relevant given the fact that the vast majority of Cuban Maroons were classified as belonging to the Congo nation (La Rosa Corzo 2003), may explain their association with Indians on the island. Images of Indians occupy a notable place within Palo Monte ritual symbols. In one cajón al muerto I attended, the Congolese and the Indian were not only described as having special affinities with one another, but they also assumed the appearance, perhaps even the identity, of the other by switching clothing:

> I've got a Congo that dresses like an Indian.
> I've got an Indian that dresses like a Congo.

Nineteenth-century paintings of the Day of Kings celebration in Cuba depicting members of the Congo nation wearing feathered headdresses also reveal their popular identification. Judith Bettelheim suggests that Palo Monte's veneration of the dead and the material spirituality of nature may help explain its reverence of the Indian as a primordial ancestral force representing land and home (2005). She argues that the implicit conflation of the Congolese and Indian, which can also be seen among the Congolese of Portobelo, Panama, during carnival celebrations and the Mardi Gras Indians of New Orleans (see Roach 1996; Restall 2005), may be linked to the intense sense of emotional loss resulting from transatlantic slavery; that is, the Indians, who were decimated by Spanish conquest, became both a proxy for lost African ancestors and a privileged loci of mystical power (Bettelheim 2005: 312).

It is not by chance that the iconic historical figures invoked in the cajón are associated with subaltern forms of knowledge either directly through their status as fortune-tellers, diviners, or sorcerers, or indirectly through their proximity to nature and the silence of the lost histories of the Indians. These ceremonies celebrate forms of knowledge discarded by modernity and resurrect the memory of vanquished histories as a source of power. Apart from its attention to subaltern histories via the memory of marginalized iconic figures, the cajón al muerto's explicit purpose, following my friends and informants, is inherently practical. The cajón al muerto, like all ritual performance, concerns the ritual management of proper forms of socialized interaction between different existential and cosmological domains. The dead need the living to both revisit the phenomenological comforts of corporeal life and to progress along the spiritual continuum between matter and spirit. "The dead," as one medium put it, "still miss their bodies." The living, on the other hand, need the dead for protection, to heal illness, and to help resolve misfortune. So, although the cajón al muerto may be considered a ritual idiom of subaltern memory, its more immediate significance to participants is as a practical medium of human-dead exchange, healing, and mutual assistance.

"Good Evening, Creole"

Ritual preparations for the cajón al muerto usually begin with the purchase of chalk, candles, cigars, flowers, special herbs and plants, perfume, rum, and the ingredients to make *caldoza*—a hearty Cuban soup made of tubers (yucca and *malanga*), pumpkin, salted pork, small green peppers (*ají*), onions, and garlic (all cajón al muerto ceremonies I attended were followed with a pot of caldoza). At times, the host may also perform a limpieza de casa, a purification ceremony that spiritually "cleanses" the house of contaminating influences. Although how this purification rite is actually performed depends on the household, those that I witnessed were performed by mayomberos, specialists in Palo Monte magic and sorcery. This was the case, for instance, at a cajón ceremony I attended in Cucuní, a shantytown section of San Miguel de Padrón in Havana.

The preparations for the cajón then began in earnest. An altar was erected in the front room of the two-room structure. It consisted of a table with a bottom shelf close to the floor. On the bottom shelf were placed the attributes of the warrior orichas—that is, Elegguá, Ochosi, Oggún, and, surprisingly, Ósun, which is almost always elevated above the rest. A white tablecloth was placed atop the table and covered with a number of objects: a small, hollowed-out coconut shell from which the dead drink rum or cane liquor, chalk, cigars, candles, a bottle of perfume, and the attributes of the bóveda—that is, seven glasses of water, one containing a wooden cross, and flowers. Alongside these objects were placed a stack of tarot-like cards and ceramic statues of a partially concealed Catholic saint, a small Buddha (the attribute, as one friend put it, of "*los chinos* [the Chinese]"), the Virgin of Regla, and a refashioned commercial doll painted black and wearing a straw hat that identified it as Congolese. Behind this heterogeneous ensemble were placed large stalks of vegetation evoking the cosmological domain of the wilderness and the Congolese Maroons who dwelled there. Around the table on the floor were placed two bottles of rum, an enamel basin containing herbal water, a fruit basket, and an adorned *garabato* (hooked or forked stick). Meanwhile, Wuicho assisted the host's husband in making offerings of rum, bread, cigars, flowers, and a lit candle to the eggun, which was outside by a small palm tree. The husband kept a small wooden enclosure outside wherein he placed his nganga, mpaka, and other ritual objects associated with Palo Monte. Similar offerings were made to the mpungu and spirits of the dead associated with these objects. In some cajón altars, so-called spiritual prendas or ngangas are placed alongside the altar. Although these prendas do not contain human remains, some participants nonetheless believe that they share the same magical properties of actual ngangas.

Inside, Wuicho and the rest of the drummers began setting up on one side of the room. I had an opportunity to ask him more about the use of wooden box drums in these ceremonies. "We use the positive energy of the wood," he explained, "wood has a percussive quality completely different than skin drums. And that's a positive energy that . . . has to call, to converse with the dead that's inside the *fundamento* [nganga]." Confused by this explanation, which indicated that during the cajón the drums somehow "conversed" with his nganga miles away in Central Havana, I asked him to elaborate. "See this in the corner?" he asked, pointing to a glass of water, a cigar, a gold button flower, and a lit candle that had been placed in the corner behind the drums and enclosed by a chalked firma. "Although some say that the *batá* drums [double-headed, hourglass-shaped drums used by Ocha-Ifá devotees] are the only percussive instruments that are consecrated, the drums used in the cajón al muerto are sworn [*jurado*] to the fundamento with rum, tobacco, and herbs in a special ceremony." The ritual "swearing" of the box drums is performed so that Wuicho's muertos know where he is at all times. The dead follow the "trail" of the drums, which emanates from special substances (presumably, material taken from the nganga) placed inside. Wooden box drums are also "raw"—that is, associated with the first slaves brought to Cuba—making them more suitable for the "material" task of calling on the dead. "The dead respond to them," Wuicho went on, "they know and enjoy their sound. They are not for the refined orichas or saints because they do not dance to the rhythms of the rumba." The dead, then, still enjoy the rhythmic clamor of urban streets or the rugged materiality of the wilderness. They long for corporeal indulgence, so they loosen up with rum, smoke cigars, and move themselves to the profane rhythms of Cuban rumba.

The majority of cajón participants are often women, and this particular performance in Cucuní was no exception. The host, María, a tall, middle-aged mulatta who had prepared at length the caldoza out back, had her own theory about this gendered dimension of ritual performance: "Women are mothers. We give birth and for that reason we know something about the spirits and the dead." Wuicho mentioned women's connection to water: "they are like Madre Agua or Yemayá, the owner of the world. There's more water than land in the world and water is life. There's more water in the body than anything else. And imagine, those black women show up there and begin to do their thing until the sun comes up!" This impromptu conversation was cut short by the recitation of prayers that officially marked the beginning of the ceremony. Most of those ceremonies I attended began around four o'clock in the afternoon and went on several hours into the night. As mentioned earlier, the prayers that begin the cajón al muerto are standard Spiritist and Catholic prayers, including the Everyday Prayer, Spiritual Prayer for the Mediums, and Our Father. The third, in fact, is often repeated over and over again between songs.

The ceremony progressed quickly from prayer to song, which is structured according to typical call-and-response patterns, and moved its attention "downward" from the Catholic saints to the dead. This particular ceremony, for example, moved from these initial supplications to Catholic and local patron saints to the so-called bush songs dedicated to Congolese spirits of the dead. All the while the participants swayed back and forth in a kind of side-to-side, two-step motion. If anyone stopped, someone else would call them out and demand that they move. Ritual motility is central to a successful cajón al muerto. "The cajón is so that the dead can come and enjoy themselves," Wuicho noted. "Who wants to go to a party where no one dances?"

Like the Pueblo Nuevo ceremony, the first and only possession of the night came when the theme shifted to water and sand: "Water, Mother Water, Mother Water, I was in the river getting sand." María, the ceremony's host, began to shake violently, rubbing her forehead in distress as if attempting to resist the dead. Wuicho's singing became more aggressive, and as he approached her, his singing grew louder still, accompanied by a finger pointed at her face. Her body would periodically relax for a few moments and then suddenly jerk back into motion, as if being shocked by electricity. Breathing heavily and pacing back and forth, Wuicho grabbed a lit candle and walked back to María (or rather, whatever had taken over her body). He passed his fingers over the flame and then over the closed eyes of the still-unknown being before him. Later, I would ask him about this procedure. His response: "When someone dies, what do they do to the eyes? They close the eyes of the dead; the dead rests with their eyes closed. So when the dead comes to visit us, their eyes are still closed and it's necessary for them to feel the clarity of the light." He went on to mention that some spirits of the dead who mount the living never open their eyes because they have "inner light." But those that are not quite so elevated still depend on their host's eyes to see.

The now-embodied spirit of the dead, a female, bozal-speaking Congolese named Francisca, introduced herself as she continued to pace nervously across the room. Most of the Congolese spirits of the dead, I should note, have the same or similar names. This is not due to a lack of imagination or some sentimental attachment to these particular names. Rather, as Wuicho explains, these names are a façade:

> It's not like that's their real name. What happened? When they brought Africans here, when they sold Africans here, in order to distinguish between them they would say, "Oh, you're Francisco, you're José, you're such-and-such." A lot of times the owners would name them after themselves. So, the slaves would say, "Ah, yeah, my name is Francisco Siete Rayos or José." But only they knew their real names. And so they would hide it. It was a way to obscure things. In reality, they didn't want to tell people their real name. Their real name was a source of power.

After Francisca quenched her thirst with a few sips of *malafo* (rum), she went around offering honey to everyone present by dipping her finger into the bottle and wiping it onto our tongues and lips. My uncertainty about the significance of this must have been clear, because one of the female participants looked at me and said, "This muerto comes with the *camino* [path] of Chola, with Ochún. She wants to sweeten us up."

Francisca's affinities with Chola or Ochún, the oricha of sensuality, love, and all things sweet, became clear in her "counsel." It is here that the often very personal and emotionally moving significance of the cajón al muerto becomes clear. This spiritual advice also reveals the way in which feminine values shape the practical benefits of the ceremony. Francisca focused almost entirely on La Mariquilla and her family. "Salamalekum," she greeted Antonio as she jerked his arms downward to rid him of any negative influences.

"Malekumsala," he responded.

"This pants [man] wants to lift his foot," she told La Mariquilla, meaning that he wanted to either leave her and/or the country. Everyone was surprised by Francisca's comment, for how could she know something so private? She warned him that this was not a good idea, that his relationship with La Mariquilla was more important than he realized and that he would not survive or be happy on his own.

The Cult of the Profane · 141
The Cult of the Profane · 141

"It's true," Antonio responded, "I've been told this before."

Francisca then began to address Caridad, still looking at La Mariquilla, "this child is intelligent and because of that you think she is mature. But this child needs more love than most. She needs her mother's hugs and kisses. She needs security." Finally, she focused her attention on La Mariquilla's older son, Miguelito. "You're a womanizer [*mujeriego*]," she told him, provoking laughter from everyone present. "This doesn't work for you," she continued, "what you look for in all those women you can find in one single woman. Open your eyes!"

I can find no better ethnographic example than this to demonstrate, following René Devisch, that beyond its evocation of elaborate symbolic regimes, cosmological depth, and even its performance and expression of visceral memories/histories, the cajón's modus operandi seems to lie in the realignment of sensory exchanges, enabling desired forms of sociality to circulate between the body, the living world, and the group (1993). The phenomenological density of the cajón lies in its ability to simultaneously touch on both the personal and social layers of existence, the present and the past, the local and the global.

The Congolese and the Indian

Though the cajón ceremonies celebrate a host of figures of varying gender and ethnic/racial backgrounds, the Congolese spirits of the dead, with the exception of those family spirits described at the beginning of this chapter, were the only ones who actually mounted participants in those ceremonies I witnessed. This, of course, may be due to the fact that my familiarity with these ceremonies was entirely confined to predominantly urban, black communities in Havana. Yet I do not think it is much of a stretch to suggest that the brutish but magically empowered Congolese slave or Maroon is the central figure in Cuba's "cult of otherness" (also see Taussig 1987). In making this claim, it would help to recall Bettelheim's argument about the conflation of the Indian and the Congolese on the island. Although there is merit to her argument, I do not feel that she carries it far enough. Just as we may see the Indian as a kind of iconic substitute for lost African ancestors (Bettelheim 2005: 312), we might just as well see the Congolese as a proxy for the lost Indian. In this particularly Cuban economy of otherness, the two are interchangeable—hence the song describing the Congolese that dresses like an Indian and the Indian that dresses like a Congolese.

This conflation of the Congolese and the Indian, however, is less common among the larger Cuban public. Particularly since the collapse of the former Soviet bloc, the symbolic privileging of Africanness in general has become increasingly central to expressions of national belonging. Since the *apertura* (opening-up) that began during the 1990s, national belonging in Cuba has increasingly been expressed in terms that tend to privilege blackness. Phenotypically white or light-skinned Cubans are now much more likely than ever before to admit the existence of black family members or, if they are lacking such, invent them. Instances of white devotees of Afro-Creole religions being mounted by the orichas and the spirits of black slaves and maroons are far from unusual in Cuba. Indeed, white Cubans have been participating in these religious formations since at least the late nineteenth century. Since the onset of the economic crisis and the government's experimentation with limited economic reform in the 1990s, which led to the redevelopment of the tourist industry, there has been, some believe, a marked increase of white participation in Afro-Creole religions. Some black Cubans have responded with skepticism:

> Now there are people whose skin color is white saying they have a grandfather who was a slave, that their grandfather was black. Now they say they're black, when before they said they were white, that their grandparents were Spaniards. (Benkomo 2000: 144)

I take this to be a remarkable reversal of Cuban duplicity with regard to race, religion, and citizenship. For centuries black Cubans have had to hide their true religious beliefs from white elites beneath a façade of Catholic saints. Now, many white Cubans are openly expressing their devotion to those same black idols that were once denounced as obstacles to modernity. Clearly, this reversal is related to the social transformations that began after the 1959 revolution, which promoted the cultures of historically oppressed, and overwhelmingly black, groups as national folklore. But this fact alone is not enough to explain the current popularity of so-called *cosas de negro*, or "black things." As Benkomo's remarks suggest, the recently intensified embrace by some white Cubans of historically black popular religions is suspicious and likely motivated by a changing economy that is characterized by tourism and thus places exotic value on the island's subaltern and largely black cultural "traditions."

The Prophetics of Revolution

CHAPTER 7

25 January 2004: Despite the confusing directions, I somehow managed to find the temple house of the babalao who had planned a massive rogación, or purification rite. One of the house's initiates had encouraged me to come to the ceremony, which was being held not far from Havana's Chinatown. A few weeks before this trip, several babalaos had gathered to read the Ifá oracle. The sign that emerged, Baba Eyiobe, stirred up panic. As one of the most ambiguous signs in the Ifá corpus, it forecasts either prosperity beyond imagination or hopeless tragedy and destruction. Word on the street was that the oracle had expressed doubts about who would actually govern the country in the coming year.

As the ritual cleansings were being performed on the forty or so participants gathered in the back patio of the house, the babalao suddenly interrupted the proceedings with an impromptu speech. Citing an Ifá myth, he had one of his assistants read a story that described how an entire African village had suffered from famine because the ports had been closed, a particularly obvious reference to the American trade blockade or embargo. Then, the babalao spoke as if in reply to charges accusing him and others of a spiritual transgression—raising ritual fees. Not only has inflation of these ritual fees made it much more difficult for cash-hungry Cubans to fulfill their religious obligations, but it has greatly increased profits from foreigners who are flocking to the island in droves and paying exorbitant sums of money to "make saint," fueling perceptions that associate ritual priest-healers and diviners such as the babalaos with the illicit entrepreneurialism and consumer aspirations of jineterismo, or hustling:

> *We Cubans . . . we're all hustlers [jineteros]! We have no other choice. The santeros and babalaos . . . they're all hustlers. We're all hustlers by necessity! And the government . . . the government's the biggest one of them all!*

Hustling has become an integral if not vital part of the Cuban economy in the new culture of resolver. And this babalao's speech had simply called attention to what is perhaps Cuba's greatest public secret by stressing that no one can claim moral purity within the new hustler economy. Everyone is implicated.

After the rogación, everyone present—their heads and faces still wet from the herbal water and goats' blood—walked down to the oceanfront with offerings to the oricha or santo Olokun, owner of the great secrets that lie within the ocean's depths. There were policemen and tourists everywhere. Although he had not applied for a permit, the babalao insisted on completing the sacrifices in public along the Malecón, near the entrance to the Port of Havana (Figure 7.1). There, in front of the tourists, lovers, jineteros, and police, he sang the praises of Olokun, offering the blood of seven roosters and a duck. My Cuban friend, a godchild of the babalao, said that spiritual corruption was the reason for holding the ceremony. There is concern that supernatural repercussions might follow morally dubious manipulations of religion, the results of an age of scarcity and moral decay. On our way back, several of the Cubans who had participated in the ceremony were exuberant. They suggested that such a ritual feeding along the Malecón was unprecedented, and they were pleased to have been a part of it.

The social anxieties addressed by the rogación and ritual feeding that day are clearly linked to the economic strangulations that occurred after the collapse of the former Soviet bloc and the subsequent tightening of the U.S. blockade (hence the ceremony's proximity to the Port of Havana). This much is obvious. The blood that spilled out into the bay, the babalao and his followers hoped, would nourish Olokun, and, in return, perhaps this oricha would then protect the participants from mystical retribution and open the ports, ending the U.S. blockade. What is perhaps less obvious, however, is that the ceremony also alluded to the unease rooted in the increasing economic and ideological promiscuity occurring between the Ifá oracle and revolutionary officialdom. The babalao who presided over the ceremony

7.1. Animal sacrifices to Olokun along the Malecón.

has been one of the most vocal critics of the revolutionary state's attempt to co-opt and nationalize the Ifá divination priesthood, not to mention those babalaos who both encourage and enable such efforts. For many years, these tensions, which had been slowly brewing since the mid-1980s, were confined to a small segment of the population who were in the know. In 2003, however, the controversy became public.

"The King Turns in His Crown Before Dying"

In January 2003, a group of over eight hundred Ifá divination priests gathered together in Havana, Cuba, to read the "Letter of the Year," an annual divination ceremony that forecasts the social, political, and economic climate for the coming year. The group of both Cuban and foreign diviners was organized by the Miguel Febles Padrón Commission (CMFP), which, since 1986, has been uniting a number of otherwise independent divination priests for the purpose of the ceremony. Although it has been performed intermittently since the time of the first Cuban babalaos, knowledge of the ceremony was until recently largely confined to the island's Ocha-Ifá (Santería) community. Since the late 1980s, however, the Ifá oracle's prophecies have been attracting the attention of both the larger Cuban public and the international press. The annual divination ceremony's increasing public visibility and contested political meanings became clear in the CMFP's 2003 reading. Aside from the usual predictions of natural disasters, social ills, and war, the CMFP's reading also made what some believed was a cryptic reference to the Comandante himself with one of the year's signature proverbs: "The king turns in his crown before dying." The proverb not only underscored the danger of talking about the revolutionary leader's death (at the time, at least), but also turned heads given the fact that the CMFP is a faction of babalaos vying for control of the ceremony with the government-licensed Yoruba Cultural Association of Cuba (ACYC). Although members of the CMFP went to great lengths to stress that the proverb was in no way a reference to the nation's revered Comandante, claiming instead that it referred to "all of humanity," the incident underscored the volatile political role of popular religion in contemporary Cuban society.

This situation has been further complicated by the increasing commodification and exoticization of Afro-Creole religions and expressive culture, which is being marketed by some for foreign tourist consumption (Hagedorn 2001). After being kept in the shadows for several decades, images of Ocha-Ifá, Palo Monte, and Abakuá ritual specialists and devotees suddenly stepped into the limelight of public marketing campaigns beginning in the 1990s. Most foreign visitors to the island will readily recognize the image of a black babalao performing divination that appears on bottles of Santero *aguardiente* (Figure 7.2); the crude depiction of a dark-skinned brujo standing before his nganga—complete with human skull and secret ideographic script—on bottles of Ta' Francisco cologne (Figure 7.3); the tourist posters with photos of dancing *íreme* masquerades from the Abakuá societies; or the pictures of happy-go-lucky female devotees of Yemayá and Ochún smiling on billboards promoting tourism—right next to others inscribed with revolutionary slogans (Figure 7.4 and 7.5). These images, along with the token visits to regime-friendly babalaos included in some tourist packages, are just a few examples of the state-organized commodification of popular religions. Afro-Creole expressive culture and history have been forced to the forefront of national politics and the socialist economy, raising questions not only about the intermingling of secular and spiritual power, but also leading to intense debates on how to define national identity.[1]

One of the most significant obstacles the revolutionary regime has faced in this regard is the increasing globalization of Cuban Ocha-Ifá and the potential threat that this poses to national identity. Beginning in the early 1990s, intellectuals, academics, and state officials began placing more of

7.2. Commercial poster advertising Santero *aguardiente.*

7.3. Commercial poster advertising "spiritual perfumes."

7.4. A billboard featuring revolutionary slogans side by side with another promoting tourism.

7.5. Tourist billboard featuring a smiling, elderly *santera* (on the left) and a younger devotee of Ochún (far right) "sharing their joy."

an emphasis on national identity than political community (that is, the revolutionary project) in order to diminish the threat that globalization and neoliberalism posed to the nation's sovereignty and self-determination (Hernandez-Reguant 2002: 105–107). This has had rather direct implications for the Ocha-Ifá community. As the number of foreign visitors interested in going through Ocha-Ifá ritual initiation—an expensive endeavor that costs anywhere from two to eight thousand dollars—continues to rise, a power struggle has emerged between practitioners, intellectuals, and state officials as they attempt to use the religion for widely divergent purposes (Ayorinde 2000: 79). In the past, the absence of an overarching institutional authority among Ocha-Ifá cults has contributed to their survival in Cuban society.[2] Now, given the increasing international popularity and economic importance of Ocha-Ifá, "there is no obvious representative among santeros and babalaos for dialogue with the state," and, "Attempts to create unifying organizations, such as the Yoruba Cultural Association, have been undermined by jealousy among rival groups of practitioners" (Ayorinde 2000: 79). The rivalry between competing Ifá ritual specialists has been most intense in the struggle for control of the annual divination ceremony, with heated exchanges and emotionally charged accusations of *interes* (economic and political exploitation) coming from both sides. The existence of rival groups of Ocha-Ifá priest-healers and their links to political power, however, are not solely the result of recent socioeconomic conditions in Cuba; they have a history that goes back to at least the turn of the twentieth century.

Ifá and the Commodification of Ritual Authority

The popular religion of Yoruba origin known as Regla de Ocha-Ifá in Cuba, or Santería, revolves around the worship of a spirit pantheon comprised of orichas or santos. Through a ritual economy defined by sacred forms of exchange and spirit possession, devotees enter into reciprocal relationships with the orichas, honoring them with praises and sacrifices in exchange for health, well-being, and spiritual protection. Ocha-Ifá temple-houses are comprised of ritual "families" linked through initiation by a common ritual godparent, a knowledgeable elder who oversees the introduction of new devotees into the religion. Although they share a common belief system, cosmology, and similar ritual practices, Ocha-Ifá temple-houses are not organized into a hierarchy ruled by an overarching authority, but rather exist relatively independent of one another. Although their relative autonomy allows for some individuation, Ocha-Ifá cults nonetheless share a fairly standardized set of religious beliefs and practices. The establishment of standard ritual protocols and common procedures for the handing over of sacred, authority-affirming ritual objects, however, did not come about without struggle. Conflict between rival groups competing for power and prestige has, in fact, been common throughout the religion's history in Cuba.

The organizational structure of the religion popularly known as Santería in Cuba is actually comprised of two somewhat distinct priestly branches: La Regla de Ocha and La Regla de Ifá. The organizational separation of Ocha and Ifá cults is based primarily on differences in the division of ritual labor to which each lay claim. The officiating priest-healers and diviners of Ifá, called babalaos (an exclusively male priestly title), control the rich and complex divination system known as Ifá, initiate devotees to a single oricha, Orula, and carry out the annual divination ceremony known as the Letter of the Year. The priest-healers and diviners of Ocha, referred to as *obá oriatés* or santeros (the position is open to both men and women), perform a less elaborate system of divination called *dilogún* and initiate devotees to numerous orichas. Whereas the Ifá cults appeal to only one spiritual authority (Orula) and attempt to monopolize spiritual power and authority through a hierarchy of heterosexual, male divination priests, the Ocha cults tend to decentralize spiritual authority by appealing to the numerous and sometimes competing interests of several orichas with a diffuse network of both male and female ritual specialists (Brown 2003: 155). Although there is more cooperation between these groups than there is tension and conflict, there have been, nonetheless, some notable power struggles both within and between the two groups throughout the religion's history on the island.

Much scholarly and popular opinion has it that the Ocha cults were derived from the Ifá cults, positing Ifá as an entirely separate religion.[3] They argue that African-born babalaos' knowledge of divination verses formed the structural and spiritual basis for Lucumí religion in Cuba (for example, see Murphy 1981).[4] Among some Ifá devotees, this linear, diffusionist narrative of the religion's historical origins in Cuba often carries with it an implicitly gendered ideology of ritual politics. Here, the male babalao plays the most influential regenerative role by symbolically fertilizing a dormant spirituality with his ritual knowledge and expertise. His authority not only derives from this "symbolic birth event," but also from his devotion to the level-headed, restrained, and just figure of Orula as opposed to the unpredictable, selfish, and assorted characters of the orichas, a distinction reflecting common perceptions about the essentialized qualities of masculinity and femininity on the island (Brown 2003: 144, 154).

Although more than ten African-born babalaos are acknowledged in ritual invocations and oral histories in Cuban Ifá temple houses, there are five that stand out as the most significant given the fact that they left behind powerful and influential ritual families that continue to exist today (Brown 2003: 76).[5] Despite the fact that they are credited with the founding of different branches of Ifá, it appears that there was a high level of cooperation among them. This first generation of babalaos soon established themselves as the ritual high priests of Lucumí religion in Cuba, which they partly achieved through claims of ritual authenticity and origin narratives that, more often than not, stressed historical continuity. The babalaos' appeals to the control over ritual power and prestige were also pursued through the controlled and strategic distribution of ritual objects known as *olofin* that serve to authenticate their spiritual authority.

Between the late nineteenth century and the first decade of the twentieth century, there were only around forty babalaos in Havana (Brown 2003: 80). By 1948, their ranks, according to William Bascom's estimates, had grown to around two hundred (Bascom 1952: 171). After the deaths of the first generation of conservative babalaos, who zealously guarded their olofin by limiting their distribution and severely restricted the entrance of new Ifá devotees in order to monopolize power, the number of Ifá divination priests grew rapidly between the 1950s and the 1970s (Brown 2003: 82). It is believed that the head babalao of each major *rama* had an olofin, and that their distribution was governed by strict rules. These formal ritual procedures, however, were often contested. Although the first couple generations of babalaos guarded their olofin to maintain their hold on power and authority, by 1945 this would all come to an end under the leadership of a powerful Havana babalao by the name of Miguel Febles y Padrón.

Miguel Febles y Padrón and Francisco "Panchito" Febles del Pino were the sons of the older, respected babalao Ramón Febles Molina. When their father passed away in 1939, his olofin went to the rightful heir, his eldest son Panchito. Shortly afterwards, however, Miguel Febles stole the olofin from his brother, who later conceded defeat. By the end of the 1940s Miguel Febles came to be regarded as a powerful babalao due to his mastery of Ifá divination, his predatory use of brujería (sorcery) to undermine his rivals, and his fabrication, distribution, and control of olofin. Febles first began manufacturing and distributing olofin to only his colleagues and godchildren, but soon he started producing and selling them en masse. Febles' most profitable period came after the triumph of the revolution during the 1980s, during which time he expanded his influence abroad in the United States and Colombia. This profitability was in spite of the abundance of rumors that accused him of fabricating and selling many sealed olofin "cans" that were actually empty and, therefore, devoid of magical power. As an authority-affirming ritual object, the olofin confers great symbolic capital on its owner(s), but by mid-century in Havana it had become "a 'commodity fetish' with a fluid 'exchange value' in the hands of Miguel Febles" (Brown 2003: 88–99).

Miguel Febles' actions tore deep rifts in Havana's babalao community, creating a crisis of spiritual authority that would continue well into the Special Period. The emergence of rival groups of babalaos and their struggle for control over the annual divination ceremony have become one of the major lines of contention defining the articulation and expression of national identity in contemporary Cuban society. As the cultural significance and role of Ocha-Ifá in the public debate regarding national belonging becomes ever more contested, state officials have not hesitated to step into the fray, attempting to capitalize on the divisions and infighting among different factions in order to serve official ideological agendas. This has, perhaps, been most clear in the current regime's support of the Yoruba Cultural Association of Cuba (ACYC), an organization attempting to nationalize the island's Ocha-Ifá community and establish themselves as the only legitimate authority controlling the annual divination ceremony.

Decentering Ritual Authority

In order to better understand the current controversy surrounding the Letter of the Year ceremony and the government's support of the Yoruba Cultural Association, a brief discussion of the revolutionary regime's relationship with the Ifá divination priesthood is necessary. Despite initial attempts by the revolutionary government to repress Ocha-Ifá religion on the island—having local police deny requests to hold religious parties (*toques*), barring devotees from membership in the communist party, launching media campaigns that disparage practitioners as criminals or social deviants, and so forth—the current regime could not resist the religion's potential political value to provide continuing popular support for the revolution or its potential to attract hard currency through tourism (Hanly 1995: 35).[6] By the late 1970s, according to Cuban ethnographer Natalia Bolívar, state functionaries began promoting several regime-friendly babalaos as folkloric attractions for foreign tourists and diplomats who paid in hard currency. These so-called *diplo-babalaos* charged in U.S. dollars, as did the government diplo-stores that sold imported consumer goods to foreign diplomats and tourists. The government took most of the money, ranging anywhere from the fifteen thousand dollars a Spanish television station once paid to film a half-hour ceremony to the at least two thousand dollars babalaos often charge to initiate foreigners. According to Bolívar, the diplo-babalaos "also put on special 'ceremonies' for foreigners, including some with bare-breasted women dancers who went into 'trances,' and eventually drew strong protests from serious believers" (quoted in Tamayo 1998). The government, then, according to Bolívar, has played a significant role in the exoticization and commodification of Ocha-Ifá religion.

By the early 1990s, after the demise of the former Soviet bloc and the end to massive inflows of subsidies, tapping into Ocha-Ifá's secret ritual economy became not only an economic, but a political necessity as well. Given the grim economic forecasts of the late 1980s and the threat of economic collapse in the 1990s, it became crucial for the revolutionary government to reenergize grassroots political support, which meant appealing to the social base that formed the core of support for the revolution—namely, the black population and the working poor. One way to do this was by tapping into the social resources of Ocha-Ifá and ensuring that the prophecies of the babalaos did not fuel public anxieties about the future. The result was a government-sponsored media campaign that promoted Ocha-Ifá as national folklore and the creation of a special government office on religious affairs, which some of the regime's critics believe attempted to recruit babalaos to work for the regime's internal security apparatus (Oppenheimer 1992: 342–52). Although these accusations are almost impossible to confirm, several of my informants do believe that the Comandante turned to the counsel of regime-friendly Ifá diviners when making difficult decisions, often jokingly referring to the "army of babalaos" that allegedly advise the regime as the "Ministry of Orula" (also see Cabrera Infante 2000; Gutiérrez 2002: 101–102).

The most obvious indication of the revolutionary regime's desire to garner the support of the Ocha-Ifá community and the babalaos in particular, however, came in 1987 when they extended a formal invitation to the Oni of Ife, the Yoruba king whose seat is the sacred Nigerian city of Ile-Ife, to visit the island. Although his visit was preceded that same year by other African dignitaries, including the Asantehene of Ghana and the Nigerian writer Wole Soyinka, the Oni of Ife's visit was the most anticipated by both the regime and the Ocha-Ifá community. Earlier that year, according to some interpretations, "the Ifá oracle . . . announced that the Comandante would die unless the Yoruba 'king of kings,' the 'great Oni' of the babalaos, traveled to Cuba and kissed the ground" (Valdes 2001: 226). The Oni of Ife's visit was arranged in 1994 by José Felipe Carneado, head of the Party's Office of Religious Affairs. The Yoruba religious leader, attended to by top government officials, including the Comandante himself, reportedly urged Cuba's babalaos to cooperate with the regime when he met with a government-selected group of them in a special ceremony at Havana's Casa de

Africa (Ruiz 1987; Moore 1995: 231). His visit, however, was not without its fair share of controversy.

Some prominent Cuban babalaos complained about their exclusion from the event, which they were forced to watch on the evening news rather than witness in person (Fernández-Robaina 2001: 52–53). Others questioned the entourage's spiritual motivations by calling attention to the disproportionate amount of time they spent striking economic agreements compared to attending to religious matters (Fernández-Robaina 2001: 90–91). But the most controversial moment of his visit came when the Oni commended Cubans for having retained what he claimed was eighty percent of the religion, and declared Cuba's Ocha-Ifá community to be "a subsidiary (*subsede*) of Ile-Ife," a comment apparently embraced by the Yoruba Cultural Association (Ayorinde 2000: 79–80). The Oni's statement infuriated some Cuban babalaos. "He was saying that we were missing things," the late Cuban babalao Lázaro Marquetti told me, "but the [Cuban] Lucumí religion is a total religion; it isn't lacking anything." Marquetti went on to mention how flamboyant he thought the Oni of Ife appeared, "with his forty wives and army of attendants, he was only really concerned with getting rich." Marquetti, at the time of my interview, had only recently resumed his activities as an Ifá divination priest. He had stopped for three years in protest of what he referred to as the "commercialization" of the religion.

Two workshops followed the Oni's visit to Cuba; one at the Casa de Africa in 1992 that hosted a debate about a return to Africa and fears of ethnic division, and another called "The International Workshop on Yoruba Culture," which held discussions on the "*yorubización de la santería*" and the return to ritual orthodoxy through the purging of syncretic elements and the placing of the religion under the dictates of the Oni of Ife (Ayorinde 2000: 80). These have been increasingly divisive issues within the Ocha-Ifá community since the Oni's visit. Fernández-Robaina, for example, notes three major tendencies and concerns within the Ocha-Ifá community in the past couple decades. First is the desire on behalf of some to organize new associations, such as the Asociación Hijos de San Lázaro, La Sociedad San Antonio, and the Yoruba Cultural Association. Secondly, there have been attempts to recuperate older ritual practices of which there are two main variants: the first seeks to rescue ritual forms typical of the colonial and republican era by limiting initiation to those in need of healing or material and spiritual improvement. This mode of selecting eligibility for initiation is intended to limit the increasing commercialization of the religion, which has led to a dramatic rise in what some believe to be unnecessary initiations. The other variant suggests the adoption of the Nigerian Yoruba mode of initiation, which only involves "seating" one oricha in the head of an initiate, rather than several as is done in Cuba. For example, Victor Betancourt—who also happens to be the youngest ranking member of the Miguel Febles Commission and the head of the Ifá Irán Lowó society—has recently begun performing the head-and-foot initiation style characteristic of early initiations on the island and believed to be of African origin. Fran Cabrera and Taiwo Abimbola, the son of Yoruba babalao and writer Wande Abimbola, founded the Ile Tun Tun society. "A reborn Ilé Ifè homeland on Cuban soil," Brown notes, "Members wear African clothes and conform to hierarchies and rituals believed to organize the Ifá order of the Ifè kingdom" (Brown 2003: 162).

Finally, some advocates are forming schools and academies in order to insure the "proper" transmission of ritual knowledge and practices. Others reject institutionalization altogether, arguing that this is a matter that should be handled by the *padrino* and his or her *ahijados* or initiates (Fernández-Robaina 2001: 2). As Ayorinde notes, the attitude of "*en mi casa mando yo* [I rule in my house]" has worked against institutionalization and unity (2000: 79). Apparently, only a minority of Cubans have shown an interest in institutionalization, ritual orthodoxy, and "re-Africanization," and it appears that the majority of these have been babalaos who like to stress the distinction between Ocha and Ifá by arguing that the latter is more African because of its ritual purity and the former is more Cuban because of its syncretism (Ayorinde 2000: 81). According to Fernández Robaina, the root cause of this return to orthodoxy can be traced to the mass exodus of Ocha-Ifá priest-healers and diviners during the Mariel boatlift and the resulting vacuum of ritual power (2003). Those babalaos who stayed are believed to have seized the opportunity to extend greater power and authority over the Afro-Creole religious community.

> Eighty percent of the *santeros* and *aleyos* felt that the general cause of these reforms, of the general tendency to return to older, more orthodox forms, was due to the interest among the *babalaos* in having a position of greater power and control over believers. . . . Everyone thought that this phenomenon had become more evident a few years after the exodus of hundreds of *santeros* and *babalaos* in the Mariel boatlift, above all with the arrival of many of them on the

island accompanied by their godchildren who counted direct contact with other Cuban, American, and African *babalochas* and *iyalochas* in their experiences. Some affirmed in a very general way that in that manner the *babalaos* began to be more popular, above all with the arrival of foreigners to make saint or initiate themselves in Ifá, so much as to receive saints that are not very well known in the United States. (Fernández Robaina 2003)

The contestation over the relative Africanness and Cubanness of Ocha-Ifá religion has had serious implications for the articulation and expression of national identity in Cuba:

If African-derived cultural practices are to reflect and validate a *national* identity (which they do), then the importance of Africa cannot be allowed to predominate. This could lead to transnational ethnic identification which could be potentially threatening to national unity. (Ayorinde 2000: 83)

The revolutionary government has responded in part to this threat to national identity by licensing and funding the Yoruba Cultural Association. Yet, paradoxically, it is the ACYC, among others, who appear to advocate transnational ritual identification with Ile-Ife, which seems to contradict efforts to promote a singularly Cuban national identity rather than a transnational one.

The Battle Over the "Letter Of the Year"

Since the onset of the Special Period, the annual Ifá divination ceremony known as the "Letter of the Year" has attracted the attention and curiosity of both the larger Cuban public and the international community. Popular interest in the ceremony's annual prophecies has come to rival if not eclipse that in the government's own socialist slogans for the year. In an era of uncertainty and scarce resources, the babalaos' annual prophetic pronouncements—for example, "Some Would Give Up an Eye to See Another Go Blind," "Contradictions Bring the Light Out of its Hiding Place," "The King Turns in his Crown Before Dying," and so forth—offer more symbolic fat to chew on than do official socialist slogans for the same years—"2006—Year of the Energetic Revolution in Cuba," "2005—Year of the Bolivian Alternative for the Americas," "2004—Year of the 45th Anniversary of the Revolution," or "2003—Year of the Glorious Anniversaries of Martí and the Moncada." The existence of multiple prophecies and infighting among various factions of babalaos, however, has not only led to a crisis in ritual authority and threatened to undermine the integrity of the annual ceremony, but it has also been further complicated by the political opportunism of forces outside the religion. As a result, Ocha-Ifá religion has become a veritable battleground of contested political meanings in contemporary Cuban society.

The Letter of the Year consists of a "ruling" or "governing sign," a "prohecy," a "governing" oricha and their "companion," a flag or banner, a particular purification rite (ebó), a list of environmental, medical, and social conditions, and a number of associated proverbs. According to David Brown, the designation of governing orichas—that is, those that will rule over matters throughout the year—has its roots in the old Afro-Creole cabildos, or mutual-aid societies that black communities were allowed to form beginning in the colonial period:

> the old cabildos' annual elections of royal "rulers" continued symbolically in the annual 1 January "Ifá Divination of the Opening of the Year," in which a male and female oricha couple—in effect, a king and queen—are selected to "govern the year." (Brown 2003: 215)

With at least two separate groups consulting the oracle, however, exactly what the governing signs, prophecies, and proverbs are, as well as who the governing orichas are, is far from clear.

Although the government officially covers the reading performed by the ACYC on national radio (Radio Progreso), most Cubans hear of the annual predictions through radio bemba, or word of mouth. Some take the prophecies seriously, while others express only mild interest. During my fieldwork, local interpretations were almost always dire. In January 2004, for example, one of the rumors circulating on the streets was that the babalaos were distressed after the annual ceremony because, as one friend put it, "they don't know who is going to govern the country this year," suggesting that a change in political leadership was imminent. Local interpretations of the prophecies for 2005 were equally ominous in tone; the dead (los eggun), my informants warned, would rule over the coming year, ensuring that the immediate future would continue to be marked by an atmosphere of uncertainty. In 2006, some interpreted prophetic warnings that "the road toward neighboring lands would grow even longer" as an indication that immigration accords between Cuba and the United States would be threatened, a situation that could not only undermine the efforts of those planning to emigrate to the United States, but could also further alienate family members separated by out-migration. I should note that these interpretations of the annual prophecies were not necessarily circulated by those who opposed the revolutionary government. Most of them came from people who, like most Cubans, temper frustrations with the country's socioeconomic difficulties by noting the success of the revolutionary government in areas such as race relations, medical care, and education. The point here is that attempts on behalf of Ifá divination priests to manage local interpretations of the oracle have been hindered by the existence of multiple prophecies from various rival groups. This is the most significant factor plaguing the annual ceremony's credibility. In 1999, for example, at least six ceremonies were performed by different groups, in addition to at least one more that was carried out in Miami (see Guerra and Loureda 1999).

After the first generation of babalaos passed away, the tradition of performing a single, annual divination ceremony was lost. As early as the 1950s, prominent devotees were complaining about the crisis in ritual authority that Miguel Febles' actions had precipitated and attempts were made to revive the institution. Just prior to the revolution, between 1950 and 1959, Bernardo Rojas brought together various factions and for almost a decade the ceremony was carried out by a single, unified group of babalaos. Soon after the revolution, after Rojas passed away, however, these groups splintered into competing factions once again. In 1976, a group of babalaos came together to form an association known as the Ifá Yesterday, Ifá Today, Ifá Tomorrow Association, but eventually this dissolved when the government rejected their request for a state license. Another attempt at unification was made several years later under the leadership of the babalao Manelo Ibáñez, who renamed the organization the Yoruba Cultural Association of Cuba (ACYC).

The ACYC was granted formal legal recognition as a cultural association by the Cuban government in 1991. It is jokingly referred to by some (and derided as such by others) as the "Ministry of Orula"—suggesting that the patron deity or oricha of Ifá divination and its priesthood have become so cozy with the political leadership on the island that they have been given their own government ministry. Since its founding, the association's Cuban Council of Elder Ifá Priests has been conducting its annual divination ceremony and distributing its official reading of the oracular decrees

7.6. The Yoruba Cultural Association of Cuba's restored mansion.

through state-run media outlets from a refurbished mansion on the pictur-
esque boulevard Paseo Martí (Prado) in Central Havana (Figure 7.6). According to the association's president, Antonio Castañeda, the ACYC had
some seven thousand registered members in 2003, one thousand of which
were babalaos. Just two years later, the number of card-carrying members
jumped to eleven thousand five hundred (Kadri 2006). Castañeda also
claims that the eldest babalaos on the island make up the ACYC's Cuban
Council of Elder Ifá Priests, who are responsible for its annual divination
prophecies.

The government's decision to support the ACYC may have been due, in
part, to the existence of a rival group of babalaos whose prophecies are seen
by some as less politically sensitive to revolutionary vulnerability. Upon
Miguel Febles' tragic death in a kitchen fire in 1986, his followers created
the Miguel Febles y Padrón Commission (CMFP). Since its founding, the
CMFP has been uniting hundreds of babalaos from within Cuba and abroad
during its annual Letter of the Year ceremony. Soon after being licensed by
the state, the ACYC began performing its own annual divination ceremony
to compete with that of the CMFP. By officially recognizing an association
of Ifá diviners interested in institutionalizing their priesthood, the state
benefits in several ways: it ensures more direct access to and information

about (for example, statistical, sociopolitical, and financial) this somewhat secretive religious community, marginalizes those groups who are uninterested in institutionalization by making them appear to be against the virtues of religious unity, guarantees some measure of control over how prophecies and activities are interpreted, provides for the appearance of religious tolerance in a country once officially declared atheist, indicates the state's commitment to its historically marginalized black communities by elevating their cultural heritage to the level of an officially sanctioned public institution, and generates hard currency by attracting religious pilgrims and foreign tourists with a thirst for the "authentic" Cuba.

The existence of various annual prophecies and competing factions has been increasingly politicized by different groups both on and off the island. Indicative of the ceremony's increasing political significance in contemporary Cuban society are the recent flurry of scholarly articles on the subject published in Cuba and abroad, many of which are included in a large section of a recent issue of the University of Havana Review.[7] Local reaction to this recent coverage has been mixed with some babalaos, such as the CMFP's Victor Betancourt, who denounces such coverage as opportunistic sensationalism (Betancourt 2003: 219). Though Betancourt addresses his comments to the international community, his criticisms of the "opportunism" that characterizes the interests of those outside the religion, whether at home or abroad, can easily be read as a veiled reference to government itself. Nonetheless, interpretations from abroad, especially in the Miami exile community, have certainly complicated matters for the CMFP. Rumors on the streets of Miami had it that the commission's sign for 2004, Baba Eyiobe, was the same one that appeared when the Comandante came to power in 1959 and that reappeared in 1989 when the commander of Cuban troops in Angola, General Arnaldo Ochoa, who many exiles believed was the only person capable of organizing a successful coup on the island, was shot and killed. Many Cuban exiles in Miami believed that the CMFP's 2004 letter predicted a major political shake-up on the island. The CMFP, of course, emphatically denies these interpretations.

Although both factions of Cuban Ifá divination priests have been preoccupied in recent years with managing public interpretations of their prophecies, the majority of their public relations efforts have continued to focus on discrediting their rivals. Today, the CMFP and the ACYC are the two main rivals struggling for control over the annual ceremony. The differences in the ritual protocols followed by these two groups appear to be minor. For the former, the youngest-ranking member is the one who takes out the letter (that is, ritually determines which sign will rule the year), whereas for the latter, it is the oldest babalao. According to the former the ceremony should be performed on the first day or during the first week of the new year, whereas the latter group believes it should be performed during the morning hours of December 31st. They also disagree as to what kinds of ritual sacrifices are appropriate for a successful ceremony. Some argue that the sacrifices should always be the same every year, whereas others argue that it depends on what Orula orders should be done, which is revealed in divination (Argüelles 2003: 210). Despite slight differences in ritual procedures, it is fairly obvious that the more important lines of contention between these two associations center around contestations over their respective claims of the power and authority necessary to control the annual ceremony. Although the conflict between these two factions is often represented as a contest between competing claims of spiritual or ritual authenticity, the struggle has increasingly been articulated in terms of economic exploitation and morality.

The sometimes heated rivalry and tensions between these two major factions of Ifá divination priests have included a number of scathing rhetorical attacks designed to undermine the spiritual capital of the other side by claiming that more than just religious concerns motivate their organizing efforts. The CMFP, for example, accuses the ACYC of submitting to the political manipulation of the government in exchange for the perks of state sponsorship (for example, a restored mansion in central Havana, state-sponsored media coverage, financial support, the sociopolitical capital that comes from state recognition, and so forth). The ACYC, however, counters these charges by accusing the CMFP of exploiting the religion for profit, a particularly thorny issue since the onset of the current economic crisis. Similar accusations of economic exploitation and political manipulation have also hindered efforts to unite babalaos across the political divide separating Havana and Miami (see Correa 1997). Antonio Castañeda, president of the ACYC, wearing a suit and tie and sitting behind a large office desk, appearing more like a businessman or politician than a divination priest, had the following to say of the rivalry between the two groups:

We have been fighting for unification for several years. . . . Today, some want to go to battle over the letter of the year. . . . They say we [the ACYC] are being manipulated by the government. But what we do has nothing to do with politics or influence. I'm still driving the same car I had before I became president of the association. I don't receive any special favors. The truth is they [the CMFP] want to exploit the religion to get rich.

Accusations of interés (profiting from religion), however, are often a matter of interpretation. After we concluded our conversation, Castañeda apologized for having postponed the interview a week before (I had been waiting to interview him for a couple of weeks). "I was in France," he boasted, "attending to one of my ritual godchildren, a wealthy French businessman who paid for the entire trip and even treated me to a brief vacation." Later, in 2008, Castañeda would take his own official seat in the National Assembly, the supreme body of state power in Cuba.

The ACYC's allegations of spiritual transgression, which denounce those who use the religion as a vehicle for profit, are thinly veiled attempts to dismiss the CMFP's babalaos by implying their participation in the illicit economic activities associated with jineterismo. Like jineteros, Castañeda represents rival babalaos as purveyors of the entrepreneurial spirit that has come to define the informal economy since the withdrawal of massive foreign subsidies that began in the early 1990s. The informal economy lies outside of formal state control and thus presents a challenge to revolutionary morals by allegedly promoting the materialistic and individualistic values associated with capitalism. By claiming that the CMFP embodies the legacy and infamous reputation of Miguel Febles, its members are spiritually discredited by association with commodity fetishism, and socially ostracized by insinuation of participation in economic activities incongruent with socialism. The CMFP has responded, in part, to charges of economic exploitation with their own counterclaims of spiritual transgression. They note that they, unlike the ACYC, have refused to be co-opted by the state, which they describe as a kind of spiritual coup that essentially enables the government to usurp the powers of Orula for both financial and political reasons.

The Dollar-Store Shrine: Or, Speculation and the Domestication of Hard Currency

31 December 2005: Just a few days following the UJC's festival featuring a mural depicting José Martí holding an effigy of Elegguá, I found myself in a local

7.7. A Santería altar (*trono*) in one of Guanabacoa's dollar stores.

chópin *(shopping), a type of store that only accepts hard currency, in Guana-bacoa. There were lots of people coming and going. The store's security guards attempted to control the flow of shoppers by only allowing them to enter and exit through one door. A sign hung on the wall of the store said, "WELCOME TO THE SECOND ENCOUNTER OF COMMERCIAL TECHNIQUES," a socialist euphemism for the end-of-the-year sale taking place there, also said to be commemorating forty-seven years of revolutionary triumph. A space had been cleared amidst the luxury kitchen items, toiletries, television sets, and outdoor furniture for a faux Santería shrine (Figure 7.7). A local folklore ensemble had performed dances for the orichas in front of the shrine that morning. Now, local residents armed with hard currency fought over the last of the highly valued plastic buckets, fans, drinking glasses, and blue jeans on sale.*

Exploitation of the Ocha-Ifá religion for profit was perhaps the most salient concern of my informants in Havana and Matanzas. Many complained that such not only represented an act of spiritual debauchery that threatened established ritual protocols, but was also causing unnecessary harm and suffering by angering the orichas. Yoel, a santero in the province of Matanzas, complained that tourism in Havana coupled with the financial disparity visible among its residents was exposing the religion to unprecedented forms of greed and corruption. Those who turned to the religion with the intention of making money by initiating tourists, he argued, were not only inflicting harm on unsuspecting tourists, but were also threatening to alienate the orichas from their true devotees on the island:

> In Havana, they bring in saints that are not known here. . . . Songs don't even exist for those saints. Everything they do is for commerce. There's this Spaniard impresario that came to Havana and received the *mano de orula* and made saint. Afterwards, the guy lost his business; one of his legs swelled up and now he has heart trouble. You know what people are saying? That he's waiting until he can come back in order to kill the person that did that to him, and he has his reason. They made him a saint that wasn't necessary. He was supposed to receive Changó, but instead they made him San Lázaro because it's the most expensive. . . . There was also this Spanish woman who made the wrong saint and, afterwards, she went bald. They talked about it on the radio in Spain. They were criticizing the religion. The woman destroyed all of her ritual belongings and now is half crazy. . . . Notice that the saints do not come like they did before. . . . They don't do the same things that they did before. They make their exceptions.

Yet the lure of hard currency has also begun to attract new initiates to Ocha-Ifá in Matanzas. The seductive power of the consumer lifestyle some see in nearby Varedero Beach seems to provoke this interest. They see in ritual initiation a way of gaining access to the tourist economy.

29 May 2003: After the "Awan de San Lázaro" or "Limpieza de Babalú Ayé" healing ceremony in the Marina barrio of Matanzas, one of the young, white participants was eager to strike up a conversation with me. Ismael worked as a tour guide for Canadian and German tourist agencies. He began explaining his involvement with Regla de Ocha. He said he kept having bad luck and eventually decided to see if the religion would change things for him. He told me he had, at first, wanted to be a child of Ochún, but after cowrie-shell divination was performed for him, they found out that Ochún did not want to be his oricha. After asking several orichas, Changó finally agreed to be his patron saint. After his initiation, he told me, he found a job as a tour guide. In fact, he credits his luck at finding a job in the tourist industry to Changó. He spoke of all the luxury consumer items he now enjoys as a result—all the

latest fashions, a seven-hundred-dollar stereo, and a cell phone. He said that
the religion had made all of this happen for him.

Allegations of religious hustling and state-organized commercialization
prompted the collective rogación and ritual feeding mentioned in the beginning of this chapter. The speech the babalao—a member of the CMFP—
made that day may have been an unacknowledged reply to the ACYC's
charges of spiritual transgression through the illicit practices associated
with jineterismo. For the state-sponsored babalaos of the ACYC to pretend
that they were not complicit or take the moral high ground by claiming
their nonparticipation in this informal economy, he seemed to be saying,
would amount to hypocrisy.

Indeed, as Martin Holbraad notes, both the recent effervescence of Ocha-
Ifá religion and the ritual inflation of fees reaching into the thousands of
dollars during the Special Period can be linked to the transformation in
everyday consumption habits during the current economic crisis (2004).
Why, in a time of economic austerity, he asks, are people willing to pay exorbitant fees for lavish ritual ceremonies and initiations? Ifá, Holbraad suggests, provides a less stigmatized arena for emergent capitalist values and
consumer desires. The recent invigoration of Ifá cults is linked to a certain
style of conspicuous consumption known as "speculation" on the island.
Speculation is defined in socialist discourse as "spurious profiteering." Yet,
in the popular imagination, speculation has more to do with consumption than production. The stereotypical image is that of a young Cuban be-
decked in designer sportswear and heavy gold chains and bracelets, a youth
looking for any opportunity to show off his new wealth through frivolous
spending on dollar-denominated beer, food, women, and fancy nightclubs.
Frivolous patterns of spending on luxury consumer items and activities,
Holbraad argues, constitute strategies of ideological contestation.

Because Ifá has always emphasized unbridled expenditure on ritual initiation, described as the "birth of a king," it provides an arena conducive to
conspicuous consumption. Moreover, religious speculation (conspicuous
consumption of ritual services) is also a local means of domesticating or
laundering the suspect wealth and hedonistic consumer lifestyle associated with the new economy. Ifá and speculation, however, are ultimately
incompatible, since their emphases on conspicuous consumption are based
on entirely different motivations. Whereas speculation allows one to tran-

scend poverty for the moment, speculation in Ifá is based on an ethos of submission and spiritual obligation to the deities and oracular authority (Holbraad 2004).

Nevertheless, the dollar-store shrine suggests that the revolutionary state itself has gotten involved in the ritual domestication or laundering of hard currency and the consumer lifestyle associated with foreign tourists that its populace is so willing to mimic.

The Prophetics of Revolution

The government's decision to support the ACYC has important political and economic implications. In part, it reflects an attempt to tap into the secret ritual economy of Ocha-Ifá. This has contributed significantly to the increasing commercialization of the religion through international marketing campaigns designed to attract foreign tourists to the island by exoticizing local practices. Of course, the ACYC is not responsible for those who choose to exploit or otherwise violate ritual protocols in the interests of profit. But their association with the state has only fueled allegations of their complicity with the government's marketing of the religion for foreign tourist consumption. What is perhaps most perplexing about the government's support of the ACYC is that it appears to be encouraging an association that promotes what some refer to as the "Yoruba-ization" of Ocha-Ifá religion on the island, that is, it advocates, according to Ayorinde, the decentering of local ritual authority in Cuba in favor of the dictates of the Nigerian Oni of Ife. It is not entirely clear what is behind such a decision, which appears to contradict the government's desire for a unified national identity since it encourages identification with a transnational ritual authority. There are, however, at least two possible implications of the government's current support of the ACYC. On one hand, it reflects the government's desire to cast these religious cults as cultural "survivals" from a remote African past, a move which attempts to displace the local foundations of ritual authority by claiming that the religion's roots lie elsewhere. This certainly fits well with the government's efforts to represent Ocha-Ifá as a kind of quaint national folklore, acknowledging the entertainment value of its myths, songs, and dance, but implicitly rejecting its contemporary vivacity by representing it as an essentially "dead" practice, valuable only as a historical curiosity.

On the other hand, through its support of the ACYC the government appears to have, at least with respect to the Ifá community, sidelined the issue of national identity for the time being in exchange for the political guarantees that control of the annual divination ceremony may bring. The "official" babalaos of the ACYC, as Hanly observes, "can be counted on to come up with their own politically correct *letra*" (2004). The use of Ifá divination to bring competing factions under one authority is not without historical precedent. In the mid eighteenth century, for example, a Dahomean king used the Ifá divination of his Yoruba neighbors "to centralize the kingdom's oracular authority by delegitimizing and controlling the dangerously 'centrifugal' and subversive tendencies of the country's multifarious *vodun* possession oracles" (Brown 2003: 115–16). The government's investment in the struggle for control of the annual divination ceremony is not only a political strategy designed to create the impression that it respects the religious faith of its citizens, but also is intended to mend the frayed edges of the body politic by encouraging the unification of multifarious religious factions and ensuring that their prophecies do not contradict the state's agenda. After all, ritual identification with a transnational religious community may appear to be less of a challenge to the legitimacy of the state's power and authority than a politically charged oracle that reflects negatively on the nation's leadership.

The Letter of the Year ceremony and the attendant infighting among various factions of divination priests struggling for control over it was initially a relatively esoteric conflict without much relevance to those outside of Cuba's Ocha-Ifá community. What was once a matter of local ritual politics, however, was suddenly forced to the forefront of nationalist politics by both the state's involvement in the conflict and the increasing global presence of the religion, facilitated in part by the redevelopment of Cuba's tourist industry. As a result, Ocha-Ifá religion has become one of the most visible battlegrounds on which struggles over how to define national identity and value in contemporary Cuban society are being waged.

Despite these struggles between different factions of Ifá divination priests, however, one thing is certain. The CMFP's objection to governmental oversight should not be confused with political discontent or opposition to the revolutionary leadership. The youngest ranking member of the CMFP, Victor Betancourt, for example, following a recent *tambor* or drumming ceremony performed at his temple-house to aid in the Comandante's recovery, was quoted by a reporter for Agence France Presse as saying that he and others truly believed that the revolutionary leader was protected by divine forces. The intimacy between the Ifá priesthood and the revolutionary state circulates, then, through both formal and informal channels. That is, it is not just formal state recognition that leads to promiscuity between ritual and state power. The revolutionary state may indeed be attempting to tap into the occult power of the Ifá oracle, but, according to Ayorinde, "some *babalawos* have even incorporated dialectical materialism into their religious discourse" (2004: 136). The blurring of the boundaries distinguishing these two kinds of power, then, also issues from the bottom up.

Epilogue

Although the Comandante has always been the subject of a baffling range of moralizing political fantasies, tales of his hidden powers and magic began circulating with a renewed intensity during the Special Period. Not only did new embellishments of old rumors circulate subterraneously in the form of whispered anecdotes and jokes, but they also surfaced as more overt public commentary in documentaries and books.[1] In his fictional autobiography *Dirty Havana Trilogy*, Cuban author Pedro Juan Gutiérrez, for instance, put to print popular rumors regarding a secret council of elderly santeros commissioned by the state during the Special Period:

> So for years I was what I was supposed to be, and proudly too, with the truth in one hand and the red flag in the other. Then came the crash, and in a few years time, everything was ashes. But a person can't drift forever. Either you find something to grab on to, or you sink. And to top it all off, then we found out that even the head of the government had his santería gods and necklaces and ten Santería elders ministering to him. (2002: 101–102)

Tales of the state's appeal to hidden powers and magic as a response to the economic crisis also circulated in the form of humorous anecdotes. Back in the summer of 2005, for example, there was a joke going around about the Comandante, Hugo Chávez, and—depending on the version—an expatriate Cuban brujo or babalao (Ifá divination priest): The Comandante goes to Venezuela. At some point, Chávez brings him to the cult house of an elderly black brujo from Cuba who has taken up residence there. When the two heads of state enter the house, the apparently awestruck brujo looks at the Comandante and, flailing his arms about in what appears to be a gesture of adulation, says something that the two political leaders mistakenly understand as, "A God! A God! A God! [*¡Un dio'! ¡Un dio'! ¡Un dio'!*]."

"No," Chávez politely interrupts, "this is the Comandante, the president of Cuba."

"A God! A God! A God!" the man repeats, still looking at the Comandante and paying Chávez no mind. Losing his patience, the Venezuelan president raises his voice,

"No! He's not God! He's the great Comandante! The leader of the Cuban revolution!" The brujo cracks a smile and begins speaking again. This time, however, his words are clear.

"It sunk! It sunk!" he exclaims. "Cuba sunk into the sea and now he wants to come here! [*¡Hundió! ¡Hundió! ¡Hundió! Cuba en el mar y ahora el quiere venir pa'ca!*]."[2]

The joke exploits the irony of a situation to poke fun at power. The image of an expatriate Cuban brujo who just cannot seem to get away from the revolutionary leader and the machinations of state resonates with many of the issues discussed here. Desperately searching for some way to revive the island's economy and, by extension, his own diminishing political capital, the Comandante travels to Venezuela, hoping that his closest ally in the region, Hugo Chávez, will provide him with some badly needed advice and assistance. But, rather than arranging an emergency meeting with his own economic advisors and political strategists, the Venezuelan president instead takes the revolutionary leader to see an elderly, black, Cuban brujo who, presumably, left the island years ago in search of better economic opportunities abroad. This suggests that the crisis facing the island is so severe that it will require an act of magic or divine intervention to bring it to an end.

In doing so, however, the joke not only resonates with popular rumors of political leaders who harness the magical powers of brujos in their hour of need, but also recalls the inherently paradoxical nature of racist fantasies in which historically marginalized social classes, despite their imagined backwardness and profound ignorance of modern ways, are believed by elite groups to be gifted with the extraordinary power to dramatically alter the course of misfortune and affliction (see Taussig 1998). Although Chávez clearly has confidence in the elderly black man's ritual prowess, he also takes him to be somewhat dense, believing that he has mistaken the secular leader of a nation for a god at the center of a cult. But the old brujo is no fool. His response is not an indication of political mystification, an apotheosis of the revolutionary leader. Rather, the old brujo sees the revolutionary leader as a mere mortal, implicitly casting him in the role a maritime maroon (*balsero*) or economic migrant. Unable to keep the country afloat, the revolutionary leader, like so many others during the Special Period, has fled the island as it sinks ever deeper into a sea of economic deprivation and moral decay. The revolutionary leader's attempt to either resurrect the economy from abroad or relocate the revolution elsewhere (both interpretations are possible) and, by extension, to save his own sinking political career, has landed him at the brujo's doorstep. The irony here is that the very ritual powers and practices that were once officially excluded from revolutionary political culture—publicly, at least—have now become the privileged sources of national renewal.

Popular Culture and the Revolutionary Cuban State

This book has focused on questions concerning the intimacy or promiscuity (Mbembe 1992) between popular culture and the state in post-Soviet Cuba. Rather than treat popular religions and revolutionary officialdom as distinct cultural spheres, I have called attention to their various entanglements. The result is an ethnography that refuses to stay put, rather moving awkwardly back and forth between different cultural arenas and practices. Yet what unites these uneasy ethnographic shifts—from everyday politics in the local barrio to the monumental powers of the socialist state, from domestic ritual space to the public stage of revolutionary political spectacle, from popular constructions of the past to the national and global projects of public memory, from the brutal realities of local economic deprivation to the emergent economies of desire and cosmopolitanism in the tourist zones—has been the effort to highlight some of the ways in which metaphorical and magical constructions of power, both popular and official, feed the moral and political imaginary in contemporary Cuban society. In particular, this book has addressed several questions regarding the role of magic in the economic, social, and political changes taking place on the island—for instance, How does the monumentality of the state inspire popular images of its hidden powers and magic? How might the state be seen as appropriating popular idioms of power in order to legitimize and reestablish its own political standing vis-à-vis its subjects? How might the state's perceived embrace of vernacular imaginaries of power, whether real or imagined, be circulating back into popular culture? How does historical memory, both popular and official, influence these constructions of power?

Revolutionary officialdom has over the years forced itself into a rather precarious position vis-à-vis popular imaginaries of power, especially those rooted in the cosmology and magic of Afro-Creole religions. Although they had historical value as a counter-ideology inherited from the colonial and slave era, these religions were also dismissed by hard-line revolutionary authorities as obstacles to socialist modernity. Their contemporary survival may have validated the structural terror of a bygone era, but they also represented the ideological vestiges or mystifications of a past made obsolete by the socialist reforms that followed the 1959 revolution. Paradoxically, then, these religions were both national cultural patrimony and anachronistic forms of mystification that would, the government believed, soon fade away with socialist restructuring. The Soviet-style Marxist agenda that the leadership originally promoted was typical of a classic top-down rationalist modernism; popular religions, like race, were mystifications of class and thus expected to fade away with the socialist reforms that would dismantle the structural foundations of the class system. They were simply out of place in a political community that privileged socialist values and scientific atheism.

The revolutionary embrace of cultural diversity by the current regime follows a different kind of strategy, one symptomatic of the "late Marxist" tendency to seize upon whatever happens to be popular at the moment and harness it to the ideological agenda of the party by calling it "Marxist" or "revolutionary." Yielding on Marx's ideological absolutism (that is, his model of religion as false consciousness), however, has allowed the emergence of other perspectives regarding the powers of the revolutionary state, or what Michel Foucault called the "insurrection of subjugated knowledges" in public discourse. The capillary nature of power becomes apparent when official discourse is complemented by a popular imaginary that reckons the revolutionary leadership's power not in terms of a "dictatorship of the proletariat" or other communist rationales for rule, but rather as an expression of the leadership's mastery of occult forces. By selectively borrowing vernacular idioms of power in an effort to revive revolutionary political fervor and nationalist sentiment, then, the state may be seen as embracing the occult model to legitimize its authority. Thus, popular (bottom-up) imaginations take hold of official (top-down) ideology and state iconography, reformulating the very notion of political power and its justification.

This point is crucial. Because power is distributed unevenly across and between societies, we tend to miss or overlook the cultural and political influences of subjugated groups on dominant sectors in favor of top-down models of cultural change. What I have attempted to demonstrate here is that cultural flows and the circulation of power in society are not governed by a strictly one-way process, but are in fact the result of reciprocal, if uneven, incursions and permutations between those who stand at the helm of a society's political machinery (the dominant sectors) and those subject to its machinations (the masses). The revolutionary Cuban state, as this ethnography shows, is making concerted efforts to domesticate and harness popular imaginaries of power and their magical capacities to the national agenda. Yet, at the same time, the revolution's reifications of these vernacular fantasies are fast being reabsorbed into the realm of popular culture, where there are then subject to further embellishment, enabling the body politic to fashion new magic out of the magical detritus of the state.

Notes

Chapter 1. The Magic of the Revolution

1. I borrow this phrase from Michael Ondaatje's book *Coming through Slaughter*, an imaginative account of the life of New Orleans cornet player Buddy Bolden. In the book Ondaatje describes how Bolden collected all of the rumors and stories he heard from people in the barbershop and on the streets and published them in a magazine: "*The Cricket* existed between 1899 and 1905. It took in and published all information Bolden could find. It respected stray facts, manic theories, and well-told lies. This information came from customers in the chair and from spiders among the whores and police that Bolden and his friends knew. *The Cricket* studied broken marriages, gossip about jazzmen, and a servant's memoirs told everyone that a certain politician spent twenty minutes each morning deciding which shirt to wear. Bolden took all the thick facts and dropped them into his pail of sub-history" (Ondaatje 1976: 24).

2. See Palmié for what is, in my estimation, the most thorough and theoretically sophisticated discussion of the Cuban nganga to date (2002, 2006).

3. See Hernández-Reguant's very informative chronicle and analysis of the Special Period (2009), much of which I paraphrase here.

4. Whereas for some Cubans the word *yuma* means "North American," others use it more broadly to designate non-Spanish-speaking tourists and/or foreigners in general. The term apparently derives from Delmer Daves' 1957 Western *The 3:10 to Yuma*. Culled from her conversations with Cuban exile Enrique del Risco, Dopico says the word "designate[s] what could not be named, ironically invoking a destination in a work of fiction that is never quite arrived at in order to signify a word that cannot be spoken. . . . Young people used this film as a signifying metaphor for the problems of naming, departure, and compromised choice" (2004: 64–65).

5. Ariana Hernández-Reguant suggests that Juan Padron's 1985 animated feature *Vampires in Havana* represents one of the grand narratives of revolutionary inventiveness and ingenuity. In the film, "European and American vampires linked to various mafias fight for the control of a secret formula, invented by a Cuban-based vampire, which would allow vampires from all over the world to expose themselves to the sun and therefore lead normal lives. This goes against European and North American mafioso vampires which want to keep all vampires in the dark so that they have no choice other than frequent the mafia-controlled underground beaches. In the end, the good Cubans win, insuring *vampisol*'s universal access and debunking the protectionism of patents and the control of foreign corporations of vital substances such as this" (personal communication).

6. Although he almost always called himself a "brujo," Arcaño is, more specifically, a spirit medium and specialist in the magical rites of Palo, an Afro-Creole religious formation historically associated with Congolese slaves and their descendants on the island. Other designations for these ritual specialists include *palero*, *ngangulero*, *mayombero*, *brillumbero*, *quimbisero*, and still other terms, the choice depending on personal preference and/or the ritual branch to which the individual belongs.

7. There are other examples of how popular culture and the state seduce and fuel each other's imaginaries in modern Venezuela. Jonathan Hill, for example, provides a fascinating account of how local shamans in the Upper Río Negro region "shamanize the state"—that is, how they construct visions of an imagined state that defines itself through the institutionalization of shamanic healing powers (2003).

8. For comparative purposes, see Rafael Sánchez's discussion of the María Lionza cult (2001).

Chapter 2. The Eye and the Tongue

1. Although I am sure that I came across this CDR graffiti somewhere in Vedado, I cannot remember exactly where. Nevertheless, most neighborhoods have some kind of graffiti or signboards alerting everyone to the presence of the CDR. The most common are simple signboards, usually depicting a figure draped in the Cuban flag and holding a machete, that state the particular CDR's number and zone. Incidentally, the head and torso of this image bear an uncanny resemblance to an eye and tongue similar to those seen in charm-images that protect from evil eye and malicious rumor and gossip. In any case, these are often accompanied by familiar revolutionary slogans such as, "Revolution in every neighborhood!" or "Long live socialism!"

2. I transcribed Riverón's joke from a pirated copy of a videotape rented from a private vendor, or local video "bank" (*banco*). The material is not copyrighted.

3. When André Breton came to Haiti at the end of 1945, his visit coincided with an exhibition of the Cuban painter Wifredo Lam and a series of lectures given by the Martiniquean poet Aimé Cesaire. From what little I have been able to gather, it appears that Breton made some such comment, possibly in jest, to Lam during this visit. Although the comment is attributed to Breton in a number of publications (for example, see Duany 1988), I have so far been unable to find the original source.

Chapter 3. The Opacity of Power

1. Actually, there were a couple of different opinions circulating at the time regarding who was really in charge. One was that the Comandante, despite his official retirement from public office, was still making the most important decisions. The other was that his brother wanted everyone to think this in order to deflect any potential public backlash against his own administration, policies, and reforms.

2. Some of the Comandante's critics suggest that his enduring grip on power has been achieved through a kind of hypnotic control over the nation itself. That is, by "mounting" (possessing) the body politic, the Comandante has virtually zombified the nation and ensured total obedience to his authority and control (Geyer 1991: 204). Although he does not suggest the zombification of the body politic, Stephan Palmié does express his awe at the way that the aging leader "moves"—or, at least, used to move—the bodies of thousands of citizens during state-organized protest marches and national celebrations. Here, it seems that the Comandante is rather possessed by the body politic (2004: 257–58).

3. Some of the earliest tales are clearly linked to patron-client networks that existed between colonial elites and black mutual-aid associations (*cabildos*) at the time. The immense financial success of the Bacardí rum dynasty, for instance, became the subject of much speculation after rumors circulated that they had allowed a local black cabildo to salute the protector gods of their home (*lares*) and perform purification rites on their property (Díaz Fabelo 1974: 105–106). Other stories relate the ruthlessness and fear inspired by particular colonial authorities to their possession of powerful magic. José Trujillo Monagas, for example, Havana's infamous second chief of police, remembered for having led an aggressive campaign against criminal delinquency that targeted and persecuted members of black ritual societies, was rumored to be a brujo who used an *mpaka* (a bull horn or gourd stuffed with magical substances and sealed with a mirror) to track down criminals and keep the disreputable elders of black ritual societies in check when Cuba was still a Spanish colony (Cabrera 1983: 208). In other cases, popular rumors offer insider accounts of the behind-the-scenes dramas unfolding during a period of political turmoil. General José Miguel Gómez, for example, the republic's second president, allegedly broke ties with the brujo he had hired as a secret advisor when the man foretold the failure of the political leader's efforts to hold on to power following a disputed election (Cabrera 1979: 208–10).

4. See Palmié (2002), Bronfman (2004), and Román (2007).

5. I borrow the image of a "Nietzchean vampire" from Walter Kirn's review of Mario Vargas Llosa's *The Feast of the Goat* (2001), a novel about the Trujillo dictatorship in the Dominican Republic. The blurb from Kirn's review is cited on the inside jacket of the English paperback edition. Also, see Georgie Geyer's *Guerrilla Prince* for an earlier use of zombie imagery to describe the power dynamics of post-1959 Cuban political culture (1991: 204). Another variant of the tale of the Comandante's nganga, following the Cuban scholar and writer Tomás Fernández Robaina, is that he allegedly buried an nganga on the grounds of the José Martí International Airport to protect him while traveling abroad (Fernández Robaina, quoted in Miller 2000: 47).

Chapter 4. Conjuring the Past

1. Arcaño, who practices a branch of the *reglas de congo,* or Bantu-derived magico-religious practices referred to as *palo monte mayombe* on the island, explicitly rejected the more vernacular term "*palero*" as a ritual title, since for him it evoked the frivolous image of "someone who plays with sticks." Although he often referred to himself as a "brujo" in those contexts where specifics were needed, he also referred to himself as a "mayombero." Both titles, for him, conveyed the serious character of his ritual work better than "palero," as well as more accurately reflecting the particular branch of *palo monte* or *reglas de congo* that he practiced. Although he gave me permission to use his real name, I have chosen to use a pseudonym so that my contextualization and interpretation of his ritual activities will not be confused with any kind of political positioning on his part.

2. All translations of Spanish are my own unless otherwise noted. The lines in Spanish were:

Lead: *¡Me voy, me voy pa'l monte!*
Chorus: *¡Suelta lo' perro,' mayoral!*
Lead: *¡No me agarra!*
Chorus: *¡Suelta lo' perro' al cimarrón!*

Although this is not typically what is referred to as a *puya,* a ritually stylized set of verbal abuses meant to incite the spirits into descending or mounting the bodies of their devotees, I was told that these song phrases were indeed meant as a provocation. "When someone doesn't want to cooperate and fights with the dead to keep them from taking over their body," Arcaño explained, "we sing that song to provoke the dead, to call them with more force." I was unable to find any documentation of the song in the published literature on Palo Monte. There is a segment, however, in Luis A. Soto and Tato Quiñones's 1991 documentary *Nganga Kiyangala: Congo Religion in Cuba* in which the song is performed. The performance I witnessed took place in Enrique ("Enriquito") Hernández Armenteros's Los Hijos de San Lázaro, a temple house located in La Jata, Guanabacoa. In the film, the song also appears to directly provoke possession. The participant falls to the ground, facedown, with his arms tightly pressed against his torso, and wiggles his way into another room, door of which is closed in front of the camera.

3. This spirit medium actually said, "*los bozales, los cimarrones,*" not only referring to those African slaves who were "just off the boat," so to speak, but also to those who had managed to escape the forced labor regime of the plantation by fleeing to and hiding themselves in the bush (*el monte*). The word "*bozal*" was a derogatory term used by Spanish slavers to refer to both newly arrived African slaves and the mangled Spanish they spoke. During the colonial period, *bozal* and *criollo* (Creole, meaning "island-born") were opposing terms in an emerging system of racialized social classification. Whereas the *bozales* were considered by the ruling class to be uncivilized brutes, the *criollos* were described in comparatively more civilizing terms since they spoke more fluent Spanish and exhibited some of the social characteristics that would come define to the emerging colony. Those religious devotees with whom I worked always described

the spirits of runaway slaves as not only being *bozales,* but *"congos."* My informants often collapsed the terms *"bozal," "cimarrón,"* and *"congo"* to refer to one and the same thing: a crude (*crudo*), brutish (*bruto*), runaway Congolese slave who made up for his lack of a civilizing demeanor with his great magical powers.

4. The poetics and politics of memory are not only of general anthropological interest (for example, see Connerton 1989), but have also received much more attention lately from scholars doing research in Africa and on the African diaspora (for example, see Apter and Derby forthcoming; Shaw 2002; Bongie 2001; Sarduy and Stubbs 2000; Brown 1999; Trouillot 1997; Fields 1994; Fabre and O'Meally 1994).

5. James was referring to the original "mother" nganga of the "Vititi Congo Saca Empeño" family of nganga, which was mounted sometime in the middle of the eighteenth century in Guanabacoa (James 2006: 56; Larduet 2002: 45). Nevertheless, James argues that this does not mean that Palo Monte as such came into existence on that date and in that location. He suggests that although it was not until Reynerio Pérez arrived in Santiago de Cuba from Matanzas with his nganga "Brama con Brama" sometime between 1910 and 1912 that Palo developed into an organized cult in that region of the country, it had in fact existed there as a "free" and "spontaneous" practice lacking an established hierarchical structure since the latter half of the sixteenth century.

6. I want to thank Jalane Schmidt for sharing with me her experience of the unveiling of Alberto Lescay's *Monumento al Cimarrón,* as well as for calling to my attention to some of the ways in which this event and others like it reveal the multiple layers of meaning embedded within the sacred landscape of El Cobre (see Schmidt 2005: 191–195).

7. Adepts of Palo Monte distinguish between two main types of nganga by using the terms "Christian" and "Jewish." Thus, a "Christian" nganga is one that has been "baptized" with holy water from a local Catholic church, and thus is allegedly used for benevolent ritual purposes. The "Jewish" nganga, however, are not baptized in this sense and are allegedly used for malevolent work. The term "Jewish," then, is only used to mean "non-Christian" in this context (see Cabrera 1979: 23, 121; Ballard 2005).

8. Nganga are constructed using either a clay pot or a tripod iron cauldron—depending on the particular *mpungu* with which it is associated—which is then stuffed with a bewildering array of vegetable, animal, and human remains, minerals, soil from various locations, certain manufactured objects, and miscellaneous other magically charged substances. The nganga is a master fetish, a composite magical device that derives its awesome fetish power by incorporating a litany of lesser magically imbued substances and spirit entities. In brief, their construction begins with the drawing of a cosmogram consisting of two perpendicular lines that form a quadrant representing the four "winds" of the cosmos in the bottom of the vessel. At the center and four extremities of this cross are placed five coins. A section of sugarcane filled with sea water, sand, and quicksilver, sealed using candle wax, is placed off to one side. The cadaver of a small dog, a petrified rock (*matari*), and human remains, usually only a cranium and bones from the hands and feet, occupy the center. Various types of tightly packed sticks (*palos*) are then arranged vertically along the perimeter of the nganga to form a kind of cordon. A variety of pungent, aromatic plant substances (for example, chiles, black pepper, garlic, onion, ginger, and cinnamon) are then sprinkled inside. Atop this are placed different kinds of

insects (for example, termites, spiders, and centipedes), the heads of birds (predatory and otherwise), nocturnal flying mammals, and reptiles (for instance the water snake or the chameleon). Soil gathered from a number of distinct locations is packed inside to keep its contents fixed, and certain man-made objects such as knives, daggers, machetes, shackles or handcuffs, and even pistols are sometimes stuck or pressed into the soil. Sometimes the sticks lining the perimeter are wrapped with cloth or plastic and the external surface of the nganga is encircled with a metal chain, procedures that are designed to further reinforce containment. The nganga is then buried, first in a cemetery and then in some undomesticated place (*el monte*), absorbing the sedimentary energies embedded in these locations. Finally, the nganga is disinterred and taken home, where the mayombero performs a set of rites designed to activate the forces residing inside. The mayombero must then "prove" (*hacer prueba*) the nganga by ordering it to perform some ritual task that, if completed, serves as confirmation of its magical efficacy and power.

9. The earliest type of *nkisi* objects remembered by Lydia Cabrera's informants, for example, were pieces of cloth or handkerchiefs—referred to variously as *macuto*, *boumba*, *sácu-sácu*, *envoltorio*, *saco*, or *jolongo*—in which were wrapped magically charged substances and spirit entities (Cabrera 1983: 124–29). Similar magical substances may have also been used to consecrate stones and human skulls, placed in more permanent structures such as tree trunks, and even ground into special powders that were then rubbed into the body through small incisions (James 2006: 29–31). In any case, given that they were small and easily concealed, it is likely that the *macutos* and similar objects were the first kind of *nkisi* used by slaves and their descendants in Cuba. What is almost certain is that the practice of placing such magical substances in the considerably larger and less mobile tripod iron cauldrons called nganga, as is the custom today, was largely the invention of urban black Creoles, perhaps to compete with the elaborate altar displays of the emerging *Ocha-Ifá* cults (Cabrera 1983: 129; James 2006: 31).

10. Cuba's colonial sugar estates were, as one French visitor to the island wrote in 1817, "theaters of frightening abuse" (Cabrera 1979: 31). Plantation owners and overseers resorted to various spectacular means of inspiring terror in order to punish their human property, but one which bears particular resonance with the above narrative is the mutilation and beheading of rebel slaves. As early as 1533, several fugitive slaves were caught and taken to Bayamo where they were "executed, quartered, and [had] their heads placed in the public plaza to serve as a lesson to others" (Barnet et al. 2003: 66). During the 1844 slave uprising in Matanzas, a free mulatto accused of conspiracy was mutilated—"his head posted in 'the most public place' of the town of his birth" (Paquette 1988: 243). A similarly gruesome scene concludes Tomás Gutiérrez Alea's famous film *The Last Supper* (1976). After taking advantage of their master's paternal affection and drunkenness by fleeing the estate, a group of slaves are eventually caught and then decapitated, their rotting heads shown sitting atop tall poles stuck into the ground as the credits roll. In 1815, a group of runaway slaves living in the El Frijol settlement in eastern Cuba used the body of one of their members killed in an attack by a slave-hunting militia for magico-religious purposes (La Rosa Corzo 2003: 181). During the second attack on the settlement the following year, the slave hunters came across, depended from a tree, a human skull

belonging to a Maroon named Ramón whose "marrow and hair were used to make false prophecies" (La Rosa Corzo 2003: 271).

11. Although I do think the significance of an nganga's soil has been overlooked in literature concerning the device, Esteban Montejo does mention its use among Congolese slaves on a sugar plantation in Flor de Sagua during the 1870s. "When the master punished a slave," Montejo recounted, "all the others picked up a little dirt and put it in the pot [an nganga]. With that dirt they were able to bring about what they wanted. And the master fell ill or some harm came to his family because while the dirt was in the pot, the master was a prisoner in there, and not even the devil could get him out. That was the Congolese people's revenge on the master" (Barnet 1994: 27–28).

12. The threat of having one's spirit of the dead caught by another sorcerer is further elaborated by the use of other magical devices that may have their roots in the historical experiences associated with Marronage. The sorcerer's "spies," for example, are two railroad spikes containing nfumbi that anchor a small chain on their doorstep. Before the performance of all major rituals, corn husks are stuffed with various powders and nfumbi, tied, and strategically placed on the street corners around the house. These magically charged railroad spikes and corn husks warn the mayombero of enemy movement by acting as his "army of spies." After the waves of government repression began during the early republican period, these mystical spies also became indispensable in protecting mayomberos from police harassment by warning them of the movement and proximity of law enforcement officers (see Bettelheim 2001).

Chapter 5. Tying the Yuma to the Stick

1. I am relying here on Juan Tomás Roig y Mesa's 1988 *Diccionario botánico de nombres vulgares cubanos* to determine both the common and scientific names of these plant materials.

2. Even though Arcaño is a mayombero, the ritual title of specialists in one particular branch of the Cuban ritual formation known as Palo, when it came to love magic he always worked with Ochún, an oricha or saint in the Ocha-Ifá pantheon.

3. I have been able to locate only two references to the use of love magic in sex tourism literature. One of these references refers to the use of obeah among Jamaican sex workers to eliminate competition or protect them from the magic of other envious sex workers. According to one, "The girls they obeah each other to make each other don't make any money." Another adds, "They go all over the island [to visit obeah men]. They don't want to see you prosper. If they see a way you can get out before them they 'fuck' you up. Even if they can't do it with obeah they do it with their mouths [presumably by spreading malicious rumors]" (quoted in Campbell, Perkins, and Mohammed 1999: 147).

4. See Anna Lidia Vega Serova's 2002 short story "Billetes falsos" for a poignant commentary on how the lure of hard currency is making some of the public secrets and banal evasiveness of the revolutionary moral community come into relief.

5. There are many more words used in relation to these magical procedures (for example, see Ortiz 1906; Lachatañeré 2004; and Cabrera 1983, 1980, 1979). Rather than attempt to list them all, I have selected the most expressive examples.

6. Similar gender associations are made throughout the circum-Caribbean and in other areas of the world where love magic is practiced. In Belize, for example, women turn to magical "methods of attachment" because there are few recourses for those who seek emotional and financial support from husbands or fathers who abandon their families. Love magic, then, provides "an outlet for the resentment and hostility many women feel toward males," which allows women to feel that they are at least magically in control, since practical control over men in such circumstances is rare (Bullard 1974: 264).

7. According to Christopher Faraone (1999), ancient Greek love magic took two basic forms: *eros* (sex) magic and *phillia* (affection) magic. Eros magic was normally associated with men, who used it to seduce women. Phillia magic was normally associated with women and was used to maintain their husband's or lover's affections. Eros magic had affinities with cursing magic; it worked by making the object of desire suffer insomnia or madness until they gave into the desirer. Phillia magic, on the other hand, had affinities with healing magic; it attempted to minimize the object of desire's passions for another person or else reduced their anger toward the practitioner. Although it is commonly held that ancient Greeks believed that females were more passionate, lascivious, and whimsical, Faraone argues that love magic actually suggests the opposite. Men turned to eros magic to heat up cold, chaste women; women turned to phillia magic to cool down men's sexual desires. But there were occasions when this structure was undermined. Courtesans, for instance, used eros magic to procure clients, assuming the male role of sexual predator. Men would sometimes use phillia magic to attract the attention of superiors, assuming the female role of reducing distraction or misdirected desire (it is feminizing, then, because it attempts to circumscribe male desire).

8. See David Graeber for a fascinating analysis of the association between love magic and fantasies of power and history in Madagascar (1997).

9. The published literature on the figure of the jinetera and her relation to tourism in Cuba is extensive. For specific discussions, including comparative literature from other parts of the Caribbean, see Cabezas (2004); Clancy (2002); Darling (2004); Díaz González (1997); Dopico (2002); Elinson (1997); Elizalde (1996); Fernández (1999); Fosado (2003); Fusco (1998); Hodge (2001); O'Connel Davidson (1999); O'Connell Davidson and Sánchez Taylor (1999); Paternostro (2000); Rundle (2001); Sanchez Taylor (2000); Schwartz (1997); Strout (1995); Valle (n.d.); and Wonder and Michalowski (2001). For comparative material on love, romance, sexual relations, and economic change, see Cole (2004), Corwall (2002), Jankowiak (1995), and Rubhun (1999).

10. These quotes are taken from commentary on a sex tourism website (www.cubanwomen-cubangirls.com) that I came across while researching this chapter (accessed March 10, 2005).

Chapter 6. The Cult of the Profane

1. My use of the term "kitschy" here is somewhat tongue in cheek. The cajón has failed to attract scholarly attention on the island or abroad for various reasons about which I can only speculate. I suspect that this inattention is at least partly due to the cajón's "kitschy" aesthetics—that is, its apparently random and tasteless appropriation of of-

ten stereotypical imagery, wrenched from its original context and represented in cheap, gaudy statuary. The cajón is not considered to be "authentic," but rather a corruption of independently existing, "legitimate" religious formations.

2. Although I am convinced that the full name of the ceremony was most likely *rumba del cajón al muerto* (see Fariñas 2002), people normally referred to it as *el cajón al muerto*, and, on a few exceptional occasions, as *fiesta espiritual al cajón* (box-drum spiritual party) or *fiesta para los muertos* (party for the dead).

3. For differing perspectives on the María Lionza cult see Taussig (1997) and Sánchez (2001).

4. I am referring here to a specific issue in the literature on popular culture and state—namely, the question of their imbrication or entanglement. See Hall (2006), Mbembe (1992)—from whom I borrow the term "intimacy"—Taussig (1997), and Sánchez (2001), whose statement regarding "the realignment of politics and domesticity" I paraphrase here.

5. Here, I borrow Davies insightful characterization of state spectacle as one of so many attempts to "disarm alterity" (2000).

Chapter 7. The Prophetics of Revolution

1. For specific examples of narrative describing the intermingling of secular and sacred power in Cuba see Bascom (1951: 17); Brown (2003: 84–85); Carbonell (1993: 198); de la Torre (2003); Díaz Fabelo (1974); Lachantañeré (2001); Melgar (1991); Miller (2000); Orozco and Bolívar (1998); and Valdes (2001).

2. I am using the term "cult" here in the strictest sense, to refer to the acephalous nature of a number of relatively small but interrelated ritual families.

3. West African antecedents more than likely had some influence on the animosity that developed between the Egbado and the Oyo and their competing ritual systems in Cuba (see Ramos 2003).

4. The Ifá-centric accounting of many scholars has largely been due to the fact that their main informants were babalaos (see Brown 2003: 147; Murphy 1981; and Cabrera 1980 [1974]).

5. The founders of these principal *ramas* or branches were Carlos Adé Bí, Remigio "Adechina" Herrera, Joaquín Cádiz, Olugueré Kó Kó, and Francisco Villalonga (see Brown 2003).

6. Religious believers were banned from the Cuban Communist Party until 1993, when the government officially reversed its policy and welcomed believers into the party (see Benkomo 2000; Salier and Hernández 2004).

7. See de Rey Roa (2002); Sigler (2005); Argüelles (2003); Betancourt (2003); González (2003); Guerra (2003); and Trimegistros (2003).

Epilogue

1. Víctor Betancourt, for example, an Ifá divination priest in Havana, appears in a documentary commenting on the Comandante's affinities with the orichas or santos

(see Erskine and O'Shaughnessy 2000). A book coauthored by Román Orozco, a Spanish journalist, and Natalia Bolívar, a Cuban anthropologist, is packed full of stories about the Comandante's relationship with Afro-Creole religions (1998). Pedro Juan Gutiérrez, a Cuban novelist, has also put to print popular rumors claiming that the Comandante seeks council from a secret group of santeros who work for the regime (2002).

2. The joke is hard to render in English because of the phonetics of Caribbean Spanish, in which the word for "god" (*un dios*) and the past tense of the verb "to sink" (*hundió*) have very similar pronunciations. This is due to the fact that vernacular Caribbean Spanish is often characterized by the omission of the consonant "s" in final syllable positions. Thus, because the "s" is dropped, "god" is pronounced "*un dio.*"

Bibliography

Abrams, Philip. 1988. "Notes on the Difficulty of Studying the State." *Journal of Historical Sociology* 1 (1): 58–89.

Acosta Reyes, Nilson. 2001. "Los sitios y patrimonios arquitectónicos de la ruta del esclavo en Cuba." *Catauro* 2 (3): 81–90.

Apter, Andrew. 1993. "Atinga Revisited: Yoruba Witchcraft and the Cocoa Economy, 1950–1951." In *Modernity and its Malcontents: Ritual and Power in Postcolonial Africa*, eds. Jean Comaroff and John Comaroff, pp. 111–28. Chicago: University of Chicago Press.

Apter, Andrew and Lauren Derby. Forthcoming. *Activating the Past: Historical Memory in the Black Atlantic*. London: Cambridge Scholars Press.

Aretxaga, Begoña. 2003. "Maddening States." *Annual Review of Anthropology* 32: 393–410.

Argüelles Mederos, Aníbal. 2003. "La Letra del Año." *Revista Universidad de la Habana* No. 258: 208–13.

Argüelles Mederos, Aníbal and Ileana Hodge Limonta. 1991. *Los llamados cultos sincréticos y el espiritismo*. Havana: Editorial Academia.

Asturias, Miguel Angel. 1963 [1946]. *The President*. Long Grove, Ill.: Waveland Press.

Austen, Ralph A. 1993. "The Moral Economy of Witchcraft: An Essay in Comparative History." In *Modernity and its Malcontents: Ritual and Power in Postcolonial Africa*, eds. Jean Comaroff and John Comaroff, pp. 89–110. Chicago: University of Chicago Press.

Ayorinde, Christine. 2000. "Regle de Ocha-Ifá and the Construction of Cuban Identity." In *Identity in the Shadow of Slavery*, ed. Paul E. Lovejoy, pp. 72–85. London: Continuum.

———. 2004. *Afro-Cuban Religiosity, Revolution, and National Identity*. Gainesville, Fla.: University Press of Florida.

Ballard, Eoghan C. 2005. "Ndoki bueno, ndoki malo: Historic and Contemporary Kongo Religion in the African Diaspora." PhD diss., University of Pennsylvania.

Baloyra, Enrique A. 1987. "Side Effects: Cubanology and Its Critics." *Latin American Perspectives* 22 (1): 265–74.

Balutansky, Kathleen M. and Marie-Agnes Sourieau. 1998. *Caribbean Creolization: Reflections on the Cultural Dynamics of Language, Literature, and Identity.* Gainesville, Fla.: University Press of Florida.

Bardach, Ann Louise. 2002. *Cuba Confidential: Love and Vengeance in Miami and Havana.* New York: Vintage Books.

Barnet, Miguel. 1983. *La fuente viva.* Havana: Editorial Letras Cubanas.

———. 1994. *Biography of a Runaway Slave.* Willimantic, Conn.: Curbstone Press.

Barnet, Miguel, Pedro Deschamps Chapeaux, Rafael García, and Rafael Duharte. 2003. "Fleeing Slavery." In *The Cuba Reader: History, Culture, Politics*, eds. Aviva Chomsky, Barry Carr, and Pamela Maria Smorkaloff, pp. 65–68. Durham: Duke University Press.

Bascom, William. 1951. "The Yoruba in Cuba." *Nigeria* 37: 14–20.

Benítez Rojo, Antonio. 1996. *The Repeating Island: The Caribbean and the Postmodern Perspective.* Durham: Duke University Press.

Benkomo, Juan. 2000. "Crafting the Sacred Batá Drums." In *Afro-Cuba Voices: On Race and Identity in Contemporary Cuba*, eds. Pedro Pérez Sarduy and Jean Stubbs, pp. 140–46. Gainesville, Fla.: University Press of Florida.

Berliner, David C. 2005. "The Abuses of Memory: Reflections on the Memory Boom in Anthropology." *Anthropological Quarterly* 78 (1): 197–211.

Betancourt, Victor. 2003. "Las incomprendidas letras de un año." *Revista Universidad de la Habana* No. 258: 221–27.

Bettelheim, Judith. 2001. "Palo Monte Mayombe and Its Influence On Cuban Contemporary Art." *African Arts* 34 (2): 36–49.

———. 2005. "Caribbean Espiritismo (Spiritist) Altars: The Indian and the Congo." *Art Bulletin* 87 (2): 312–30.

Bolívar Arostegui, Natalia and Carmen Gonzalez Diaz de Villegas. 1998. *Ta Makuende Yaya y las Reglas de Palo Monte.* Habana: Ediciones Union.

Bongie, Chris. 2001. "A Street Named Bissette: Nostalgia, Memory, and the *Cent-Cinquantenaire* of the Abolition of Slavery in Martinique." *The South Atlantic Quarterly* 100 (1): 215–57.

Booth, William. 2009. "The Mystifying Life and Many Deaths of Cuba's Talisman." *Washington Post*, February 7th.

Borges, Dain. 1992. "Machiavellian, Rabelaisian, Bureaucratic?" *Public Culture* 5 (1): 109–12.

Botín, Vicente. 2009. *Los funerales de Castro.* Barcelona: Editorial Ariel.

Bourdieu, Pierre. 1990. *The Logic of Practice.* Stanford: Stanford University Press.

———. 1991. "Delegation and Political Fetishism." In *Language and Symbolic Power,* pp. 3–67. Cambridge: Harvard University Press.

Brazeal, Brian. 2007. "Blood, Money, and Fame: Nagô Magic in the Bahian Backlands." PhD diss., University of Chicago.

Brennan, Denise. 2004. *What's Love Got to Do with It? Transnational Desires and Sex Tourism in the Dominican Republic*. Durham: Duke University Press.Bronfman, Alejandra. 2004. *Measures of Equality: Social Science, Citizenship, and Race in Cuba, 1902–1940*. Chapel Hill: University of North Carolina Press.

Brown, David H. 1989. "Garden in the Machine: Afro-Cuban Sacred Art and Performance in Urban New Jersey and New York." PhD diss., Yale University.

———. 2003. *Santería Enthroned: Art, Ritual, and Innovation in an Afro-Cuban Religion*. Chicago: University of Chicago Press.

Brown, Karen McCarthy. 1999. "Telling a Life: Race, Memory, and Historical Consciousness." *Anthropology and Humanism Quarterly* 4 (2): 148–54.

Brown, Vincent. 2003. "Spiritual Terror and Sacred Authority in Jamaican Slave Society." *Slavery and Abolition* 24 (1): 24–53.

Bulit, Ilse. 2007. "Fidel y su aché." http://www.insurgente.org/modules.php?name=New s&file=article&sid=1091 (accessed December 2007).

Bullard, M. Kenyon. 1974. "Hide and Secret: Women's Sexual Magic in Belize." *Journal of Sex Research* 10 (4): 259–65.

Cabezas, Amalia L. 2004. "Between Love and Money: Sex, Tourism, and Citizenship in Cuba and the Dominican Republic." *Signs* 29 (4): 987–1,015.

Cabrera, Lydia. 1979. *Reglas de Congo: Palo Monte Mayombe*. Miami, Fla.: Ediciones Universal.

———. 1980. *Yemayá y Ochún*. New York: C. R. Publishers.

———. 1983. *El monte*. Miami, Fla.: Colección de Chichirekú.

Cabrera Infante, Guillermo. 2000. "Santeros Link Castro's Future to Elian." *Miami Herald*, April 17th.

Campbell, Shirley, Althea Perkins, and Patricia Mohammed. 1999. "Come to Jamaica and Feel All Right: Tourism and the Sex Trade." In *Sun, Sex, and Gold: Tourism and Sex Work in the Caribbean*, ed. Kamala Kempadoo, pp. 125–56. Lanham, Maryland: Rowman and Littlefield Publishers.

Carbonell, Walterio. 1993. "Birth of a National Culture." In *Afrocuba: An Anthology of Cuban Writing on Race, Politics, and Culture*, eds. Pedro P. Sarduy and Jean Stubbs, pp. 195–203. New York: Ocean Books.

Casa del Caribe. 1997. "Monumento al Cimarrón." http://www.cultstgo.cult.cu/caribe/Festival/cimarron.htm (accessed October 6, 2006).

Castañeda, Jorge G. 1998. *Compañero: The Life and Death of Che Guevara*. New York: Vintage Books.

Castellanos, Isabel Mercedes. 1990. "Grammatical Structures, Historical Development, and Religious Usage of Afro-Cuban Bozal Speech." *Folklore Forum* 23 (1&2): 57–84.

———. 2001. "A River of Many Turns: The Polysemy of Ochún in Afro-Cuban Tradition." In *Osun Across the Waters: A Yoruba Goddess in Africa and the Americas*, eds. Joseph Murphy and Mei Mei Sanford, pp. 34–45. Bloomington: Indiana University Press.

Childs, Matt D. 2004. "Expanding Perspectives on Race, Nation, and Culture in Cuban History." *Latin American Research Review* 39 (1): 285–301.

Cino, Luis. 2005. "Nganga con garras." http://www.cubanet.org/CNews/ y05/mayo5/05a10.htm (accessed February 5, 2006).

Clancy, Michael. 2002. "The Globalization of Sex Tourism and Cuba: A Commodity Chains Approach." *Studies in Comparative International Development* 35 (4): 63–88.

Colás, Santiago. 1995. "Of Creole Symptoms, Cuban Fantasies, and Other Latin American Postcolonial Ideologies." *Publications of the Modern Language Association* 110 (3): 382–96.

Cole, Jennifer. 2004. "Fresh Contact in Tamatave, Madagascar: Sex, Money, and Intergenerational Transformation." *American Ethnologist* 31 (4): 573–88.

Comaroff, Jean and John Comaroff. 1992. *Ethnography and the Historical Imagination.* Boulder, Col.: Westview Press.

———. 1993. "Introduction." In *Modernity and its Malcontents: Ritual and Power in Postcolonial Africa.* eds. Jean Comaroff and John Comaroff, pp. xi-xxxvii. Chicago: Chicago University Press.

———. 1999. "Occult Economies and the Violence of Abstraction: Notes from the South African Postcolony." *American Ethnologist* 26 (2): 279–303.

Comité Cubano de "La Ruta del Esclavo." 2001. "Informe de 'La ruta del esclavo' en Cuba." *Catauro* 2 (3): 41–52.

Connerton, Paul. 1989. *How Societies Remember.* Cambridge: Cambridge University Press.

Constable, Nicole. 2003a. *Cross-Border Marriages: Gender and Mobility in Transnational Asia.* Philadelphia: University of Pennsylvania Press.

———. 2003b. *Romance on a Global Stage: Pen Pals, Virtual Ethnography, and "Mail-Order" Marriages.* Berkeley: University of California Press.

Correa, Armando. 1997. "Discordia divide a santeros." *El Nuevo Herald*, January 15th.

Corwall, Andrea. 2002. "Spending Power: Love, Money, and the Reconfiguration of Gender Relations in Ado-Odo, Southwestern Nigeria." *American Ethnologist* 29 (4): 963–80.

Couliano, Ioan. 1987. *Eros and Magic in the Renaissance.* Chicago: University of Chicago Press.

Daniel, Yvonne. 1991. "Changing Values in Cuban Rumba: A Lower-Class Black Dance Appropriated by the Cuban Revolution." *Dance Research Journal* 23 (2): 1–10.

Darling, Lynn. 2004. "Havana at Midnight." In *Traveler's Tales: Cuba*, ed. Tom Miller, pp. 254–63. San Francisco, Cal.: Traveler's Tales.

Davies, Catherine. 2000. "Surviving (on) the Soup of Signs: Postmodernism, Politics, and Culture in Cuba." *Latin American Perspectives* 27 (4): 103–21.

de Certeau, Michel. 1984. *The Practice of Everyday Life.* Berkeley: University of California Press.

de la Torre, Miguel A. 2003. *La Lucha for Cuba: Religion and Politics on the Streets of Miami.* Berkeley: University of California Press.

Derby, Lauren. 1999. "The Dictator's Two Bodies: Hidden Powers of the State in the Dominican Republic." *Etnofoor* XII (2): 92–117.

de Rey Roa, Annet Aracelia. 2002. "(Re)-Construcción de discurso africanista entre babalawos y santeros cubanos." In *América Latina y el Caribe: Realidades sociopolíticas e identidad cultural*, eds. Silke Helfrich and Marina Sandoval, pp. 66-73. San Salvador, Spain. Ediciones Heinrich Boll.

Devisch, René. 1993. *Weaving the Threads of Life: The Khita Gyn-eco-logical Healing Cult among the Yaka*. Chicago: University of Chicago Press.

———. 1999. "Sorcery and Fetish." In *The Law of the Lifegivers: The Domestication of Desire*, eds. René Devisch and Claude Brodeur, pp. 57–89. Amsterdam: Hatwood Academic Publishers.

Díaz Fabelo, Teodoro. 1974. *Diccionario de la lengua Congo residual en Cuba*. Santiago de Cuba: Casa del Caribe.

Díaz González, Elena. 1997. "Tourismo y prostitución en Cuba." In *Cuba, Impacto de las crises en grupos vulnerables: Mujer, familia, infancia*, eds. Elena Díaz, Tanía Carmen León, Esperanza Fernández Zegueira, et al., pp. 3–8. Habana: Universidad de la Habana.

Diène, Doudou. 1994. "The Slave Route: A New International Project." *UNESCO Courier* October: 29.

———. 1998. "The Slave Route: A Memory Unchained." *UNESCO Sources* 99: 7.

———. 2000. "Editorial." *The Slave Route Newsletter* 1 (September): 1.

———. 2001. *From Chains to Bonds: The Slave Trade Revisited*. New York/Oxford/Paris: UNESCO/Berghahn Books.

Dopico, Ana Maria. 2002. "Picturing Havana: History, Vision, and the Scramble for Cuba." *Nepantla: Views from South* 3 (2): 451–93.

———. 2004. "The 3:10 to Yuma." In *Anti-Americanism*, eds. Andrew Ross and Kristin Ross, pp. 47–68. New York: New York University Press.

Duany, Jorge. 1988. "After the Revolution: The Search for Roots in Afro-Cuban Culture." *Latin American Research Review* 23 (1): 244–55.

Elinson, Hannah. 1997. *Cuba's Jineteros: Youth Culture and Revolutionary Ideology*. Cuba Briefing Papers Series 20. Georgetown University: Center for Latin American Studies.

Elizalde, Rosa Miriam. 1996. *Flores desechables: ¿Prostitución en Cuba?* Habana: Casa Editoria.

Emery, Amy Fass. 1996. *The Anthropological Imagination in Latin American Literature*. Columbia: University of Missouri Press.

Erskine, Rosalind and Hugh O'Shaughnessy. 2000. *Fidel Castro: Big Man, Small Island*. Princeton, New Jersey: Film for the Humanities and the Sciences.

Fabre, Geneviève and Robert O'Meally. 1994. *History and Memory in AfricanAmerican Culture*. New York: Oxford University Press.

Fagen, Richard. 1969. *The Transformation of Political Culture in Cuba*. Stanford: Stanford University Press.

Faraone, Christopher. 1999. *Ancient Greek Love Magic*. Cambridge: Harvard University Press.

Fariñas. 2002. *Cajón al muerto*. Havana: Envidia 7049.

Fernández, Nadine. 1999. "Back to the Future: Women, Race, and Tourism in Cuba." In *Sun, Sex, and Gold: Tourism and Sex Work in the Caribbean*, ed. Kamala Kempadoo, pp. 81–89. Lanham, Maryland: Rowman and Littlefield Publishers.

Fields, Karen. 1994. "What One Cannot Remember Mistakenly." In *History and Memory in African-American Culture*, eds. Geneviève Fabre and Robert O'Mealley, pp. 15–163. Oxford: Oxford University Press.

Flikke, Michelle Tisdel. 2006. "Cuban Museums and Afro-Cuban Heritage: Fragments and Transition in Daily Life." PhD diss., Harvard University.

Fosado, Gisela. 2003. "The Exchange of Sex for Money in Cuba: Masculinity, Ambiguity, and Love." PhD diss., University of Michigan.

Foucault, Michel. 1977. *Discipline and Punish*. New York: Vintage Books.

Fraser, Nancy. 1989. *Unruly Practices: Power, Gender, and Discourse in Contemporary Social Theory*. Minneapolis: University of Minnesota Press.

Fuentes, Norberto. 2009. *The Autobiography of Fidel Castro*. New York: W. W. Norton & Company.

Fuentes Guerra, Jesus. 2002. *Nzila ya mpika (la ruta del esclavo): Una aproximación lingüística*. Cienfuegos: Ediciones Mecenas.

Fuentes Guerra, Jesus and Armin Schwegler. 2005. *Lengua y ritos del Palo Monte Mayombe: Dioses cubanos y sus fuentes africanas*. Madrid/Frankfurt: Iberoamericana/Vervuert.

Fundación Fernando Ortiz. 2001. "Special Issue on 'La Ruta del Esclavo.'" *Catauro* 2 (3).

Fusco, Coco. 1998. "Hustling for Dollars: *Jineterismo* in Cuba." In *Global Sex Workers: Rights, Resistance, and Redefinition*, eds. Kamala Kempadoo and Jo Doezema. New York: Routledge.

Gainza Chacón, Miguel A. 2006. "De la Nganga Viva, la Mpaka y los manos mágicos de un escultor." http://www.caribenet.info/pensare_06_gainza_lescay.asp?1 = (accessed October 9, 2006).

García Márquez, Gabriel. 1968. *La novela en américa latina: Diálogo*. Lima: CMB, Universidad Nacional de Ingeniería.

———. 1975. *The Autumn of the Patriarch*. New York: Harper & Row.

———. 1982. "The Solitude of Latin America." http://nobelprize.org/nobel_prizes/literature/laureates /1982/marquez-lecture-e.html. (Accessed September 15, 2007).

———. 1985. "Big Mama's Funeral." In *Collected Stories*, pp. 197–214. New York: Perennial Classics.

———. 2005. "A Personal Portrait of Fidel." In *Fidel: My Early Years*, pp. 11–25. Melbourne, Australia: Ocean Press.

Geertz, Clifford. 1977. "Centers, Kings, and Charisma: Reflections on the Symbolics of Power." In *Culture and Its Creators: Essays in Honor of Edward Shils*, eds. Joseph Ben-David and Terry Nichols Clark, pp. 150–71. Chicago: University of Chicago Press.

Geschiere, Peter. 1997. *The Modernity of Witchcraft: Politics and the Occult in Postcolonial Africa*. Charlottesville: University of Virginia Press.

Geyer, Georgie A. 1991. *The Guerilla Prince*. Boston: Little, Brown & Company.

González, Flavia. 2003. "El legado de los ancestros." *Revista Universidad de la Habana* No. 258: 176–81.

González García, Rigoberto. 2000. "Tata Kuyere Nkisi: El rey de los espíritus." *Del Caribe* 33: 110–16.

González-Whippler, Migene. 1992. *The Santería Experience*. St. Paul, Minn.: Llewellyn.

Gordy, Katherine. 2006. "'Sales + Economy + Efficiency = Revolution?' Dollarization,

Consumer Capitalism, and Popular Responses in Special Period Cuba." *Public Culture* 18 (2): 383–412.

Graeber, David. 1997. "Love Magic and Political Morality in Central Madagascar, 1875–1990." In *Gendered Colonialisms in African History*, eds. Nancy R. Hunt, Tessie P. Liu, and Jean Quataert, pp. 94–117. Oxford: Blackwell Publishers.

Guerra, Rosa María de Lahaye. 2003. "Del oráculo y la profecía: La letra del año." *Revista Universidad de la Habana* No. 258: 206–207.

Guerra, Rosa María de Lahaye and Zardoya Loureda. 1999. "Las letras del año." *Catauro* 1: 118–38.

Gutiérrez, Pedro Juan. 2002. *Dirty Havana Trilogy*. New York: Harper Collins Publishers.

Gutiérrez Alea, Tomás. 1976. *La Última Cena*. Havana: Instituto Cubano del Arte e Industria Cinematograficos.

Hale, Lindsay L. 1997. "Preto Velho: Resistance, Redemption, and Engendered Representation of Slavery in a Brazilian Possession-Trance Religion." *American Ethnologist* 24 (2): 392–414.

Hall, Stuart. 2006. "Popular Culture and the State." In *The Anthropology of the State*, eds. Aradhana Sharma and Akhil Gupta, pp. 360–80. Malden, Mass.: Blackwell Publishing.

Hanly, Elizabeth. 1995. "Santería: An Alternative Pulse." *Aperture* 141: 30–37.

———. 2004. "Santería Discussion Stirs up Passions." *Miami Herald*, April 17th.

Hayes, Kelly E. 2007. "Black Magic and the Academy: Macumba and the Construction of Afro-Brazilian Religious Orthodoxies." *History of Religions* 46 (4): 283–315.

Helg, Aline. 1995. *Our Rightful Share: The Afro-Cuban Struggle for Equality, 1886–1912*. Chapel Hill: University of North Carolina Press.

Hernández-Reguant, Ariana. 2002. "Radio Taino and the Globalization of the Cuban Culture Industries." PhD diss., University of Chicago.

———. 2006. "Havana's Timba: The Macho Sound of Black Sex." In *Globalization and Race: Transformations in the Cultural Production of Blackness*, eds. Kamari Clarke and Deborah A. Thomas. Durham: Duke University Press.

———. 2009. "Writing the Special Period: An Introduction." In *Cuba in the Special Period: Culture and Ideology in the 1990s*, ed. Ariana Hernández-Requant, 1–18. New York: Palvgrave-Macmillan.

Hertz, Robert. 1960. *Death and the Right Hand*. Aberdeen: Cohen and West.

Hill, Jonathan. 2003. "Shamanizing the State in Venezuela." *Journal of Latin American Lore* 21 (2): 163–77.

Hodge, Derrick G. 2001. "The Colonization of the Cuban Body." *NACLA Report on the Americas* March/April 34, 15: 20–30.

Holbraad, Martin. 2004. "Religious 'Speculation': The Rise of Ifá Cults and Consumption in Post-Soviet Cuba." *Journal of Latin American Studies* 36 (4): 643–64.

———. 2005. "Expending Multiplicity: Money in Cuban Ifá Cults." *Journal of the Royal Anthropological Institute* 11 (2): 231–54.

Howes, David. 2003. *Sensual Relations: Engaging the Senses in Culture and Social Theory*. Ann Arbor: University of Michigan Press.

Jackson, Michael. 1996. "Phenomenology, Radical Empiricism, and Anthropological Critique." In *Things As They Are: New Directions in Phenomenological Anthropology*, ed. Michael Jackson, pp. 1–50. Bloomington: Indiana University Press.

James Figarola, Joel. 1996. "La Brujería Cubana: El Palo Monte." *Revista Mexicana del Caribe* 2: 100–37.

———. 1999. *La muerte en Cuba*. La Habana: Ediciones Unión.

———. 2006. *Cuba, la gran nganga: Algunas prácticas de la brujería*. Santiago de Cuba: Ediciones Caserón.

Jankowiak, William. 1995. *Romantic Passion*. New York: Columbia University Press.

Kadri, Francoise. 2006. "La santería gana más adeptos extranjeros." *El Nuevo Herald*, October 10th.

Kantorowicz, Ernst H. 1957. *The King's Two Bodies: A Study in Medieval Political Ideology*. Princeton: Princeton University Press.

Kennedy, William. 1976. "A Stunning Portrait of a Monstrous Caribbean Tyrant." *The New York Times*, October 31st.

Kutzinski, Vera M. 1993. *Sugar's Secrets: Race and the Erotics of Cuban Nationalism*. Charlottesville: University of Virginia Press.

Lachatañeré, Romulo. 2004. *El sistema religioso de los afrocubanos*. La Habana: Ciencias Sociales.

Lago Vieto, Angel. 2001. "El Espiritismo en la Región Oriental de Cuba en el Siglo XIX." *Del Caribe* 35: 72–79.

Laguerre, Michel S. 1998. "The Voodooization of Politics in Haiti." In *Blackness in Latin America and the Caribbean*, Vol. II, eds. Arlene Torres and Norman E. Whitten, pp. 495–539. Bloomington: Indiana University Press.

Larduet, Abelardo. 2001. "Reynerio Pérez en el panorama de las creencias de origen bantú en Santiago de Cuba." *Del Caribe* 34: 114–15.

———. 2002. *Nganga: Centro de culto palero*. (Unpublished Manuscript).

La Rosa Corzo, Gabino. 2003. *Runaway Slave Settlements in Cuba: Resistance and Repression*. Chapel Hill: University of North Carolina Press.

Lefort, Claude. 1986. "The Image of the Body and Totalitarianism." In *The Political Forms of Modern Society*, ed. John B. Thompson, pp. 292–306. Cambridge: Massachusetts Institute of Technology.

Lewis, Oscar, Ruth Lewis, and Susan Rigdon. 1977. *Living the Revolution: An Oral History of Contemporary Cuba*. Urbana: University of Illinois Press.

MacGaffey, Wyatt. 1986. *Religion and Society in Central Africa: The Bakongo of Lower Zaire*. Chicago: University of Chicago Press.

Martinez-Alier, Verena. 1974. *Marriage, Class and Colour in Nineteenth-Century Cuba: A Study of the Racial Attitudes and Sexual Values in a Slave Society*. Cambridge: Cambridge University Press.

Mason, Michael Atwood. 2002. *Living Santería: Rituals and Experiences in an Afro-Cuban Religion*. Washington, D.C.: Smithsonian Institution Press.

Matibag, Eugenio. 1996. *Afro-Cuban Religious Experience: Cultural Reflections in Narrative*. Gainesville, Fla.: University Press of Florida.

Matory, J. Lorand. 2005. *Black Atlantic Religion: Tradition, Transnationalism, and Matri-*

archy in the Afro-Brazilian Candomblé. Princeton, New Jersey: Princeton University Press.

———. 2007. "Free to Be a Slave: Slavery as Metaphor in the Afro-Atlantic Religions." *Journal of Religion in Africa* 37: 398–425.Mauss, Marcel and Henri Hubert. 1972. *A General Theory of Magic*. London/New York: Routledge.

Mbembe, Achille. 1992. "The Banality of Power and the Aesthetics of Vulgarity in the Postcolony." *Public Culture* 4 (2): 1–30.

McCalister, Elizabeth. 2002. *Rara! Vodou, Power, and Performance in Haiti and Its Diaspora*. Berkeley: University of California Press.

Melgar, Ricardo. 1993. "Los orishas y la ciudad de la Habana en tiempos de crisis." *Cuadernos Americanos* 5: 165–84.

Menéndez, Lázara. 2002. *Rodar el coco: Proceso del cambio en la santería*. La Habana: Editorial de Ciencias Sociales.

Merleau-Ponty, Maurice. 1962. *Phenomenology of Perception*. London: Routledge.

Miller, Arthur. 2004. "A Visit With Castro." *The Nation* 278 (2): 13–17.

Miller, Ivor. 1995. "Belief and Power in Contemporary Cuba: The Dialogue Between Santería Practitioners and Revolutionary Leaders." PhD diss., Northwestern University.

———. 2000a. "Religious Symbolism in Cuban Political Performance." *The Drama Review* 44 (2): 30–55.

———. 2000b. "A Secret Society Goes Public: The Relationship Between Abakuá and Cuban Popular Culture." *African Studies Review* 43 (1): 161–88.

———. 2004. "The Formation of African Identities in the Americas: Spiritual 'Ethnicity.'" *Contours* 2 (2): 192–222.

Mitchell, Timothy. 1990. "Everyday Metaphors of Power." *Theory and Society* 19: 545–77.

Moreno Fraginals, Manuel. 1976. *The Sugarmill: The Socioeconomic Context of Sugar in Cuba, 1760–1860*. New York: Monthly Review Press.

Murphy, Joseph. 2001. "Yéyé Cachita: Ochún in a Cuban Mirror." In *Osun Across the Waters: A Yoruba Goddess in Africa and the Americas*, eds. Joseph Murphy and Mei Mei Sanford, pp. 87–101. Bloomington: Indiana University Press.

O'Connell Davidson, Julia. 1999. "Sex Tourism in Cuba." *Race and Class* 38: 39–48.

O'Connell Davidson, Julia and Jacqueline Sánchez Taylor. 1999. "Fantasy Islands: Exploring the Demand for Sex Tourism." In *Sun, Sex, and Gold: Tourism and Sex Work in the Caribbean*, ed. Kamala Kempadoo, pp. 37–54. Lanham, Maryland: Rowman and Littlefield Publishers.

Ondaatje, Michael. 1976. *Coming Through Slaughter*. New York: Vintage Books.

Oppenheimer, Andres. 1992. "Courting the Babalaos." In *Castro's Final Hour*, pp. 338–55. New York: Simon & Schuster.

Orozco, Román and Natalia Bolívar. 1998. *Cubasanta: Comunistas, santeros y cristianos en la isla de Fidel Castro*. Madrid: El País Aguilar.

Ortiz, Fernando. 1956. "La secta conga de los 'matiabos' de Cuba." In *Libro jubilar de Alfonso Reyes*, ed. Alfonso Reyes, pp. 308–25. México: Dirección General de Difusión Cultural.

———. 1985. *Nuevo cataura de cubanismos*. La Habana: Editorial de Ciencias Sociales.

———. 2001. *Los Negros Brujos*. La Habana: Editorial de Ciencias Sociales.

Padura Fuentes, Leonardo. 2001. *Adios Hemingway y La cola de la serpiente*. Havana: Ediciones Unión.

Palmié, Stephan. 2002. *Wizards and Scientists: Explorations in Afro-Cuban Modernity and Tradition*. Durham: Duke University Press.

———. 2003. "Comments on *The Iconization of Elián González*." http://divinity.uchicago.edu/martycenter/ . . . /o72003/response_palmie.pdf. *(Accessed March 23, 2009)*.

———. 2004. "Fascinans or Tremendum? Permutations of the State, the Body, and the Divine in Late-Twentieth Century Havana." *New West Indian Guide* 78: 229–68.

———. 2006. "Thinking with Ngangas: Reflections on Embodiment and the Limits of 'Objectively Necessary Appearances.'" *Comparative Studies in Society and History. 48 (4): 852–86.*

Paquette, Robert L. 1988. *Sugar Is Made With Blood: The Conspiracy of La Escalera and the Conflict Between Empires over Slavery in Cuba*. Middletown, Conn.: Wesleyan University Press.

Paternostro, Silvana. 2000. "Sexual Revolution." *The New Republic* (July): 10–17.

Pérez Sarduy, Pedro. 2001. "In Living Memory." http://www.afrocubaweb.com/pedroperezsarduy/inlivingmemory.htm (accessed October 6, 2006).

Pérez Sarduy, Pedro and Jean Stubbs. 2000. "Introduction: Race and the Politics of Memory in Contemporary Black Cuban Consciousness." In *Afro-Cuba Voices: On Race and Identity in Contemporary Cuba*, eds. P. Perez Sarduy and J. Stubbs, pp. 1–38. Gainesville, Fla.: University Press of Florida.

Ramos, Miguel W. 2003. "La División de la Habana: Territorial Conflicts and Cultural Hegemony in the Followers of Oyo Lukumí Religion, 1850s-1920s." *Cuban Studies* 34 (1): 38–70.

Restall, Matthew. 2005. *Beyond Black and Red: African-Native Relations in Colonial Latin America*. Albuquerque: University of New Mexico Press.

Roa, Ramon. 1950. *Con la pluma y el machete*, Vol. 1. La Habana: Ministerio de Educación.

Roach, Joseph. 1996. *Cities of the Dead: Circum-Atlantic Performance*. New York: Columbia University Press.

Roche y Monteagudo, Rafael. 1925. *La policía y sus misterios en Cuba*. Havana: La Moderna Poesía.

Roig y Mesa, Juan Tomás. 1988. *Diccionario botánico de nombres vulgares cubanos*. Havana: Editorial Científico-Técnica.

Roman, Reinaldo. 2007. *Governing Spirits: Religion, Miracles, and Spectacles in Cuba and Puerto Rico, 1898–1956*. Chapel Hill: University of North Carolina Press.

Romberg, Raquel. 2005. "Ritual Piracy or Creolization With an Attitude." *New West Indian Guide* 79 (3&4): 175–18.

Rubhun, I. A. 1999. *The Heart is Unknown Country: Love in the Changing Economy of Northeast Brazil*. Stanford: Stanford University Press.

Rundle, Mette Louise B. 2001. "Tourism, Social Change, and *Jineterismo* in Contemporary Cuba." The Society for Caribbean Studies Annual Conference Papers 2. http://www.google.com/search?hl=en&ie=ISO-8859-1&q=%22Tourism%2C+Social+Ch

ange%2C+and+Jineterismo+in+Contemporary+Cuba%22. (Accessed October 3, 2009).

Sahlins, Marshall. 2004. "The Iconization of Elián Gonzalez." In *Apologies to Thucydides: Understanding History as Culture and Vice Versa*, ed. Marshall Sahlins, pp. 166–93. Chicago: University of Chicago Press.

Sánchez, Rafael. 2001. "Channel-Surfing: Media, Mediumship, and State Authority in the María Lionza Spirit Possession Cult (Venezuela)." In *Religion and Media*, eds. Hent de Vries and Samuel Weber, pp. 388–434. Stanford: Stanford University Press.

Sanchez Taylor, Jaqueline. 2001. "Tourism and 'Embodied' Commodities: Sexual Tourism in the Caribbean." In *Tourism and Sex: Culture, Commerce, and Coercion*, eds. Stephen Clift and Simon Carter, pp. 41–53. New York: Pinter.

Sanders, Todd and Harry G. West. 2003. "Introduction: Power Revealed and Concealed in the New World Order." In *Transparency and Conspiracy: Ethnographies of Suspicion in the New World Order*, eds. Harry West and Todd Sanders, pp. 1–37. Durham: Duke University Press.

Sandoval, Mercedes C. 1983. "Santería." *Journal of the Florida Medical Association* 70 (8): 620–28.

Schmidt, Jalane. 2005. "Cuba's Rival Rituals: 20th-Century Festivals for the Virgin of Charity and the Contested Streets of the 'Nation.'" PhD diss., Harvard University.

Schwartz, Rosalie. 1997. *Pleasure Island: Tourism and Temptation in Cuba*. Lincoln: University of Nebraska Press.

Sharma, Aradhana and Akhil Gupta. 2006. *The Anthropology of the State: A Reader*. Malden, Mass.: Blackwell Publishing.

Shaw, Rosalind. 2002. *Memories of the Slave Trade: Ritual and the Historical Imagination in Sierra Leone*. Chicago: University of Chicago Press.

Sigler, Bret. 2005. "God, Babalawos, and Castro." In *Capitalism, God, and a Good Cigar: Cuba Enters the Twenty-First Century*, eds. Lydia Chávez and Mimi Chakarova, pp. 207–21. Durham: Duke University Press.

Singleton, Theresa. 2001. "Slavery and Spatial Dialectics on a Cuban Coffee Plantation." *World Archaeology* 33 (1): 98–114.

Soto, Luis A. and Tato Quiñones. 1991. *Nganga Kiyangala: Congo Religion in Cuba*. New York: Latin American Video Archives.

Stoller, Paul. 1994. "Embodying Colonial Memories." *American Anthropologist* 96: 634–48.

Strout, Jan. 1995. "Women, the Politics of Sexuality, and Cuba's Economic Crisis." *Socialist Review* 25 (1): 5–16.

Sutton, David. 2004. "Ritual, Continuity, and Change: Greek Reflections." *History and Anthropology* 15 (2): 91–105.

Tamayo, Juan O. 1996. "Afro-Cubans Say Catholics Have Slighted Their Religion." *Miami Herald*, January 12th.

Taussig, Michael. 1980. *The Devil and Commodity Fetishism in South America*. Chapel Hill: University of North Carolina Press.

———. 1987. *Shamanism, Colonialism, and the Wild Man: A Study in Terror and Healing*. Chicago: University of Chicago Press.

———. 1992. "Maleficium: State Fetishism." In *The Nervous System*, ed. Michael Taussig, pp. 111–40. New York: Routledge.

———. 1997. *The Magic of the State*. New York: Routledge.

———. 1998. "Folk Healing and the Structure of Conquest in Southwest Colombia." In *Blackness in Latin America and the Caribbean*, Vol. I, eds. Arlene Torres and Norman E. Whitten, pp. 445–500. Bloomington: Indiana University Press.

Teski, Marea and Jacob Climo. 1995. *The Labyrinth of Memory: Ethnographic Journeys*. Westport/London: Bergin and Garvey.

Thompson, Robert Farris. 1983. *Flash of the Spirit: African and Afro-American Art and Philosophy*. New York: Random House.

Toscano Segovia, Dax. 2004. "Fidel: Indoblegable frente al imperialismo." *Granma*, November 19th, http://www.granma.cu/espanol/2004/ noviembre/mar23/indoblegable-apartado-e.html (accessed February 10, 2006).

Trimegistros, Hermes. 2003. "Concepto 'Letra del año.'" *Revista Universidad de la Habana* No. 258: 214–15.

Trouillot, Michel-Rolph. 1997. *Silencing the Past: Power and the Production of History*. Boston: Beacon Press.

———. 2001. "The Anthropology of the State in the Age of Globalization." *Current Anthropology* 42 (1): 125–38.

Tylor, Edward B. 1974. *Primitive Culture*. New York: Gordon Press.

Valdés, Nelson. 2001. "Fidel Castro, Charisma and Santería: Max Weber Revisited." In *Caribbean Charisma: Reflections on Leadership, Legitimacy and Populist Politics*, ed. Anton Allahar, pp. 212–41. Boulder, Col.: Lynne Rienner Publishers.

Vega Serova, Anna Lidia. 2002. "Billetes falso." *La jornada semanal* No. 405, December 8th, http://www.jornada.unam.mx/2002/12/08/sem-lidia.html (accessed March 8, 2006).

Vidal, Sylvia and Neil L. Whitehead. 2004. "Dark Shamans and the Shamanic State: Sorcery and Witchcraft as Political Process in Guyana and the Venezuelan Amazon." In *Darkness and Secrecy: The Anthropology of Assault Sorcery and Witchcraft in Amazonia*, eds. Neil L. Whitehead and Robin Wright, pp. 51–81. Durham: Duke University Press.

Whitfield, Esther. 2002. "Dirty Autobiography: The Body Impolitic of Trilogía sucia de la Habana." *Revista de Estudios Hispánicos* 36 (2): 329–51.

Wirtz, Kristina Silke. 2004. "Santería in Cuban National Consciousness: A Religious Case of the Double Moral." *Journal of Latin American Anthropology* 9 (2): 409–38.

Wonder, Nancy A. and Raymond Michalowski. 2001. "Bodies, Borders, and Sex Tourism in a Globalized World: A Tale of Two Cities, Amsterdam and Havana." *Social Problems* 48 (4): 545–71.

Index

Page numbers in italics refer to illustrations.

www.ingramcontent.com/pod-product-compliance
Lightning Source LLC
Chambersburg PA
CBHW032349280326
41935CB00008B/510